Praise for *Who...*

"Take a dozen scholars who have all written books on some aspect of the life of the historical Jesus. Have them meet annually for a decade poring over articles that each one writes on his area of specialty, looking for any possible flaws. Publish the revised results on both sides of the Atlantic in a major monograph and receive wider scholarly feedback. Then commission the co-chair to write a succinct, readable digest of the results, and the result is Darrell Bock's *Who Is Jesus?* Here is the most important counterpoint available in print to the fanciful Jesuses of the skeptical fringe, and a must read!"
—Craig Blomberg, Ph.D., Distinguished Professor of New Testament, Denver Seminary

"If people with different convictions about Jesus use shared rules that everyone can agree on, what basic matters might we conclude about Jesus? Drawing on the work of many fine scholars and based on some of the best historical scholarship, *Who Is Jesus?* advances a solid picture of many essential contours of who Jesus was. Well-written, enjoyable to read, and driven by informative arguments, the book offers many excellent insights, some of them new even to the academic discussion."
—Craig S. Keener, author of *The Historical Jesus of the Gospels* and professor of New Testament at Asbury Theological Seminary

"Who is Jesus? Our culture has a vast array of ideas about this question. How would a historian evaluate the evidence? Darrell Bock summarizes the work of twelve scholars who met over a decade looking at a dozen key events in the life of Jesus. Based on the most patient and painstaking historical research, this book is as gripping as a good detective novel. The Jesus who emerges is a unique figure, with an attractive humility and an authority that invites and inspires. *Who Is Jesus?* is a must-read for anyone who wants to know the truth about history's most intriguing and divisive figure."
—Brian S. Rosner, Principal of Ridley Melbourne

"We live in a world where amateur speculation about the life of Jesus is commonplace. Rarely does a true specialist take the average person behind the scenes to see how these investigations are done. Darrell Bock is one of the leading 'History of Jesus' scholars in the United States today. In this lucid and compelling volume, Bock invites us into his seminar on 'Jesus Studies' in order to show how scholars weigh evidence for events or sayings in Jesus' life. He presents the data with meticulous care, provides the extra-biblical resources that clarify the meaning, significance, and uniqueness of the event, and then provides a well-reasoned conclusion. For any serious student of the gospels, this is the book to own."

—Gary M. Burge, Ph.D., professor of New Testament at
Wheaton College and author of *The New Testament in
Antiquity, Jesus and the Land*, and *Jesus and the Jewish Festivals*

"One of the most important and groundbreaking projects over the past few decades has been the work of the Jesus Group of the Institute for Biblical Research. Unfortunately, their conclusions published in the massive tome are beyond the technical expertise of many readers. Darrell Bock has put the reading public in his debt by distilling this important work down to a clear, concise, and engaging format. *Who Is Jesus?* is a must read for pastors and laypeople alike—for anyone interested in the truth about the historical Jesus."

—Mark L. Strauss, professor of the New Testament, Bethel
Seminary, San Diego, and author of *Four Portraits, One Jesus*

"*Who Is Jesus?* is a treasure trove of easily accessible, first class scholarship—the outcome of one of the most thorough research projects on the Jesus of history to date. Clearer than other accounts, it focuses on the rules behind the scholarly quests for the historical Jesus, 'rules that were not made by the church, nor for the church.' The main events of Jesus' ministry are here scrutinized. It is the kind of popularly written book you want to put into the hands of students of all levels. The book reads like an open-ended dialogue, engaging the major players in the field, grappling with the questions of skepticism, and approaching these through a warm and open horizon of evangelical faith."

—Tomas Bokedal, lecturer in New Testament, King's College, University of Aberdeen, Scotland

"Anyone interested in finding out about the search for the historical Jesus will find wise guidance in this book. Darrell Bock has explained technical, academic discussions in clear, concise, and fair ways and made them accessible to a general audience. He shows why these discussions are so important, how decisions are made, and how the most important events in Jesus' life reveal his identity, his purpose, and his authority."

—Klyne Snodgrass, professor of New Testament Studies, North Park Theological Seminary, and author of *Stories With Intent*

"As co-chair with Darrell Bock of the IBR Jesus Group that produced the technical version of these essays, I am pleased to see how well Darrell has summarized the results of our work. He has captured the essence of these chapters and expressed them in such a way as to be easily understood by the nonspecialist and layperson. He has also shown how historical-Jesus research need not be a threat to a layperson's faith, but can rather enhance and inform it. This book is highly recommended for laypersons to better understand Jesus and how this field of research can expand their understanding."

—Robert Webb, co-chair of the IBR Jesus Group and editor of the *Journal for the Study of the Historical Jesus*

WHO IS JESUS?

LINKING THE HISTORICAL JESUS
WITH THE CHRIST OF FAITH

DARRELL L. BOCK

 HOWARD BOOKS
A DIVISION OF SIMON & SCHUSTER, INC.

NEW YORK   NASHVILLE   LONDON   TORONTO   SYDNEY   NEW DELHI

Howard Books
A Division of Simon & Schuster, Inc.
1230 Avenue of the Americas
New York, NY 10020

First Howard Books trade paperback edition September 2012

HOWARD and colophon are trademarks of Simon & Schuster, Inc.

For information about special discounts for bulk purchases,
please contact Simon & Schuster Special Sales at
1-866-506-1949 or business@simonandschuster.com.

The Simon & Schuster Speakers Bureau can bring authors to your
live event. For more information or to book an event contact the
Simon & Schuster Speakers Bureau at 1-866-248-3049 or
visit our website at www.simonspeakers.com.

Designed by Kyoko Watanabe

Manufactured in the United States of America

10 9 8 7 6 5 4 3 2 1

Library of Congress Cataloging-in-Publication Data
Bock, Darrell L.
    Who is Jesus? : linking the historical Jesus with the Christ of faith / Darrell L. Bock.
        p.   cm.
    Includes bibliographical references (p.).
    1. Jesus Christ—Historicity.   2. Jesus Christ—Person and offices.   I. Title.
    BT303.2.B535 2012
    232.9'08—dc23   2012001352
ISBN 978-1-4391-9068-5
ISBN 978-1-4391-9519-2 (ebook)

To my wife, Sally.
To my children and spouses:
Ray & Elisa Laird
Chris & Lara Stone
Stephen Bock
To my two grandsons:
Aidan & Toby Laird

May you always grow to appreciate
the link between the Jesus
of history and the Christ of
faith.

CONTENTS

WHO IS JESUS?

Jesus by the Rules

And the Rules Were Not Made by the Church

Y EARS AGO, one of my older siblings, a lawyer who loves history, was very skeptical about what we could know about Jesus. We would go back and forth in various settings. He would raise his questions. Why do accounts about the same event have differences? How can we really determine what took place? Like a good lawyer, he would press the issue. He would not let me get away with superficial answers. How could we really know how or why to take a detail seriously? Simply saying it was in the Bible was not an answer enough.

I would engage him and try to answer his questions, and we would try to sort out what we had heard from what we could believe. Because we had mutual respect for each other's views, we had a good conversation. But it was not easy. Sometimes there was the sense we were playing by different rules. I had a regard for Scripture. My brother had natural historical questions. And there were the many things he had read about and heard from people who taught at well-known schools who raised questions about some of the things I believed. Our conversation lasted many years—we would regularly resume it, picking up old threads of a previous conversation or sometimes taking up fresh questions based on the latest things we had heard.

Our conversation now spans decades. I have come to appreciate the questions he raises and how to think about discussing them. He has come to have a much higher appreciation for Jesus and what we can know about him as a matter of history. Together we have helped each other gain a deeper understanding of Jesus.

In part, this book is about that kind of conversation. How can we talk about Jesus in the public square? How can we talk about the Bible as it relates to this conversation, especially as a historical document and with people who question Scripture? How do Scripture and the person of Jesus fit with what many people think about history? Is there really a way for both sides, those who treat the Bible with some historical skepticism and those who treat the Bible as trustworthy, to have this conversation and have it go somewhere other than stalemate?

✦ ✦ ✦

The historical study of Jesus is controversial, complex, and captivating—controversial because of the array of conclusions made about him as a historical figure; complex because it involves working with ancient sources, a pre-modern culture, and claims about divine activity (never an easy topic for discussion); and captivating because whether a person embraces Jesus or not, no one can deny that his life has impacted our world, whether that impact is seen as positive or negative. But in order to talk about Jesus within popular culture, there has to be some common ground, some mutual agreement over what we can really know about Jesus and how we know it, or at least, how to have such a conversation when so many views about Jesus exist. This book starts in a place that says public conversation about Jesus can be profitable, even when we start where the church often does not—with skepticism.

Culture's Quest for Jesus

A key part of the public conversation about Jesus involves the historical study of Jesus. This is a study that plays by its own rules— rules that were not made by the church, nor for the church. To appreciate this part of the conversation and how it works, we need to know how the game is played. I will introduce those rules and their rationale shortly, but first we need to see where these rules came from and why.

The Beginning of "Quests" for Jesus

The quest for the historical Jesus, as it is often called, began when some said the church's portrait of Jesus was too covered over with later-formulated doctrine to tell us who Jesus really was. So skeptical people formed rules to challenge the church's take on Jesus. These rules come from a mixture of tools that Jesus historians regularly use in trying to confirm a historical event as well as issues that the nature of our sources about Jesus raises. In its earliest days, and even now, much historical study of Jesus served to challenge the church's confession of Jesus. Almost any Easter or Christmas we can see television shows or read news reports about findings that are supposed to change the way we have seen or should see Jesus.

Both people of faith and people who challenge faith sit at the table and debate who Jesus is and how we can know who he was. As you might expect, sometimes the discussion is heated. Can these diverse students of Jesus have a conversation without claiming that one has to accept all the church believes in order to discuss Jesus? That is part of what historical Jesus study attempts to do.

The wide array of views about Jesus can be confusing to many, whether secular or religious. A fresh take on that conversation—what it can and cannot achieve—is also what this book is about.

The Quests for Jesus and Lessing's Ditch: Is the Real Jesus Even Knowable?

The First Quest

The first quest for the historical Jesus reaches back into the late seventeenth century. Looking at differences in the texts and questioning whether the Bible was giving us history alone, scholars set out to distinguish between the real historical Jesus and what they called "the Christ of faith," a figure many of the originators said was not the real Jesus but a later construction of the early church. The initial discussion was rooted in a deep skepticism about what the Bible said about Jesus. The goal of getting us back to a truly historical Jesus often led to a moralist turn, with Jesus becoming one prophet among many the world has hosted. It became common to argue that there was a vast difference between the *Christ of faith* and the *Jesus of history*. This gap eventually became known as Lessing's ditch because the German enlightenment scholar Gotthold Ephraim Lessing (1729–1781) used the picture of a ditch to describe the difference between the two portraits. The portraits, the biblical one and the historical one, were that distinct.

Lessing's goal was to get back to Jesus as he was, not layered with later ideas about him. The claim was that the gospels really did not give us the real Jesus. He had to be rooted out of the sources through all kinds of historically based questions. No longer could a person simply say, "The Bible tells me so." Or if they did, there was a good chance that their claim would be dismissed as naïve or unscientific. Lessing's ditch not only argued for a gap between the Christ of faith and the Jesus of history; it also placed a huge space between people who sought to converse about who Jesus was and is.

Some said we could never cross Lessing's ditch. This was said most famously by Rudolf Bultmann (1884–1976), who argued that we could not get back to Jesus as he was.[1] For him and many others like him, "ditch" was too small a gap to adequately describe what Lessing claimed. It was more like a canyon. We cannot find the real Jesus, he argued, at least not in the gospel sources that present him. If Jesus is to be found, he has to be reconstructed historically.[2]

But not everyone was so completely skeptical; many tried to bridge the gap between the Christ of faith and the Jesus of history. These bridge builders argued there was a way to cross Lessing's ditch, and they have tried to construct a way through. Not all skepticism is strictly negative but can lead to good questions and fresh answers.

These discussions first started in the late seventeenth century when miracles began to come under serious challenge, differences between accounts of the same events were noted, and issues were raised about the claims of Jesus. There were no rules for judging the events of the scriptural accounts, just subjective judgments about what Jesus had likely done. The array of portraits led Albert Schweitzer in 1906 to publish a work on this phase of Jesus study and to critique it as far too subjective and detached from the original Jewish context of Jesus' work. He argued that the vast array of distinct Jesus portraits produced up until that time were methodologically flawed. Most agreed with Schweitzer's analysis of work done over a period of more than a century. His book and critique marked the end of this first period of the quest for the real Jesus. This initial period was in many ways the most skeptical.

The "No Quest" Period

Then came what is often called the "no quest" period, which spanned the first five decades of the twentieth century. In fact, this is a very poor name for the period, because a lot of writing was done about the historical Jesus during those years. What seemed to be missing, however, was any unified method of approach, any methodical way of engaging the issues. Each writer continued to see the Jesus he or she wanted to see and constructed him on the basis of what seemed best to the author. It was in this period that Rudolf Bultmann argued that we could know next to nothing about the historical Jesus. His influence is why some call this the "no quest" period. It was a period when many thought nothing could be gained by going down this path. Others disagreed and continued to work in this area.

The Second Quest

In 1953, the prevalent skepticism changed. One of Bultmann's students, Ernst Käsemann, who had become a professor himself, argued that we could know more about Jesus than his famous mentor had claimed. He argued for trying to separate later Greek strata from the original, more Hebrew/Aramaic layers of the tradition as a way in. He also argued that studying the development of the tradition as it told and retold given events could give clues as to what was more original. This area of study is known as Form Criticism. It argued that stories were passed on with a variety of certain kinds of structures (forms). Variations of the forms might yield clues as to what was original with the story and what was not. This historical use of Form Criticism was always a debated feature of its use. Vincent Taylor, an English scholar, wrote in the 1930s that as helpful as Form Criticism was as a literary tool to analyze the outline of a story, it was worthless as a historical tool, which is how the new (or "second quest") Jesus scholars wanted to use it. Nevertheless, it is in this period the rules began to emerge as a means of giving some structure to the effort and overcoming the criticism being leveled against Form Criticism.

As Käsemann was proposing a fresh look at Jesus study, new archaeological finds changed the map and understanding of the first-century religious environment of Jesus. The finds at Qumran on the Dead Sea known as the Dead Sea Scrolls surfaced between 1947 and 1956 but were slow in being published and even slower to be more fully evaluated. This library of texts came from a community that had separated from official Judaism and the temple, and had moved out into the desert in the mid–second century BCE (Before Common Era; used in place of BC) to await God's vindication on their behalf. They remained there until the Romans rolled through in the same war that led to the temple's destruction in 70 CE (Common Era; used in place of AD).

Eventually, scrolls were found in eleven different caves. Scholars have labeled these scrolls with the letter Q, preceded by a cave number and followed by a manuscript number, so they can be easily identified as ancient sources from Qumran. So, for example, 4Q174 is manuscript number 174 from cave 4 at Qumran. These manuscripts gave us unprecedented insight into Judaism of the period in the very locale where John the Baptist and Jesus also worked. The scrolls also began to undercut the idea that we could easily separate Greek ideas from Jewish ones, a key premise of the second quest. The reason was that this separatist Jewish sect— which was anti–Greek culture in attitude—had many expressions that had been thought to be a unique reflection of Greek culture.

Other means of evaluating the Jesus material needed to be found.

The Third Quest

With the publication of the scrolls, it became clear that Judaism was far more complex in the time of Jesus than had been previously appreciated. With these finds we now had more means by which to study the ancient beliefs. In addition, other older Jewish works became more accessible in English translation. As a result, scholars began to better appreciate how these works shaped discussions about the Hebrew Scriptures. Thus a new quest (often called the third quest) emerged in an effort to understand Jesus in the setting called Second Temple Judaism. This was the Judaism of which Jesus had been a part growing up. This Judaism, with its emerging diversity of views reflected in the Dead Sea finds and other ancient sources, was the theological context of his audience.

In 1945, yet another set of texts was found, at Nag Hammadi in Egypt. These texts, though containing later materials, included other gospel texts that described Jesus. Many of those other gospels that appear in TV specials and on the news came from this find. These texts also drew a lot of attention and added to the discussions about Jesus and how others saw him in the earliest centuries. They were generally not as important to the development of the third quest, but have come to have a role in reflection about Jesus as the quest progressed. Their discovery added to the complexity of the conversation. Now there were many different kinds of Jesus to discuss based on the ancient sources.

Such dramatic new finds propelled the third quest. It began to emerge in the 1960s, especially as the Dead Sea Scrolls came to be appreciated more and more. By the 1980s, some scholars were writing from a third-quest viewpoint and challenging the second-quest approach. Unlike the second questers, they did not start by trying to peel away at the texts of the gospels, but by trying to understand the historical setting in which Jesus lived. This meant playing not only with an eye to the rules but also to a cohesive presentation of Jesus that fit into this emerging background of what was happening in the first century. Third-quest scholars began to ask how Jesus' actions and teachings would be understood and whether they could fit together well in such a setting. This reversal of the starting point also went back to a premise Albert Schweitzer had stated: if you are to understand Jesus, it must be out of his Jewish environment and the audience he challenged.

This book reflects a third-quest approach. It argues that a person of faith can sit at the table with people who abide by historical Jesus study rules and still have a conversation about who Jesus was. This can be done without forcing people to accept at the start of the conversation everything many believers hold. The third-quest approach argues you can play the game by these rules and still move toward a better historical understanding of Jesus that also explains the faith of his earliest followers.

You can cross the canyon.

You can even show how it can be done, tracing the steps to get there. Doing so does not absolutely prove who Jesus was. There is too much judgment in the process for that. However, it does argue that a strong case can be made for appreciating who Jesus was through the sources we have.

THE STUDY THAT STANDS BEHIND THIS BOOK

Over the period of a decade (1998–2008), an international group of Jesus scholars met for one weekend each summer to take a close look at twelve core events in the life of Jesus. (One could make a longer or shorter list, but the twelve the group chose were events we regarded as significant and corroborated as likely to have occurred for reasons I shall show.) We met in such varied locales as Chicago, Dallas, Tübingen, and Jerusalem. The final meeting in Jerusalem was to wrap up our work and to produce eight thirty-minute TV shows on our study for Day of Discovery. In any year, we had six to eight scholars present out of the entire pool of fifteen participants. I organized and co-chaired this fresh look at Jesus "by the rules" with Robert Webb. Robert has taught at various schools in Canada and is the editor of the *Journal for the Study of the Historical Jesus*, published out of Sheffield, England. Eleven of the group wrote essays. All the participants were members of the international OT-NT scholarly organization known as the Institute for Biblical Research (IBR), which meets annually each November at the Society of Biblical Literature meetings held in the United States.

We were known as the IBR Jesus Group. Each participant had already written an internationally recognized, full technical study on Jesus. By "technical," I mean that all the ancient data and debate about events that come from the study of Jesus is laid out for the reader. The initial study was more than 800 pages long. In the end, we argued that a person can play by many of these historical rules and still appreciate that the gist of these events has been faithfully rendered to us in our earliest sources.[3] By "gist," we mean that despite the variety in the details among the various accounts, we can affirm that the core event is reflective of what took place. You can get a good glimpse of Jesus, even if you start by asking more skeptical questions.

This result is surprising in a world where often playing by the rules results in a very deconstructed Jesus and a skeptical take on the sources. The conclusion is that very careful and detailed study shows that the historical Jesus and the Christ of faith are not as disconnected as Lessing and many others have claimed.

WHY THIS BOOK?

Our Goal

Who Is Jesus? is meant to be an accessible treatment of the results of our technical study.[4] The world of historical Jesus studies is fascinatingly complex, and my purpose is to disclose the roots of the debates that swirl around whether or not we can know who he was, as well as offer twelve events well known to those who believe in Christ that can be considered authentic to the historical Jesus.[5]

Most historical Jesus studies argue that there is a chasm between the Jesus of history and the Christ of faith. Depending on who does the study, that chasm is either crossable or not. For some, the gap's nature makes crossing it difficult at best. Others cross it with more confidence and land in various places regarding Jesus. According to these studies, Jesus may be a moral teacher, a prophet, a misguided leader, the messiah, or in some sense the Son of God.

Historians and Jesus scholars all have their own conclusions on which events recorded in the gospels are truly historical. Such a diversity of results about what we can say about Jesus leaves many people asking: How do people negotiate their way through such a variety of conclusions from a wide array of experts? If experts who give their academic lives to study this cannot agree, what does that mean for the rest of us?

My hope is to take you on a historically rooted journey that explains the rules by which most scholars play the historical Jesus game, along with explaining how the conversation works. Then I will argue that we can get a solid glimpse of the historical Jesus and the Christ of faith. Using the same rules many historical Jesus scholars work with, we can determine how Jesus saw his mission. The trip involves a careful look at the world Jesus lived in—dealing with the history, customs, cultural clues, and archaeology that inform what Jesus was about. We cite many texts (some familiar, others less so) to illuminate the background and context of what Jesus said and did. We try to paint the canvas of what the world was like and how they saw things in Jesus' time by actually introducing you to ancient texts that describe what some in Jesus' time thought about certain issues.

The Key to the Rules: Looking for Corroboration and Examining the Historical Environment

By examining Jesus this way, we make the case—not using rules of the church, but rules rooted in a much more skeptical approach to Jesus. These rules argue that we cannot speak without corroboration. This means that most of the gospel of John is not usable, since a great majority of it is singularly attested, as well as half of Luke and a quarter of Matthew. (This rule shows nicely that the church is not responsible for these stipulations.)

And, as we proceed through the events, you will see many references to Jewish texts outside of the Old Testament as reflective of the values of this third quest. We shall name the works, identify the passages, and even cite a few texts so the point of background is clear. What you will hear are the many different voices in the Judaism of Jesus' time speaking. This material provides a way to see what Jesus might have been getting at with his Jewish audience. The Jesus Seminar in the '90s worked more out of a Greek background, reflecting the second quest. Our decade-long study worked from premises of the third quest. But both quests play by the rules.

The bar we have to cross for historical Jesus study is a high one. We have to think like a prosecutor making a case in court. There might be DNA from the scene, but is it relevant DNA, contaminated DNA, or DNA from another time and place? Historical Jesus study pulls us into such deliberation of the evidence. But before we look at the evidence, we begin our quest with a look at the rules. I invite you to pull up a chair and engage in the conversation—just like my brother and I have—and discover how fascinating historical Jesus discussion can be.

I

The Rules:

Getting Ready to Play

RULES MAKE a difference. They determine what can and cannot work in a game. Just take soccer and football. In one of the
great ironies in American sports, soccer (appropriately called
football in most of the world) allows use of the feet but not the
hands; while American football hardly uses the feet at all in rela-
tion to possession of the ball. The difference involves the rules of
the two games.

So also in Jesus studies, there are rules that apply in order to
make a corroborative case for the historicity of the accounts and,
as a result, to understand what Jesus said and did. These rules
are technically called the "criteria for authenticity." [1] They test
whether we can show a text to have its roots authentically in the
actual events in Jesus' life. Where the church allows the gospel
texts to stand as witnesses for Jesus without such corroboration
(because these texts are included in the canon that makes up
Scripture), in historical Jesus studies, we have to make a historical
case for any event or saying that is tied to Jesus. Like soccer and
football, different rules make for a different game: the church uses
faith, and historical Jesus studies use *corroboration*.

Theological vs. Historical

One of the earliest rules involved setting aside claims or qualifying claims of divine activity for what was called a more rational approach to Jesus. Rather than working from heaven or through a claim about divine revelation to get the story, one worked from the earth. This was done in three ways.

First, some said we cannot speak of God at all as a historical matter, but that speaking of him is a theological matter—and theology is different from history. Since divine activity cannot be validated, it must be left off the table of history. The most skeptical form of this view argues that God is a human construct or that history and God have nothing to do with each other. In this most radical form, little conversation is possible. Wherever God is said to act, something else is going on, not divine activity.

A *second* approach argues that history and theology are distinct, but both address distinct realities within events. Historians address only what humans *do* and can show only what humans did. If God is to be included, it has to be understood as a matter of faith and is theology, not history. This second view contends that history has limitations and that God is real; so whenever God is addressed, we have moved from discussing history to treating theology. Think of this view as erecting a kind of secular wall in the discussion of history. Those who hold to it argue that history is not equipped to make theological judgments.

However, there is a *third* view that contends that a person must still be open to God and the possibility of his working in history. You may not be able to *prove* absolutely that God acted, but the historical work shows that the most likely explanation for an event is that God acted as claimed by some involved in the event. Even if absolute proof of divine activity cannot be established, a case can be made for the likelihood of events rooted in divine activity.

In the origins of the historical approach to Jesus, rationalism becomes the key over any form of theism. Our mind and its judgment become the key arbiters in the game. This is where understanding the rules and the nature of the game is important. The church in general does not handle this topic as historical Jesus scholars do. In the church, *faith* relies on God's guidance and inspiration when it comes to the gospels, both the writing and canonization. But in this particular kind of historical discussion, claims of divine activity are ruled out, or bracketed off to the side. A case has to be constructed for the claim of divine activity, so we have to rely on the historian's toolbox, that is, *corroboration*.

CORROBORATIVE SUPPORT REQUIRED

Historical Jesus study requires corroborative support and validation for claims. This means that singularly attested materials are largely set aside (even though they might contain real information about Jesus). "Singularly attested material" means accounts that are told from only a single source, even if others used that source. There are complicated ways singularly attested material can be brought in at a later stage of study, but for the most part, much of what is uniquely attested is set aside for lack of corroboration. Lack of corroboration simply means that there is no confirmation that what these single sources attest is true or not. This is a key limitation of the corroborative process because it can well be the case that a singularly attested event took place. One just cannot corroborate that it did.

This chapter seeks to explain the rules that we shall be applying to the twelve key events we study in subsequent chapters. These are the rules most historical Jesus scholars use.

Rule 1: Multiple Attestation of Sources

At the core of technical gospels study are the sources that one argues stand behind the gospels. Luke 1:1–2 tells us about traditions, oral and written, that he was aware of as he wrote his gospel. Verse 1 speaks of written materials, while verse 2 describes those who as eyewitnesses and ministers of the Word verbally passed on material about Jesus. Scholars refer to these kinds of sources in doing their work. There are written sources and oral traditional materials. These traditions are said to come from eyewitnesses. That is important, but in historical Jesus discussion, the credibility of that source, even if it is early, has to be established. The claim alone is not enough.

The First Source—Mark

Although scholars debate the exact order of the writing of the gospels (as is the case with many matters in scholarly discussion), most Jesus scholars see Mark as the first one written. They name his work as one of the sources, if not the key source, for understanding the historical Jesus. Almost all of Mark is also found in Matthew or Luke. More than that, the other gospels follow an outline of events very parallel to Mark. These facts point to Mark's importance. So Mark is our first key source.

The Second Source—Q

The second source commonly appealed to is called Q. This single letter stands for the term *source*, because the German word for "source," *Quelle*, begins with the letter Q. This source is hypothesized (posited as likely) because some 220 verses of Jesus' teaching are shared between Matthew and Luke—almost 20 percent of each of these gospels. Most scholars believe that Matthew and

Luke did not use each other in writing their gospels. For example, the accounts of Jesus' birth are quite different in the two gospels. Matthew's Sermon on the Mount (Matthew 5–7) differs significantly from Luke's Sermon on the Plain (Luke 6:20–49). Matthew has five key discourse units, but Luke lacks some of these.

The accounts about Jesus' appearance after the resurrection differ in their locale, with Luke highlighting Jerusalem and Matthew, Galilee. So the theory goes, if Luke did not use Matthew and vice versa, where did those 220 verses come from? The argument is they shared a circulating traditional source of some type, which has never been found, that had similar teaching in it. The idea is that something has to explain the size of this agreement and overlap, even if we have never found such a written source.

In calling Q a source, we are not committing to the idea that Q is only a written source, a source reflective of oral tradition, or a mixture of the two. Variations on all of these positions exist when it comes to Q. The point is only that Matthew and Luke share a strand of tradition that circulated in the church without having used each other. So Q becomes the second source.

Other Sources

Material unique to Luke becomes our third key source. It is often called simply L. Material unique to Matthew is the fourth source. It is called M.

John's gospel counts as a source; but as we noted in the last chapter, most of its material is unique and so it is not frequently used as evidence because it cannot be easily corroborated. In the view of many, the best we can do is to use John carefully as it might lend support to what is also present elsewhere. Others will use John more extensively and bring in other types of arguments beyond corroboration to utilize what it presents. Material from Paul's letters or from one of the other New Testament epistles can also count as a source, but it is rare that specific events of the gospels also appear here. (These are usually very limited references to the Last Supper, transfiguration, crucifixion, and resurrection.)

Potentially, other materials, such as other gospels outside the Bible, can be counted as sources when there is reason to believe the materials might go back to the events of the authentic Jesus. However, this historical link often is quite disputed, because the pedigree of these extrabiblical gospels in going back to the earliest apostolic circles is even less clear than with the biblical gospels, whose apostolic roots are also often discussed. So these extrabiblical materials are used only in a limited way in historical Jesus study.

Rarer still, but able to count as well, is testimony from near contemporary non-Christian sources, such as the first-century Jewish historian Josephus, or the early second-century Roman historians Suetonius and Tacitus, who together testify multiple times to the fact that Jesus lived in first-century Galilee and died at the hands of Rome (see discussion in rule 5 below). But for most scholars, the key sources used for historical Jesus studies are four: Mark, Q, L, and M.[2]

Multiple attestation argues that if a saying, teaching, or theme is attested in multiple sources, then it has a better chance of being authentic, that is, of going back to authentic events in the life of Jesus. Note how the rule guides a historian's judgment about an event. A historian cannot say outright that this event took place, nor does this prove all the details. This kind of history does not work that way. It makes judgments about events and their relationships based on how it views the sources that describe those events. The rationale here is that the more widely distributed an idea is across the independent levels of the tradition, the more likely it is to be old and reflective of actual events. The independence of the sources from one another means that no one of them created this event, but rather the event stands attested across distinct pieces of the tradition and is older than a given source.

Multiple attestation is one of the most important of the rules, since it is most obviously connected to the idea of corroboration. We will see it applied to many of the events we'll consider, but a straightforward example involves the words of Jesus at the Last Supper, which are attested in their gist in distinct versions in Mark (Mark 14:22–25) and by Paul (1 Corinthians 11:23–26). These constitute multiple sources for the reporting of this event. Within these multiple sources, there are two versions of the wording. Matthew's version is like that in Mark, and Luke's is like that in Paul, but these only count as two source streams despite the repetition in four texts. (Remember we are not counting how many passages the material appears in, but how many distinct source strands attest to it.)

RULE 2: MULTIPLE ATTESTATION OF FORMS

This rule is a variation on multiple attestation. Here the issue is not sources but the literary shape of the story or saying, which is known as a *form* in scholarly study. Forms include miracle stories, discourse teaching ranging from proverbs to parables, pronouncement accounts (where the key goal in telling the account is presenting a saying at the end of the account called the pronouncement), and stories designed to elevate the stature of Jesus. When a theme or event shows up in multiple forms, then it again is seen to be widespread in the tradition and thus more likely to go back to Jesus. We use this rule when verifying Jesus' association with tax collectors and sinners—a theme that appears in discourses, miracles, and pronouncements.

RULE 3: VARIOUS FORMS OF DISSIMILARITY

The next rule is more radical in its approach, so radical that variations on it have emerged. Dissimilarity argues that if a saying or event corresponds neither to the Judaism of the time (called Second Temple Judaism) nor to the early church, it is likely to go back to Jesus. The early church is seen as referring to the beliefs of the first few generations of the faith (say, up to approximately 100 CE, the date most take to be the latest for the writing of any of the gospels).

Sometimes this criterion is called double dissimilarity because the case for authenticity is said to apply only when the Jesus element is distinct from *both* Second Temple Judaism and the early church. The logic is that neither Judaism nor the early church can be responsible for this material since there is no match with either. This makes sense, but it turns out that very little material makes it through both ends of this sieve. These dissimilar elements may end up presenting to us the *unique* Jesus, but much of what Jesus did also had connections either to the diverse beliefs within first-century Judaism or to the early church, if not to both settings. Jesus could not have been so detached from his cultural and religious context that much of what he said was unrelated to it. This is why this rule is seen as so radical. The point reminds us that failure to meet a criterion is not necessarily evidence that something *did not take place*. Failure to meet a criterion simply means *that way of seeking corroboration is not attained*.

Some scholars have reworked the rule in an effort to make it more realistic to Jesus' participation in a first-century setting. The most common of these reformulations argues that if an account has distinctive elements from both Judaism and early Christianity and yet looks like something that forms a bridge between them, then that is likely to be authentic. This has been called either "double similarity/dissimilarity" or the "continuum approach." Here the logic is that we can see a line between where we start with an idea and where we end up. Jesus is seen as the middle figure in the movement.

Double dissimilarity can be used to corroborate Jesus' saying to allow the dead to bury the dead. Both Judaism and the early church continued to bury people, and even though Jesus' remark is seen as hyperbolic, it is seen as something stated so powerfully against the normal cultural grain that it goes back uniquely to him. The continuum approach could be used to corroborate Jesus' parable of the prodigal son, which although singularly attested, portrays the return of the unfaithful in Israel in a way Judaism would not espouse—as we find represented in the resentment of the elder son, who might reflect the attitude of the Pharisees.

RULE 4: EMBARRASSMENT

This next rule is also important because it argues that the church would not have created certain stories, because they have an element of embarrassment to them that would not have been a created or made-up detail. The embarrassing point in the story would ring true because it was a real part of the event. In such cases, it is usually either Jesus or major early church figures who are presented in an unfavorable light.

A simple example is the very fact of Jesus' crucifixion, which requires he be seen as some type of criminal in order to have faced such an execution. Another example is the existence of Judas and his betrayal as one of the Twelve whom Jesus chose. The embarrassing feature here is that Jesus is seen normally as making good choices. In a sense this is a negative criterion because it says the church would never have made this one up, so it must have happened.

RULE 5: CRITERION OF REJECTION AND EXECUTION

Events that explain how Jesus was rejected by Jewish authorities and crucified by the Romans are likely to be authentic. One of the best-attested events in Jesus' life is his crucifixion. Even the Roman historians Tacitus (*Annals* 15.44) and Suetonius (*Claudius* 25.4) attest to Rome's execution of Jesus, as does the first-century Jewish historian Josephus (*Antiquities* 18.63–64). So how did we get to such a death? Many scholars believe Jesus' act in the temple is said to meet this criterion.

✦   ✦   ✦

These are the key rules, but others exist to supplement them. They are not as highly regarded in helping make judgments, but are sometimes applied here and there, especially as supportive reasons for authenticity.

RULE 6: COHERENCE

This rule argues that anything that coheres with or is consistent with material judged as authentic on the basis of the key rules is also a good candidate for authenticity. The weakness of this rule is that a judgment on consistency involves a good measure of subjectivity, depending on the interpreter. However, it is a rule that may allow a singularly attested element to be accepted.

RULE 7: ARAMAIC OR HEBREW TRACES

This rule argues that material that reflects Aramaic roots may point to authenticity. The logic here is that Jesus likely spoke Aramaic as his primary language. However, the gospels come to us in Greek. So if we find traces of Aramaic (or even Hebrew, its linguistic cousin) within a tradition dominated by Greek, then we can know something has been translated and could well go back to Jesus. The problem here is that Aramaic is also the language of Jesus' earliest followers. So it is not a given that if something has

Aramaic traces it must be rooted in what Jesus said. So often it is the case that this rule does not work on its own, but is tied to another rule to strengthen the case for authenticity.

RULE 8: PALESTINIAN ENVIRONMENT

This rule argues that if something fits the customs and life of first-century Palestine, then it is likely to be authentic. However, this rule is like the last one. Jesus' followers also lived in this environment, so accounts from them could just reflect the general life of the time and not be distinctive in pointing to Jesus. So this rule, when it is applied, is often used to supplement other rules.

RULE 9: INHERENT AMBIGUITY

This rule argues that the early church would have been explicit about who Jesus was or what he did, so if it invented a statement or event about Jesus, it would be clear, not ambiguous. If, however, a statement or an event has inherent ambiguity within its meaning, then it is less likely to have been made up by the church. In other words, the church was more likely to be clear than ambiguous in its affirmation of Jesus. This less-well-known rule is one we will appeal to often, as we will see when we get to Peter's confession at Caesarea Philippi and when we discuss the story of Jesus arriving in Jerusalem. This was a rule our group formulated as a part of its work, since in many of the events we will cover, the presentation of who Jesus is was more implicit than explicit. If a person were to argue that the event was created by the early church to declare clearly who Jesus was, then such a claim would not be ambiguous. So ambiguity points to authenticity.

Rule 10: Historical-Cultural Plausibility

This criterion argues that what is authentic must fit into a Second Temple Jewish setting of the early first century and yet show an influence on the early church not entirely in line with the church's major tendencies. This rule is close to the continuum approach we saw earlier under dissimilarity. Jesus' ministry focused on Jews in Israel, and the general lack of overt outreach to Gentiles fits this rule. The activity fits Jewish concerns and the context out of which Jesus emerged, yet it does not line up with the church's later clear emphasis on its Gentile mission.

The Rules as a Group

As was already suggested, these rules are not ironclad. Meeting one or a few of them does not guarantee the general acceptance of a piece of Jesus material as authentic. They serve more as guides; the more rules that apply to a saying or event, the stronger the case for corroboration.

However, these rules and their logic are so debated among scholars that some doubt whether any work based on the rules takes us anywhere. Such doubt can come from conservatives, who do not like any questioning of the gospel tradition, or from those more liberal, who doubt such rules are really clear guides. So this way of discussing the historical Jesus is not unanimous in its acceptance, in part because the rules are not perfect guides by any means.

The problem is that without such rules, making judgments about the material can become either a complete matter of faith or an exercise in complete subjectivity. How else can we begin to make a case for or against a saying or event unless we have some set of standards with which to weigh it? We would be forced to choose faith or personal preference. The advantage, then, of some rules to work with is that a case for corroboration can be made without appeal to purely theological claims (even though theological claims are sometimes valid), which opens up the possibility of conversation with someone whose theological convictions may differ from our own. The rules also serve as a check on the whim of the interpreter about what he or she may think Jesus is likely to have done or about what the church is likely to have created. So although we can see that the rules involve judgment and are neither ironclad nor comprehensive in their logic, they can be useful.

CONCLUSION ON RULES

So these ten rules are the ones many Jesus scholars use. As you can see, there are many judgments involved in what sayings and events can show and how these rules apply. The only way to really see how the game is played and how the conversation proceeds is to look at specific events, apply the rules to them, and see how the rules work. So we approach our core task with these rules in hand. We shall look at a dozen key events, apply these criteria, and see what we may be able to learn about Jesus by looking at things through this particular lens. We begin with John the Baptist and his association with Jesus.

2

John the Baptist:

Washings, a Prophet, and Jesus

Our survey of events will proceed in a fixed structure:

1. We begin each event by considering if any rules would open the door for seeing the core of the event as authentic.
2. Then we examine the common objections raised about the event. Often in looking at the objections, key issues of background and the cultural context will surface.
3. Next we shall consider how the relevant background opens up the event and what it means for understanding Jesus.

Our effort will be a little like putting together a puzzle—each event will yield a piece contributing to the portrait.

We start with John the Baptist and the baptism he called Israel to experience.[1] There are two parts to this event: John's ministry of baptism and the report of heavenly remarks to Jesus. We consider each part separately. First, let us consider the case for John baptizing Jesus and why such washings matter.

The Rules That Apply to the Baptism

Multiple Attestation

John's baptism of Jesus is multiply attested. First, Mark 1:9–11 describes the baptism, and it is usually agreed that Matthew 3:13–17 and Luke 3:21–22 are taken from Mark's account. So this is one source. (The exchange between Jesus and John before the baptism in Matthew is singularly attested, so it does not possess the corroboration the act of baptism does.) Also suggestive of a baptism, although not presenting it, is Q. Texts in Matthew and Luke show John preaching repentance and discussing a stronger one to come (Q: Luke 3:7–9, 16–17 = Matthew 3:7–10, 11–12). This text also seems to presuppose a meeting between the two. John is seen as pointing to someone else. Why narrate a tradition pointing to someone unless there was an encounter or anticipation of such a one? That is, why would the gospel writers mention John's preaching and the prophesying of one to come, unless they had met at some point? This point, however, is not a given. When an encounter becomes multiply attested in yet another text, then the case becomes stronger. So we turn to a third text and source.

John 1:29–34 also points to an encounter, although it also does not narrate the specific baptism event. Instead, John's gospel notes that John the Baptist pointed to the one to come when John saw the Spirit residing on Jesus as an indication that he was God's chosen one. John serves here as a witness to Jesus. When we use the gospel of John in this way, we are agreeing with most scholars today that John's gospel is independent of the Synoptics, even if he is aware of elements of the Jesus story that Matthew, Mark, and Luke tell. Interestingly, the Baptist's act on behalf of Jesus also appears in the extrabiblical *Gospel to the Hebrews,* as reported in Jerome's discussion of a fragment from that text (Jerome, *Commentary on Isa* 11:2).[2] It attests to the coming of the Spirit tied to the heavenly response, but in ways that point to sources beyond those gospels.

Adding all of this together, we have witnesses from Mark, John, and the *Gospel of the Hebrews*, plus a likely allusion to the event from Q. However, of these texts, only Mark's version gives us a description of the event of baptism. So four sources point to the event, but only one source describes it.

Embarrassment

Multiple attestation is not the only rule that speaks to the authenticity of Jesus' baptism—we can also consider the criterion of embarrassment. Why would Jesus submit to a baptism *by John* and *for sin*? The early church believed Jesus was sinless, and the submission to John's baptism might make it look like Jesus is a lesser figure than John, needing something from John's ministry. As the last note indicated, the *Gospel of the Nazareans* had Jesus refuse to be baptized. Matthew also has a brief discussion pointing to the sense that something is not quite right because John initially refuses to baptize Jesus. To deal with that tension, Jesus tells John to baptize him for the sake of righteousness. The gospel of John also shows some signs of handling this issue delicately by focusing on John's witness of the heavenly response to Jesus versus pointing to the baptism itself (John 1:29–34). So John's baptism of Jesus shows up but often in ways that provide some distance between John and Jesus. This rule says the church would not make that event up and put Jesus in a position that might make him look inferior to John. If this event never happened (as some skeptics claim), then why put Jesus in such a position?

OBJECTIONS

Despite the above considerations, objections to whether John ever baptized or met Jesus do exist.[3] *First,* some argue that there is a movement between the sources that diminishes John's role. This is said to raise a question about the event. *Second,* objectors argue that the description of John's baptism in the first-century Jewish historian Josephus does not have the same thrust as the gospels' description (*Antiquities* 18.117)[4]—Josephus discusses John as one who called Israel to virtue and presents the baptism as a washing for purification. *Third,* there is evidence that followers of John the Baptist continued to exist in the period after Jesus (Acts 19), which some argue wouldn't have happened if John met Jesus and pointed to him.

To our group, these objections argue for too much. On the first point, the discussion and variety of details about what John's relationship to Jesus was—witness or baptizer—does not point to a non-meeting. Rather, it suggests an encounter that needs to be explained. That writers choose to highlight one idea or another does not deny the presence of an event, but speaks to the variety of ways in which it was understood.

On the second point, Josephus' mention of virtue and baptism is simply putting Jewish practice in Greek philosophical terms for his non-Jewish audience. That Josephus makes no mention of a John-Jesus connection is not surprising, because Josephus is writing to the Romans and wants to minimize any sources of rebellion against Rome, limiting the blame to religious Zealots who clearly acted against the empire. The Zealots' violent attitude is something neither John nor Jesus advocated. Josephus was living in the emperor's home and was trying to explain to the Romans that not all Jews caused Rome's problems with Israel, but only a select few.

The third objection does make an explicit identification by John of Jesus seem more problematic. However, it ignores a later text involving John (Q: Matthew 11:26 = Luke 7:18–23), where John asks for assurance that Jesus is the one to come, expressing doubt as John sits in prison. The question is a natural one, since Jesus hardly brought the note of victory John had anticipated would come with the one he had pointed to as God's hope. This text pointing to the Baptist's doubt also fits the criteria of embarrassment. It makes John look like a doubter and Jesus' ministry look like it was not what it should be in this prophet's mind. Would the early church make up that tension? It also assumes there was a time when John made an identification of Jesus as God's chosen one. However, near the end of his life, John is now questioning the identification, possibly because the style of Jesus' ministry did not entirely match what John had expected. If John could question whether Jesus was the one, perhaps some of John's followers came to the conclusion that Jesus had not brought what John (and they) had anticipated. Jesus' answer urges John to again embrace the identification and reassures him, but others may not have been so inclined.

These objections do not seem so formidable as to preclude a meeting with John and a baptism by him that also generated much explanation.

THE EVENT AND WHAT IT MEANS

John is known as the Baptist, or "the one who baptized," for a reason. A citation from the Jewish historian Josephus tells us in *Antiquities* 18.117 that John "exhorted the Jews to practice virtue and act with justice toward one another and with piety toward God, and so to gather together by baptism." John was calling on people to share in a corporate act of cleansing before God. Josephus then becomes a witness to John's activity and helps secure this event as one of the most certain things we know about Jesus' preparation for ministry.

The act of washing is related to rites of purity. Though common in ancient religions, such washings are not common today. In first-century Judaism, there were several types of washing. Leviticus 14–15 describes a series of various washings the Law called Jews to perform. Why washings were required is noted below. Of course, some Jews were more "Law observant" than others. This is why different groups existed within Judaism: from the Pharisees, who strictly observed the Law and built traditions around it, to Sadducees, who did not add to the Law with traditions, to those at Qumran, who were also very strict in observing the Law and adding to it. Still other Jews were less scrupulous in observing such acts, but *everyone* knew such washings were to be done and what they meant.

The Purpose of Washings

A Law-abiding Jew washed hands as a way of removing uncleanness that was seen to taint what he touched and render him unsuitable as a person to draw near to God. Being unclean was another way of saying "common," that is, not appropriately set apart and prepared to see God. This is different than washing simply for hygiene. A person immersed the body in a washing to remove ritual uncleanness just as he washed another's feet as a sign of respect. So these washings were an appropriate preparation to see God. Since we are at the Jordan River (Mark 1:5, 9–10), John's washing involved an immersion.

In Judaism, for a washing to count, the water had to be "living," that is, it had to be flowing (Leviticus 14:5–6, 50–52). The Greek word for *baptized* actually means "to dip," like one colors cloth by dipping it in dye. Our English word *baptism* is simply a transliteration of the Greek term.

John's Baptism

What John was doing, however, was a new kind of washing, not previously prescribed in the Scripture the Hebrews followed. It was a onetime washing that signified a person's readiness for God to come in final deliverance. In this way, it differed from the washings prescribed in Leviticus in preparation for the temple or the washings that involved Gentiles developed later, to signify that non-Jews were ready to enter covenantal relationship to Israel's God. This was a new rite for an approaching new era, taking place completely removed from the temple.

Our sources tell us several things about John's baptism.

First, it was about repentance.[5] This suggests that in John's view the people were not walking properly with God. Such a view would not have been uncommon, because the Jews would have believed, as is written in Deuteronomy 28–32, that the reason Rome—or any foreign nation—was in the land was because of the sin of the people of Israel.

Second, it led into forgiveness. Mark 1:4 (= Luke 3:3) calls it a "baptism of repentance" and links it to "forgiveness of sins." Now, older Judaism associated sin and repentance (Isaiah 55:7) but did not necessarily tie a response to a specific rite or washing. The newer thing in Judaism was to tie this all to a washing. At the Dead Sea community at Qumran, located farther south down the Jordan River from where John was baptizing, purification was tied to a washed heart, required for the washing to truly count (1QS 3:6–9). 1QS is an ancient text that gives rules about how this Qumran community lived together. Where normally it had been a sacrifice that accompanied a turning back to God, now some in Judaism were arguing such a turn should require a washing. Verses 8–9 read, "Through an upright and humble attitude his sin may be covered, and by humbling himself before all God's laws his flesh can be made clean. Only thus can he really receive the purifying waters and be purged by the cleansing flow." Since those who lived at Qumran no longer attended rites at the temple, this substituted for the role of sacrifices made in Jerusalem. Usually it was sacrifices, not washings, that were the rites more commonly tied to seeking forgiveness. Although new, the tie of washing to cleansing was clear to all Jews.

Third, the rite made one ritually clean. Ritual cleanliness was required to meet God in an acceptable manner. Being *unclean* was distinct from being *in sin*, though there is some overlap, since sexual immorality made one unclean (Leviticus 18) and was also a sin. But a person could be unclean from having a flow of blood, the wrong kind of bodily emission (Leviticus 15), touching a corpse (Numbers 19), or touching other unclean things. The unclean person was not able to go to the temple until they had been washed and made ritually clean. Again, hygiene had nothing to do with this washing; it was a spiritual act.[6]

Fourth, John pointed to the era to come, as well as to the deliverer, by calling for this washing (Q: Matthew 3:11 = Luke 3:16; Mark 1:8; John 1:26–27). Pointing to this era also involved pointing to the deliverance tied to it and the hope of a delivering figure. This makes the washing eschatological—John is invoking the end times by pointing to this deliverance. This was more than John declaring that God was coming in final deliverance, because he compares himself with this figure, saying he is not worthy to untie the thong of his sandal (Mark 1:7; Q: Matthew 3:11 = Luke 3:16). This is an important remark. John was seen as a prophetic figure, one high on the religious vocational ladder. Yet in all his glory, this prophet was not worthy of this act—which was something Hebrew slaves were told not to do for masters because untying the sandal was seen as too demeaning (*Mekilta*, *Nezekin* 1 on Exodus 21:2).[7] John's remark suggests that the greatness of the one to come is of another order. Even a prophet is not worthy enough to do a demeaning act of a slave in comparison with him. When John doubts later in life, he asks if Jesus is the one to come, pointing to the expectation of a great and powerful delivering figure (Q: Matthew 11:3 = Luke 7:19). Note how the theme of this point about not being worthy is multiply attested.

The reference to the coming baptism by the Spirit and fire is important as well. It points to a "purging" of people—some are gathered like wheat for storage; others are burned. This is the Spirit doing a work of judgment and restoration/preservation, which fits with Jewish expectations of the end, when a final judgment separates the righteous and unrighteous (Daniel 12:2; *1 Enoch* 95–100).

Fifth, those who partook in this baptism were saying they were ready to be identified with God's people. A person did not engage in this baptism merely for his own personal salvation, but to join others who shared this eschatological hope and expectation. To share in John's baptism is to say, "We are ready for you to come and deliver us, God. We stand together in hope and expectation."

All that John did here took place away from and outside the temple in Jerusalem. Miles away, at the Jordan River, he acted independently of the priests who gave sacrifices for the nation and helped with some forms of cleansing. Those priests had nothing to do with what John was doing. They did not authorize him to do it. He did not ask them. This independence is part of what made John a prophet in people's eyes. His program came from God. My colleague Robert Webb published a full dissertation on John the Baptist, describing John as a "leadership popular prophet" because he formed a movement.[8] His baptism pointed to a prepared people. Josephus tells us it caused Herod Antipas to worry about John's social influence.

Jesus Accepts John's Baptism

All of this is important to what it means when Jesus accepts baptism from John. When Jesus partakes in John's baptismal rite, Jesus is accepting for people the key points and direction that John proclaims, including the call for accountability to God, in a new era and powerful figure. Jesus' act of being baptized by John endorses John's ministry and what it represents. This is backwards from the way people of faith normally think of the association between John and Jesus. Normally we think of John endorsing Jesus—after all, that is what we read from Mark, Q, and John, but it is important to recognize the reverse is also true. Everything John's message offered was preparatory to what Jesus would offer. Everything John stood for was affirmed by Jesus when he shared in the rite that stood at the hub of John's ministry.

There is another reason this is so important. Some historical Jesus scholars want to argue there are two strands in the Jesus tradition—a wisdom element and an eschatological-apocalyptic element. In the wisdom strand, Jesus tells us how to live before God like a prophet exhorts people or as proverbs teach. In the eschatological-apocalyptic strand, Jesus serves as part of the delivering drama himself as he reveals how God will defeat evil and hidden forces that oppose the divine will. Apocalypticism is where judgment and salvation take place, as the righteous are vindicated and the wicked get their just reward. The argument by some goes that Jesus taught the wisdom strand, but that the eschatological-apocalyptic strand is an addition by the early church not tied to Jesus. The results of the Jesus Seminar of the 1990s leaned heavily in the direction of making this distinction.

However, if what we are tracing in this chapter is true, namely that Jesus submitted to a baptism by John and endorsed his ministry by doing so, then Jesus was affirming the direction of John's eschatological-apocalyptic way of seeing the program of God. In other words, the Jesus Seminar got this wrong. In doing so, it left out an important half of the Jesus story.

In saying Jesus agreed with John, we do not mean Jesus saw the details of the future exactly as John saw them—which is why John later asks for assurance that Jesus is the one. However, Jesus' participation in baptism does mean that John and Jesus shared the expectation of accountability and judgment that John preached, embracing ideas such as a figure to come, cleansing, repentance, and a final deliverance that would distinguish between two types of people.

So understanding washings is important to understanding John and his connection to Jesus. Understanding how this washing was about the end-times story is even more important. It was unique to John's washing that it was eschatological and apart from the temple. When Jesus got baptized by John, he was signing on and living into that story. It was announcing the arrival of a new era and a fresh way of approach to God. It was signing on to the ministry of renewing a people in need of returning to her roots in a faithful walk with God.

THE RULES THAT APPLY TO THE HEAVENLY VOICE AND THE OBJECTIONS

The rules that help corroborate the heavenly voice in the baptism story illuminate how this discussion differs from the way the church embraces the story. Most in the church simply accept that if Scripture says so and the event happened, then the voice as part of that event also happened. But what of those who might distinguish the two parts of the scene and argue that John may have baptized Jesus, but that is all we can corroborate?

In reply, it is interesting to note that all the remarks about *multiple attestation* with regard to the event of baptism apply to this very detail. In the multiply attested baptismal event, there also appears the account of a dove descending with a voice speaking to Jesus and identifying him as "my Son."

Nonetheless, the objections to these details intensify.

Objections about the Voice from Heaven at John's Baptism

The basic issue of how directly a heavenly voice is involved in the story engages a key question we often meet in the gospels: How does one handle transcendent or extraordinary claims? Those who doubt them will immediately dismiss this material as created by the church. They likely will call them mythic or legend and compare them with other accounts in other cultures that have such elements. Even some who are open to divine activity might raise questions.

There are three main objections to this part of the story. *First,* the voice's remarks are similar to early church theology, especially the clear affirmation about Jesus as Son. *Second*, the voice also explains why Jesus is baptized by John when John is seen as a lesser figure by the church. John Dominic Crossan, who was one of the chairs of the Jesus Seminar, calls this detail "theological damage control."[9] In other words, John did baptize Jesus, but the interpretation of that event was added later to deal with the seeming submission Jesus gives John here. *Finally*, the two explicit allusions to Psalm 2:7 and Isaiah 42:1 in the heavenly remarks (when the voice speaks of "my Son in whom I am well pleased") combine the portrait of king and Servant of God that some say presents Jesus in a theologically sophisticated manner. Such sophistication is a part of early church reflection, not a real event.

Factors in Response to the Objections

Beyond the core worldview issue of divine activity's historicity, there are other factors that serve as a reply to these objections. There are four elements in Jesus' ministry presentation that seem to assume a moment like this. *First*, Jesus tied the presence of the Spirit with evidence of the presence of the kingdom hope linked to his ministry. This theme is *multiply attested* (Q: Matthew 12:27–28 = Luke 11:19–20; Mark 3:28–29 = Matthew 12:31–32 = Luke 12:10; L: Luke 4:16–21). *Second, coherence* would apply, as almost all scholars accept that Jesus spoke of God as his Father in a way unprecedented for Judaism (Mark 14:36 = Matthew 26:39 = Luke 22:42; Q: Matthew 11:25–27 = Luke 10:21–22). A claim of an authenticating experience about Jesus as Son, like the one tied to baptism, coheres with this other data. *Third*, it was common for prophets to have a sense of call to their role, what is often called a vision call, so *historical-cultural plausibility* would apply. Isaiah's call in Isaiah 6 is an example. If Jesus' experience fits this pattern, then a call event is no surprise. (Of course, those who question this would argue that it is why such a story was created, to fit the pattern, thus demonstrating how the same ideas and textual data can be presented to fit different worldviews in contrasting ways. This is why we get debates on some features.) *Fourth*, the symbol of the dove with the Spirit has never had a good explanation for its origin. This detail is *dissimilar* to the Jewish religious background, nor is there clear precedent for it elsewhere. It seems to be a completely new association. In the early church, the dove symbol itself does not appear in the New Testament outside the gospels and belongs only to this scene in them. So it is not a fixed, emphasized feature of the early church. This meets the dissimilarity criteria.

These four factors suggest that the objections to the voice are not convincing. Jesus is likely to have had a call experience, and his ministry and remarks about the Father point to a sense of intimacy with God that could well have come from such an experience. The detail also coheres with the general frame of the baptismal event, where John points to the nearness of kingdom hope and to one to come who is greater. In addition, at his baptism John received a clear sign that the one to come was Jesus.

This opening event is important in that it sets the table for what comes later in the ministry of Jesus. When Jesus gets baptized, he affirms John's call and message. In turn, the voice from heaven affirms Jesus, and Jesus begins his own ministry. Jesus identified with the need for cleansing of the people called by John, and issued his own call to the people to repent. But more than wisdom was required to walk with God—what was needed was a renewed heart, something the stronger one would give when he brought the Spirit of God with the new era.

3

The Choosing of the Twelve:

The Authority to Restore

Symbols can be powerful. Consider the different meanings and emotions that the Statue of Liberty evokes for both Americans and the world at large. Lady Liberty stands at the door of our largest city saying welcome. In her are encapsulated the values and goals of a community. So it is with Jesus' choosing of his twelve disciples—what this meant and why he did it shed light on who Jesus was and what he intended to do.[1] As we look at Jesus' choosing of the twelve disciples, we see that Jesus was actually making a statement about the kind of community he sought to bring about. So we will look at the historicity of this event, why some doubt that Jesus chose twelve disciples, and what it means if he did.

As we discuss this historical detail, we will come upon a key point this study as a whole makes—that Jesus often revealed more about who he was by what he did than by what he said. Anyone appreciating the meaning of his actions in context can understand the message. Choosing twelve sent a signal. Like flashing a V-for-victory sign, the number twelve was no accident. The number spoke without needing words.

THE RULES THAT APPLY TO THE CHOOSING OF THE TWELVE DISCIPLES

The key texts naming the twelve disciples are Mark 3:16–19, Matthew 10:2–4, Luke 6:14–16, and Acts 1:13. This tradition is rooted in Mark, even though there are some variations in the lists so that they are not exactly the same.

Historical-Cultural Plausibility

Historical-cultural plausibility applies here, as tying teachers to followers is common in the ancient world. It shows that the teacher is establishing a movement or a school of thinking. In Judaism, listing the names or even the qualities of famous disciples of a teacher is a common practice. For example, in the late second century CE, the *Mishnah* lists not only some of the famous students of Rabbi Yohanan ben Zakkai, but also some of the qualities of his students (*Abot* 2:8–14).[2] The lists we have of Jesus' twelve disciples give only names in most cases, though with a few of the names we get a nickname or additional description to give us a sense of the breadth of Jesus' choice when we put the entire group together.

So Matthew is a tax collector while one Simon is a Zealot. As contemporaries, they would have been on opposite sides in terms of beliefs about how Israel should function in relationship to Rome. Matthew was cooperating with Rome, while Simon would have sought to incite resistance to Rome. So the group Jesus brought together covered a wide range of views that existed in first-century Israel.

Multiple Attestation

Multiple attestation also applies to the naming of the twelve. Beyond Mark's listing of the twelve noted above, Q also discusses the disciples, simply referring to them as a group with the number of members (Matthew 19:28 = Luke 22:30). Material unique to Matthew, Luke, and John also names the grouping the Twelve (Matthew 11:1, 20:17, 26:20; Luke 8:1, 18:31; John 6:67, 70; 20:24). In fact, the grouping also appears as "the Twelve" when they are only eleven after Judas' death and before he was replaced in Acts 1. This use of "Twelve" to refer to what is temporarily eleven happens twice—in the traditional listing of the resurrection appearances in 1 Corinthians 15:5, and again in Acts 1:13. So the grouping is *multiply attested*. This multiple attestation also extends to *forms*, as the twelve are noted in narrative (Mark, Acts), sayings from Q and John, a catalogue (Mark and the use by the author Luke in Acts), and in a traditional creed (1 Corinthians).

Embarrassment

The criterion of *embarrassment* also applies here in the case of Judas, who always appears in the last slot in the catalogue of names. He is noted as one of the Twelve when he betrays Jesus (Mark 14:43). The point is—Why would the church invent an internal betrayer unless there was one? This detail does not have the look or feel of a created detail, especially with a Jesus who is believed to be infinitely wise in the church. As John Dominic Crossan puts it, Judas "is too bad to be false."[3] This presence of Judas among the group has a corollary, since Judas was a part of this special group of disciples only during Jesus' time in ministry. The twelve predate Jesus' death and the time of the early church.

The Lack of Development about the Figures Named

Besides historical-cultural plausibility, multiple attestation, and embarrassment, an argument that falls outside any of the rules also has merit.[4] It is that despite the naming of each individual of the group, we actually know very little about most of them. If the church had made up the group and its importance, we'd expect more than we have about most of these people, as well as more about what they did as a group in the early church. However, we do not have any of this. They appear in the formula of 1 Corinthians 15:3–5, appear in Acts 1:12–26 only to disappear after Acts 6:2, and make one appearance in Revelation 21:14. Thus, if this is a detail created by the church, next to no use was made of it. That is very unlikely.

So in sum, there are several good reasons to claim that the choosing of a special group of disciples, as well as the fact that they numbered twelve, stands on good historical ground.

Objections

Objections to the existence of the twelve disciples appear in four arguments made most famous by the Jesus Seminar.[5] *First*, to try to nullify the impact of multiple attestation, the Seminar claims that the presence of material in Q belongs to a hypothesized late third stage of development in that source. It also notes that the twelve disciples are not mentioned in the *Gospel of Thomas*, *Didache*, Clement of Rome's letter to Corinth known as *1 Clement*, or in the letters of Ignatius. These are all late first-century or early second-century sources. *Second*, they claim the eschatological meaning of the number twelve is a reflection of the early church, not Jesus. *Third*, they state that the presence of the Twelve is a product of editorial work by Mark himself and that Judas is a fabrication according to "many scholars."[6] *Fourth*, the lists of the Twelve do not entirely match.

Of these objections, we think only the last raises a serious issue.

On the first objection, the attempt to challenge multiple attestation by arguing for a late insertion in Q is tied to a theory of the development of Q that is far too speculative. We have to reconstruct Q from what we have in the gospels. Because we have no explicit example of it, its existence is questioned, even though I have argued it is likely. However, to speculate on how this reconstruction itself developed is full of additional suppositions that are even harder to substantiate. And then there is the argument from silence, which scholars generally do not find compelling.

On the second objection, we discussed the authenticity of an eschatological dimension to Jesus' ministry in our discussion of John the Baptist. The eschatological interpretation of the twelve disciples is that they represent a reconstituting of Israel with the disciples symbolizing its original twelve tribes. Jesus' act points to a rebuilding of Israel around new leaders, announcing the arrival of the new era. Jesus identified with the view that God was doing a new thing, a theme central to John's teaching. This detail shows how discussion links events together in the debates about Jesus. What we learn about one event can help us sort out what is going on elsewhere.

The third objection also is speculative, for it is hard to check Mark's editorial work when we do not have his sources. As for the claim about scholars, E. P. Sanders says, "A vast majority of scholars is in favour of the basic historicity of the Twelve."[7] The Seminar's handling of Q and Mark have the appearance of special pleading.

The key remaining objection involves the lists of names in four passages (Mark 3:16–19, Matthew 10:2–4, Luke 6:14–16, and Acts 1:13). These lists show much consistency alongside some variation. Peter is always first. Peter, the sons of Zebedee (James and John), and Andrew are always the first four, but not always in the same order. Philip, Bartholomew, Matthew, and Thomas are always the second set of four, but again not always in the same order. James, son of Alphaeus, is in all the lists in the lead position of the last section of four. There is a Simon the Cananean also called Simon the Zealot who appears in all four lists. Judas is always last, except in the list in Acts, where he has died and so is not listed. The remaining oddity surrounds the names Thaddaeus (Mark and Matthew's list) and Jude, son of James (the lists of Luke and Acts). First of all, this difference may suggest Luke's list is not simply taken from Mark, but comes from a distinct source. Now it is likely that Jude, son of James, is Thaddaeus and that the choice not to use Judas was to prevent confusion with the more infamous Judas. Two sets of names are not uncommon in Jewish circles. One can quickly think of Peter/Cephas, Saul/Paul, as well as the likely but less clear case of Matthew/Levi. Gaston notes that the differences actually reflect not the creation of the Twelve by the early church, but an institution established by Jesus early enough that it generated distinct traditional listings.[8] This remark is an appeal to our rule of multiple attestation, since if the tradition existed in multiple forms with overlaps, it shows that the Twelve existed and their naming circulated in various forms not controlled by a single creative event.

So again the objections to historicity of the choosing of the twelve are not so compelling.

MEANING OF THE CHOOSING OF THE TWELVE

The most commonly accepted explanation for the choosing of the Twelve is to replicate the picture of the twelve tribes of Israel and thus symbolically depict her restoration and unification (Matthew 19:28; Luke 22:29–30). The roots of this connection go back to the most common use of *twelve* in the Hebrew Bible, namely for the sons of Jacob/Israel who in turn form the twelve tribes of the nation (Genesis 42:13, 32; 49:28), but also other symbolic acts that involve twelve pieces to represent the nation (twelve pillars: Exodus 24:4; twelve stones on the high priest's breastplate: Exodus 39:14; twelve bowls: Numbers 7:84; twelve bulls, rams, lambs, or goats: Numbers 7:87; twelve staffs: Numbers 17:17; cutting a prostitute into twelve pieces: Judges 19:29; Ahijah's cutting the robe into twelve pieces: 1 Kings 11:30–31). So the association of the number with the nation is common—most formalized upon acceptance of the covenant (Exodus 24:4) and entry into the land (Joshua 4:1–20). Even the Dead Sea community enlisted a similar symbolism, as it had twelve leaders serving alongside three key priests (1QS 8:1 among several texts from Qumran).

The number twelve, however, does not show up in any eschatological contexts in the Hebrew Scripture. It is a way to talk about Israel as a people, not an Israel to come. The twelve Jesus chose became in effect leaders of a new community that also saw itself as a faithful remnant, longing to experience God's promises. In other words, there is something old here and something new. The old pictured a remnant tied in continuity to the twelve tribes of Israel; the new was designed to take the nation in a fresh direction as this group proclaimed the arrival of a new era of God's old promise. That promise is now realized and tied to Jesus' kingdom proclamation.

The idea of restoration or renewal reflects the new era context of Jesus' message. This call evoked the idea of the renewal to faithfulness of tribes, expressed in the Hebrew Bible and Second Temple Judaism. The image of gathering the dispersed or raising up the tribes appears in future-hope contexts in Isaiah 11:11–12, 49:6, and 63:17. Jeremiah also has this theme (3:19, 29:14, 30:3, 31:7–10, 32:36–41). Ezekiel announces this in several texts tied to his famous picture of the resurrection of dry bones in Ezekiel 37 (36:8–11, 37:19). Ezekiel follows this image with a full picture of restoration in chapters 40–48, with 47:13 noting the unification of the tribes. Amos 9:14 speaks of God "restoring my people." Other prophets follow suit (Micah 2:12, 4:6–7; Zephaniah 3:19–20; Zechariah 10:8–10). This hope lived on in the Second Temple period, extending to the time of Jesus, including passages from Sirach 36, which speaks of this hope of regathering, especially verses 18, 19, and 21, which mention Jerusalem and Zion spe-

cifically. *Testament of Judah* 25:1–2 looks to a restoration of the
twelve tribes with each one named. *Testament of Benjamin* 10:7
also speaks of unification. All of these Second Temple texts likely
come from before the time of Jesus. These later texts show how
many Jews held this hope that Hebrew Scripture had generated.
It is restoration of hope in line with covenant that is in view here.

So what did the Twelve do? They heard some teachings of
Jesus privately, including access to inside discussion of his parables (multiply attested: Mark 4:10, 10:32–34; John 6:67; Mark
11:11, 22:14). Jesus sent out the disciples to announce what God
was doing through him (multiply attested: Mark 3:14; Matthew
10:1; Luke 6:13; Q: Matthew 10:1 = Luke 9:1–6; some uniquely
Matthean material in Matthew 9:35–11:1). Their activity is re-
stricted mostly to Galilee and Israel, most vividly portrayed in
Matthew 10:5–6. In that text Jesus tells the Twelve, "Go only to
the lost sheep of Israel." So part of the point here is that the bulk
of Jesus' own ministry and that of the Twelve focused on Israel.
Initially, Jesus sought to regather his own through the Twelve, and
one day he promised that the Twelve would sit in judgment over
the twelve tribes of Israel (Q: Matthew 19:28 = Luke 22:28–30).
This promise and its focus on Israel either are authentic to Jesus
or are an early interpretation of his ministry, as we have seen
how Jesus' ministry was focused on Israel and how the role of the
Twelve was not emphasized in the early church. Jesus points to a
symbolic picture of Israel's renewal and ultimate covenantal restoration. The call of Jesus through the Twelve invites participation
in God's renewed covenantal hope.

One can even consider tying this imagery to John's baptism
location. It is likely that in getting baptized in the Jordan, those
who came to John entered from outside Israel and crossed over
into the land to picture the renewal his washing represented.
These associations evoke parallels with Joshua's entry into the
land, a second entry for the new era.

All of this has a political, social, and spiritual edge to it. To establish a new line of leaders, proclaim a fresh message, and evoke the need to reconstitute the people is a critique of the nation's current religious leadership. The nation needed new shepherds, with Jesus being the chief among them. Politically, socially, and spiritually, Israel was wayward. Jesus had come to get the nation back on the right path. The Twelve would help in this cause, as those who best knew what Jesus taught.

SUMMARY

Jesus initially had a ministry focused on restoring Israel to covenantal faithfulness, and his call was to participate in the new covenantal things God was bringing. Jesus brought a fresh rule with fresh leadership and a fresh dynamic. All of this was a challenge to the established leaders of the faith. There were two trains on this track, and they were headed in opposite directions. The choosing of the Twelve shows us that Jesus was making a claim over his own people, a new way of liberty in contrast to how they were currently being led. There would either be a turning to go in the same direction . . . or a great collision.

4

Jesus' Associations with Tax Collectors and Sinners:

The Scandal of Jesus' Relationships and Table Fellowship

THIS CHAPTER considers a theme rather than an event.[1] Through the picture of Jesus' table fellowship with the rejected of society, we see an important aspect of what Jesus did and taught. For most historical Jesus scholars, it is one of the least controversial parts of Jesus' ministry, though there are still some who challenge its historical credibility. It also represents an area our culture easily associates with Jesus. But the popular understanding often tells only a part of the story, missing along the way some key points of what Jesus was trying to show. What is the true meaning of Jesus' scandalous relationships with tax collectors and sinners?

THE RULES THAT APPLY TO JESUS' TABLE FELLOWSHIP WITH SINNERS

Most scholars do accept that Jesus associated with sinners.[2]

Multiple Attestation and Forms

Once again, we have *multiple attestation*. We have several texts that involve meal scenes or debates over Jesus' associations. They include sources from Mark (Levi's banquet, Mark 2:13–17 = Matthew 9:9–13 = Luke 5:27–32), from Q (Jesus as glutton and drunkard, Luke 7:31–35 = Matthew 11:16–19; the sinners' response to John as precursor to Jesus, Luke 7:29 = Matthew 21:32), and from L (the sinful woman anoints Jesus in Luke 7:36–50; sayings introducing three parables about the lost returning, Luke 15:1–2; a parable of the Pharisee and tax collector, Luke 18:10–14; and Zacchaeus, Luke 19:1–10). Once again several strands of the tradition yield such accounts. In fact, the attestation is not only of source streams but also involves *multiple forms* with narrative (Mark 2:13–17; Luke 7:29–35 and 19:1–10), sayings (Luke 7:29, 31–35), and parable scenes (Luke 15:1–2, the complaint from the Pharisees, introducing three parables and thus also a controversy story; 18:10–14).

Double Dissimilarity

The criterion of *double dissimilarity* also applies. Here Jesus' practice is clearly distinct from the general approach of Jewish piety not to eat with sinners. However, it also is distinct from the meal emphasis we get in the early church, where the meal recedes in significance in comparison with sitting down to partake in the Lord's Supper. This Last Supper emphasis came to dominate the new community's corporate gathering and meal. Some of these

Supper meals developed rules to exclude some types of sinners from the table, so that the practice was dissimilar to Jesus'
practice as seen in the gospels (1 Corinthians 11:27–32; *Didache*
9:5, 10:6, 14:2). Although the difference is motivated by distinct
settings, since Jesus is reaching out to outsiders and the meal is
for those in the community who have affirmed a desire to reflect
righteousness, the difference is important in pointing to distinct
emphases between many gospel meals and church practice.

Embarrassment

We can also apply the criterion of *embarrassment*. Why would the
church make up a story that leads to cultural questioning of Jesus'
piety unless it was true?

So this theme fits multiple rules for testing authenticity.

OBJECTIONS

In general, the objections to this scene fit into two categories.

Objection: Greco-Roman Cultural
Roots with the Symposium Meal

Dennis Smith has argued that the meals described are Greco-
Roman in their cultural roots, reflecting the symposium meal so
popular in that context.[3] Interestingly, these meals, which often
had table talk on major life questions, are seen as so popular that
Jews also held similar kinds of exchanges around their meals.
Thus, the presence of a meal is not the point of the objection.
Rather the claim is that the symposium reflects a cultural context
outside of the Judaism that Jesus' ministry reflected, showing it
was added later, after the time of Jesus, to make him look more
Greek. However, the fact that such meals with conversations

took place in Judaism makes determining whether we have a symposium or not very difficult. What distinguished the Jewish meal from the Greek one was that these Greek meals were often much more rowdy than the Jewish ones, with much more uncontrolled drinking and other—usually sexual—activity. Those who question these scenes argue that the gospel writers added the parts involving Jesus' controversial associations. Why the church would create such associations when none supposedly existed is not clear, especially when the act was so countercultural.

Objection: Exaggerated Labeling of the Participants

Another objection sees the theme using exaggerated labeling of the participants. It is said that these exaggerations really involved a negative characterization of women present at such meals, so that sinners and other fringe people were not really there.[4] In this argument, what we had were women who now have been labeled as tax collectors and sinners. Again, it is not clear why the gospel writers or early church would create such additions later. What had really changed to lead to such a move?

Now, it is precisely the claim of the addition by gospel writers that the rule of multiple attestation is designed to test. This rule says that the more widespread a theme is across traditions and forms, the more likely the theme is to be older than any of the evangelists, since the sources are independent of one another. Meeting this rule at least suggests that these passages are not the creation of any evangelist.

The claim that we are dealing with hyperbolic expressions that refer only to women is less than convincing because in these texts and sayings, groups of women are not even in view. The list of participants in these gospel scenes includes tax collectors, a single sinful woman, and people grouped under headings such as tax collectors and sinners. In other words, the alluded-to group (women), which is the point of the hyperbole, is not even in the stories that are supposed to refer to them! So these general objections fail.

However, one could question the authenticity of the specific scenes we have noted. Are there objections to the specific scenes?

Objection: Meal Would Not Have Been Controversial Enough

Perhaps the only substantive objection to Levi's meal is whether it really would have been controversial enough to cause a stir among the Pharisees or Jewish leaders who heard about it. To answer this question, we have to consider how sources out of this pious Jewish culture (or later descendants of that culture) would have seen tax collectors and sinners.

It is slightly later Jewish sources that are of help to us here. The Jewish *Mishnah* is a rabbinic collection of oral tradition on matters pertaining to Jewish practice, written in the late second century CE. This book deals with a variety of topics in Jewish religious practice and collected opinions on disputed issues or on new questions about law and practice that the Hebrew Scriptures do not cover directly. The abbreviation *m.* introduces citations from one of the sections in this work, each of which covers a topic of concern.[5] Because the *Mishnah* records traditions, the material is older than the time of its writing. The only question is how much older.

Tax collectors (also called toll collectors) worked for Rome and gathered a variety of tolls for the world empire, including citizen (poll) taxes and sales taxes. The tax collectors' close association with Gentiles made them unpopular among Jews loyal to Israel and pious Jewish identity. They were seen as too close to Gentiles, and being in constant contact with them risked the ritual uncleanness that prevented fellowship with God for the pious Jew. In *m. Tehar* 7:6, an explanation reads, "If tax collectors entered a house, [all that is within it] becomes unclean." Even if they claim not to have touched anything, they are not to be believed. Ritual cleanliness or purity is an issue we already noted in discussing the washings of John—to be unclean was to be unable to associate with God in the temple, and uncleanness resulted from coming into contact with something unclean. Here the tax collector himself is seen as automatically unclean. Discussed in the same context are thieves and Gentiles, also indicating a lack of respect for this vocation. In *m. Baba Qamma* 10:1, one does not accept charity from a tax collector. The refusal to take alms, a highly regarded act in Judaism, is also an indication of the lack of regard the pious had for them. Other Jewish traditions from the *Tosefta* and *Talmud*, even later in date, also show this concern about association and warn about such associations (*t. Demai* 3:4; *b. Bekorot* 31a).[6]

So, if these traditions are old, and that is likely, pursuing such associations would have been seen as suspect. What about sinners? By the pious, like the Pharisees, they would have been seen as less than faithful to the Law and unfaithful covenant partners because of their violation or indifference to pious practices. In fact, John Meier defines them as "people who intentionally rejected the commandments of the God of Israel, as those commandments were understood by Jews in general, not just by an elite group of puritans."[7] For the pious, such unfaithfulness put the entire nation at risk of displeasing God. God will not acquit the guilty (Exodus 23:7; Nahum 1:3). Even Proverbs 17:15 in the Hebrew Scripture warned, "He who justifies the wicked and condemns the righteous are both alike an abomination to Yahweh."[8] At Qumran, the pious Jews of the Dead Sea complained about those who pronounce the guilty innocent and the innocent guilty (*Damascus Document* 1:19). Unrighteousness was seen as a personal affront to the honor of God. It was not merely religious preference that was at stake but social order, upholding morality, and God's honor. So their indifference mattered.

Sanders calls the story about Levi's banquet and the Pharisees' complaint unrealistic, even though he regards as historical that Jesus had such associations.[9] He says the Pharisees would not be "policing Galilee to see whether or not an otherwise upright man ate with sinners." This objection is a caricature of the scene. All that is needed to trigger the question about why Jesus eats with such questionable people is a report that he had done so or the development of a reputation for doing so, not the literal pursuit of a reconnaissance effort.

Jesus likely had such meals. It would have been controversial, but not because Jesus was reaching out to sinners. All pious people hoped that sinners would repent and welcomed those who did. There was something more significant in what Jesus was doing. This we shall clarify when we look at the significance of these meals.

The sayings on Jesus being a glutton and drunkard are a prime example of the criterion of embarrassment. Such charges surfaced because of Jesus' meals. This practice was so common for Jesus that even he commented on the negative reaction (the theme is multiply attested in sources and forms: Levi story: Mark 2:13–17 = Matthew 9:9–13 = Luke 5:27–32; Q: Jesus' Parable of the Complaining Children: Matthew 11:16–19 = Luke 7:31–35). Why make up such a charge if one did not have to do so and unnecessarily incur cultural critique? Not only this, but it is made up in a way that John the Baptist looks more pious on the surface than Jesus! It is hard to see a scenario where the early church would have made up this charge and comparison.[10] It is a complaint about Jesus' associations. The same problem with associations applies to the specific scenes of the sinful woman who anoints Jesus and to Jesus' conversation with Zacchaeus. That such associations are a virtue, not a vice, goes back to Jesus. In fact, the gospels describe an array of negative reactions to the type of thing Jesus does here.[11] The background helps us to see the point Jesus was making about God reaching out to those others rejected, while different views about how to relate to these people fueled why the leaders challenged Jesus' acceptance.

MEANING OF JESUS' ASSOCIATIONS WITH SINNERS IN TABLE FELLOWSHIP

The cultural background begins to make clear how tax collectors and sinners were seen and what Jesus is doing. Rather than moving from righteousness to fellowship, or requiring one to be clean before making association, Jesus reverses the direction. In the old view, there was a fear that uncleanness trumps cleanliness. Jesus' view differed. Fellowship with the sinner can inspire the sinner into righteousness. In addition, Jesus' clean presence triumphs over any potential uncleanness tax collectors and sinners bear. This change of perspective represents an initiative from God to cleanse.

Jesus Drew Sinners to God

God reaches out to those in spiritual need, as the parables of Luke 15 argue and the parable and narrative of Luke 7 and 19 show.

In Jesus' culture, people sat at the table with those they accepted. Consider these examples from the Hebrew Scripture: the imagery of God preparing a place for those allied to him, even in front of one's enemies (Psalm 23:5); the complaint of a person who is betrayed by one he had supped with (Psalm 41:9). An exception to sitting to show acceptance was to sit in the hopes of bringing judgment—Proverbs 25:21–22 suggests that one can eat with an enemy; but doing so "heaps burning coals on his head," a picture of judgment. Jesus' sitting did not involve this more adversarial take on table fellowship, as his engagement of sinners sought to draw them to God. Luke 5:27–32 says Jesus came as a physician to heal and bring sinners to repentance. So there was challenge present in Jesus' sitting that did not ignore scriptural concerns about righteousness, but his style was to draw sinners to God, not simply reject them.

In the period a century or so before the time of Jesus, it was common in Judaism to exhort one not to eat with sinners and to heavily criticize them. Those who did not practice the Law were described as "sinners and lawless people" (1 Maccabees 1:34; 2:44, 48). Improper observance of the Law led to a rebuke of sinners as it says in *1 Enoch* 82:4–7. *Psalms of Solomon* weighs in from a Pharisaic-like perspective against the Sadducees (1:8, 2:3, 7:2, 8:12–13, 17:5–8). Tobit 4:17 says that a person can give alms, but "give none to sinners." Stated more negatively, the book of Judith rebukes the people and warns of judgment if one eats with sinners and does not pay attention to Jewish practice. At Qumran, meals had to involve purity separation from sinners (1QS 5:2, 10–11, 14–18; *Damascus Document* 6:14–18). In several of these texts, "sinners" does not mean flagrant lawbreakers that all would recognize, but those whose practices did not correspond to the particular reading of the Law within certain Jewish religious parties. The sheer variety of passages in several Jewish works shows how widespread this attitude was in Judaism.

Also, the very moral tenor of symposium meals suggests that this meal model of the Greco-Roman world was not what was present here. These Greek meals often came with revelry and excessive drinking—Plato and Xenophon discuss such meals with austerity in their works that share the name *Symposium*, but other writers wrote satires about the partying that took place in them (Petronius, *Satyricon*; Juvenal, *Satire* 5).

To sit at table with someone was to affirm friendship. In fact, if one takes the saying in Matthew 9:12–13 that concludes Levi's meal as reflecting what Jesus is doing, then he is like a physician prescribing medicine for the sick. James Dunn considers this saying the one with the strongest credibility among the sayings in this setting.[12] It is important here to see that Jesus does not sit at the table and merely accept those on the fringe. He challenges them to live differently or mentions forgiveness as a motivation for the sinner's response, which assumes a reaction to previous sin. This is the point of his medicine illustration about his work being like that of a physician. People go to a doctor because they recognize they are sick and need what the doctor can offer to make them better. This also is reflected in Zacchaeus' response in Luke 19:8. Where he defrauded before, he will repay fourfold, fulfilling the sanction of the Law in paying back a wrong (Exodus 22:1). The parable Jesus tells about the sinful woman who anointed him says that her love is a response to forgiveness (Luke 7:41–44). These points come from the Marcan and L traditions. So they are multiply attested.

Jesus sitting at the table was an invitation to share in the relief he brought for a fresh need of God. Fellowship called for righteousness. The cleansing presence of Jesus challenged the unclean to take what the doctor had to offer. They embraced in faith the forgiveness Jesus offered. People were motivated to live differently as a result. The call was not to get oneself right and then come to God, but to take what was being offered to get right. This reversal of order meant that turning to God was not done away with or irrelevant. Rather it was seen as a response of gratitude to God's initiative to forgive. All of this implies a ruling and an authority in Jesus' distinct judgment about how a person should approach God. It suggests that Jesus himself has something fresh to offer and the ability to give it.

Why This Difference Is Important

As we apply this difference to Jesus, two things stand out. *The first key difference* is that Jesus is no moralist. He is not saying, "Straighten your life out and then God will accept you." Rather, Jesus taught that God is inviting people *to change* in a context of acceptance and forgiveness, or better, to let God change them.

On the other hand, unlike our culture's picture of Jesus—that Jesus simply accepts people without conditions and without any call to change—everything about the illustrations surrounding these scenes pictures people who have been impacted by God's acceptance to become different people as a result of colliding with God's grace. Whether we look at the sinful woman's devotion, Zacchaeus' turn to reply, or Jesus' remark about dispensing medicine to the sick, the point is that on the other end of God's acceptance is a response of love that also leads one to draw near to God. This involves responding to God more honorably than before this encounter. Appreciation of forgiveness leads to righteousness. Gratitude to God leads to spiritual change.

That Jesus' way engendered this response shows his way was not moralism nor blind acceptance, but a way rooted in the fresh presentation of God's grace. This different way stood at the center of what he was trying to show. It made his teaching distinctive in the face of what much of pious Second Temple Judaism was teaching. It also shows that the Jesus we see in these texts is not merely the social prophet often characterized by our culture. Both differences, how Jesus differed from the Judaism surrounding him and how he differs from the common contemporary portrait of Jesus, are important to getting a grasp on the historical Jesus.

Jesus shows God's initiative in reaching out to those in spiritual need. Whether taught in parables like those in Luke 15, stated as a goal of mission as in Luke 5:32 or 19:10, or enacted in how he treated others as in the case of Levi, the sinful woman, and Zacchaeus, Jesus shows that those who are "lost" need not remain there. Two texts summarize all of this. First, Luke 5:32 compares Jesus' actions to the work of a physician who brings healing. Second, Luke 19:10 says Jesus came to seek and save the lost. These are like the kinds of mission statements that corporations give to state their business goals. At the very least, they tell us how the church saw Jesus' mission; but as statements of Jesus, they also indicate why his ministry had the tone and character it did.

As Blomberg says, it is with the belief that gracious holiness can be contagious that "Jesus 'mixes it up' with the notorious and riff-raff of the world. Scarcely fearing that he will be morally or ritually defiled by them, in many instances he winds up leading them to God and to true ceremonial and spiritual wholeness. Or to put it more succinctly, holiness not impurity turns out to be the most contagious."[13]

The second key difference is that at the center of the challenge stands Jesus' authority as one who can reveal God's will, communicate God's acceptance, and give God's grace. He has the right and position to define how a central religious concept such as repentance works. There is more than divine wisdom and proverbial teaching at work in Jesus. What he is doing assumes a level of authority that involves more than being a mouthpiece for God. He represents a kind of change for things while he calls Israel into renewal. Some of what he is doing and saying is without parallel and precedent in Judaism.

So, for example, is what Jesus does or asks for in terms of response to his acceptance and forgiveness. In Jesus' teaching, nothing requires going to the temple and participating in the cult there. This direct manner of access to God also may have raised some eyebrows among the leadership. It is yet another reason they had concern for what Jesus was doing. He was messing with their rules of spirituality and practice; rules those leaders held came from God at Sinai. And to a degree those rules did have their origin there. So what was going on and how could things be changing? What gave him the right to do this? Who gave him such authority? Jesus' ministry raised such troubling questions. Other key events will explain what was going on.

5

Jesus and the Sabbath:

Authority and the Sacred Calendar

THIS CHAPTER also treats a theme versus a specific event.[1] We will be looking at Jesus' attitude toward and observance of the most sacred day of the Jewish week, the Sabbath. This special day was set apart for rest and contemplation of God, a day whose existence was rooted in a picture of creation and whose observance was commanded in the Ten Commandments. It was ordained to be a day of rest with no labor. The Sabbath takes its place among the key distinct elements of Jewish practice alongside the one temple, the special calendar of feasts, the unique division of clean and unclean foods, the covenantal self-understanding of Israel's uniqueness through divine election, and circumcision.

In other words, the Sabbath was a big deal.

A NOTE ON LAW IN THE TIME OF JESUS

In coming to such a central area of Jewish practice, it is important to understand that there was not a single Jewish approach to the Sabbath, just as there was not a single view of the Law.

Oral and Written Tradition as
a Development of Law

There were both a written and an oral law working alongside each other in Judaism as the Law developed to function in fresh contexts. The written text set the parameters and the oral law applied it in the new context. This meant that some things said to be in the Law were not written down in the Hebrew Scripture, but may have grown out of it. The fact that a ruling grew out of the Law and was not explicitly stated in it was not seen as a problem. Neither was such supplemental activity seen as adding to the Law by many Jews. Among the major religious groups in Judaism, only the Sadducean religious party questioned doing this. In *Life of Moses* 2.215–16, Philo, Jewish philosopher of the first century BCE, describes attending the synagogue on the Sabbath as a command of the Law. However, there is no such written law, in part because synagogues did not yet exist when the Law was written! This specific practice is an extension of the idea that the Sabbath is a day of rest to contemplate God, and in Philo's time this was done at the synagogue.

The connections were so much a part of life at that time that an oral law could be presented as an absolute responsibility or obligation. We can see and understand the logic of this kind of development out of the Law. Oral tradition often became written tradition as well. A Jewish work like *Jubilees*, which predates Jesus, gives evidence of rewriting law. Such an act was not always seen or understood negatively but was quite common and acceptable among certain Jewish groups.[2] For example, *Jubilees* 2:25–33 extends the Law of the Sabbath to specifically prohibit the preparation of food or drink. It also added a prohibition against carrying anything in or out of the house on this day. This process of legal reflection eventually became formalized after the time of Jesus and produced the famous rabbinic works of the *Mishnah* (late second century) and *Talmud* (fifth to sixth century). These texts collected the discussion on such issues, including the debate over various opinions, and left them in written, not just in oral, form.

Varying Expression of Laws about the Same Topic

Thus, different Jewish groups expressed such rules in different ways with differing details. The Law called Jews to rest on the Sabbath day, but the Jews were interpreting the meaning of this in new contexts and viewing it as the Law. So the Sabbath was a day of rest, but exactly how that worked was not precisely the same from place to place or group to group. One group might define precisely what was allowed, while another might not have a specific rule. So at Qumran, cattle were allowed to roam in pasture for two thousand cubits (three thousand feet) on the Sabbath (*Damascus Document* 11:5–6), while the *Mishnah* says that cattle can be led only as long as they do not carry a load (*m. Shabbat* 5:4). Interestingly, at Qumran, a walking limit of one thousand cubits (fifteen hundred feet, or about a mile) applied to people when they were outside the city. And different groups would have different rules for the same concern. So at Qumran, the strict Essenes would not allow anyone to help an animal give birth on the Sabbath nor rescue it if it fell into a pit. Neither could they rescue a person who fell into a reservoir (*Damascus Document* 11:12–17). On the other hand, later Pharisees argued that one could give medicine and aid to a seriously ill person on the Sabbath (*m. Yoma* 8:6). This kind of practice and deliberation is often characterized as "legalism," but seen from within Judaism, it was simply attempting to be faithful in carrying out what God had commanded. These rules were seen to extend the command's application into life as it was in the first century. The detail to which this was contemplated showed how important it was—a matter of being faithful to one's calling and identity.

Nothing illustrates this more vividly than the famous "forty less one" text from the *Mishnah*, *Shabbat* 7:2. I cite it here in full to show how detailed and wide in scope these rules could get. The example is reflective of the kind of concerns Pharisees would have had, since the *Mishnah* is a descendant of Pharisaical points of view. Here is the citation:

The generative categories of acts of labor [prohibited on the Sabbath] are forty less one:

(1) he who sows, (2) ploughs, (3) reaps, (4) binds sheaves, (5) threshes, (6) winnows, (7) selects [fit from unfit produce or crops], (8) grinds, (9) sifts, (10) kneads, (11) bakes; (12) he who shears wool, (13) washes it, (14) beats it, (15) dyes it; (16) spins, (17) weaves, (18) makes two loops, (19) weaves two threads, (20) separates two threads; (21) ties, (22) unties, (23) sews two stitches, (24) tears in order to sew two stitches; (25) he who traps a deer, (26) slaughters it, (27) flays it, (28) salts it, (29) cures its hide, (30) scrapes it, and (31) cuts it up; (32) he who writes two letters, (33) erases two letters in order to write two letters; (34) he who builds, (35) tears down; (36) he who puts out a fire, (37) kindles a fire; (38) he who hits with a hammer; (39) he who transports an object from one domain to another—lo, these are the forty generative acts of labor less one.[3]

Although the "forty less one" is an example from one group, what Jewish groups did agree on was that the Pentateuch (the books of Moses: Genesis, Exodus, Leviticus, Numbers, Deuteronomy) set the parameters for the Law. Pharisees and Essenes extended this through oral law. Sadducees generally did not develop an oral tradition outside these five biblical books. So some groups were more particular than others. The result was that Sabbath practices might not be the same in all locations and various groups debated the right way to do things. Nonetheless, despite the differences, all groups honored the Sabbath in some way. It was a precious and sacred day.

These historical realities show that the Sabbath Law in Jesus' time was a "moving target."[4] It depends on where we ask the question and with what group. However, what Jews shared was a concern that God be honored in some way on this special day. Such observance was seen as an important part of being faithful to God and being a faithful Jew, regardless of specific differences among the various Jewish groups. All of this variation makes historical judgments about specific practice in this area difficult work.

The Rules That Apply to the Sabbath Texts

Multiple attestation is once again a key criterion in discussion about this theme. Mark gives us the account of plucking grain on the Sabbath (Mark 2:23–28 = Matthew 12:1–8 = Luke 6:1–5) and the healing of the man with the withered hand (Mark 3:1–6 = Matthew 12:9–14 = Luke 6:6–11). Material unique to Luke also has Sabbath healings (L: Luke 13:10–17, 14:1–6). John has unique Sabbath controversies in John 5:1–47 and 9:1–41.

Dissimilarity also seems to be in play. On the early church side, there is little evidence of specific disputes defending the Sabbath. On the Jewish side, Jesus' Sabbath actions created a reaction among some Jews because his actions seemed to be distinct from their general approach to the Law regarding this day.

The rules of multiple attestation and dissimilarity point to the idea that Jesus' Sabbath activity produced a reaction from some Jews. The theme is deeply embedded in the tradition and is likely historical. In general, this is accepted as a part of the portrait tied to Jesus' ministry, but there is more dispute over specific events.

A look at specific texts yields specific objections to which we now turn.

OBJECTIONS TO SPECIFIC SABBATH EVENTS

In this section we examine a few Sabbath events and deal with objections one event at a time.

On the Grain-Plucking Event

There are some differences in the account of the plucking of grain on the Sabbath that cause some to question it as an authentic event. Matthew's version has three illustrations where there are exceptions to a law and then a remark about the Son of Man on the Sabbath (Matthew 12:5–7). Matthew's additions of God desiring mercy over sacrifice and the priest working the temple on the Sabbath are singularly attested, so we shall not examine them. Mark and Luke have only the one example of David and the shewbread, along with the remark about the Son of Man being Lord of the Sabbath.

Matthew, Mark, and Luke all refer to the example of David and his soldiers eating the shewbread, which the law did not permit; eating the shewbread was limited to priests (1 Samuel 21:2–10). This is not a Sabbath incident in Scripture, but simply an example of the Law not being followed for a reason of need.

Objection: Not Valid for Sabbath Controversy

Some object that this example is not a relevant reply. There is no evidence in Jewish sources that this event was seen as taking place on the Sabbath.[5] Meier sees a problem in this Jesus event since there is no indication of dire need in the disciples' act to pluck the grain.[6] In other words, it does not meet the standard.

However, in rabbinic analogous thinking, what can apply in

one sphere can apply in another. So Jesus, citing an exception to the law for need, can point to a similar kind of exception for Sabbath practice. More than that, the Samuel passage also does not allude to dire need but simply to supplying a meal because no other bread was present where the priest was. So basic need, not dire need, fits the example. The Jewish rabbi Israel Abrahams says that "Jesus differed fundamentally from the Pharisees in that he asserted a general right to abrogate the Sabbath law for man's ordinary convenience, while the rabbis limited the license to cases of danger of life."[7]

In fact, one could argue that the example with David is a worse violation, since sacred bread was at stake. The grain the disciples took was generally available and not set apart for any special purpose. In fact, on other days of the week, the Law clearly gave them the right to the grain (Deuteronomy 23:25). In the Pharisees' view, their act violated something like *m. Shabbat* 7:2 because it involved reaping and threshing. Jesus' analogy says that since even sacred bread can be eaten under certain conditions, so can common grain on the Sabbath.

Stating the analogy at a more personal level, the argument is, if priests can make a call that violates the Law, how much more can such a judgment be made by the one sent by God to bring the kingdom. This argument sets up what is said at the end of the passage, "The Son of Man is Lord of the Sabbath." The argument is more connected than Meier's random stitching together of the illustrations claims.

Other Objections: Abiathar Reference, the Watching of Jesus, and the Loose Linkage of the Arguments

A second objection is that the shewbread event is associated with Abiathar, when Ahimelech is the priest in 1 Samuel. This designation in Mark does not appear in Matthew or Luke's version. For Meier, this misidentification and lack of Sabbath parallel in the shewbread example speak to creation of the scene by the early church.[8] Third, Meier also questions the Pharisees keeping watch on Jesus on the Sabbath. Finally, he argues that the passage is a sewing together of diverse early-church texts on the Sabbath. These are all fair observations and questions. So what can be said in response?

The Abiathar reference may be nothing more than a less-than-precise reference to the section of 1 Samuel, since the text did not have chapters and verses then. Another option argues that the Greek reflects an Aramaic idiom equal to "in the time of Abiathar the High Priest," so the point is not that Abiathar was the High Priest when this took place, but that he was alive at this time.[9] In this case, the different detail could point to either a literary or idiomatic expression, not necessarily a created event.

On the issue of whether the Pharisees would keep watch on Jesus, arguably Jesus would have become someone worth watching to the extent that he was becoming controversial and drawing crowds (though not necessarily yet a concern, so much as a subject of interest). There is nothing in the passage that suggests the disciples were on a long journey and not a short Sabbath walk. Nor is there a suggestion that the disciples were alone on this trek. It may also be that we have an example of literary collapsing or simplification in the story. The Pharisees do not follow and complain, but complain when they see what Jesus had done.[10] This is all squeezed into a simple account of the dispute.

Meier's final objection was that the early church stitched this passage together using diverse texts. The following points suggest the integrity of this text. (1) The kind of action present here is multiply attested in the parallels from Luke 13 and 14. (2) There is no clear indication for this issue of plucking grain or laboring on the Sabbath being of such a concern that the early church would create such a story. (3) Jesus comparing his position with David's occurs again in Mark 12:25–27.

A technical note to consider as well: in many places, the wording of Matthew and Luke matches that of Mark.[11] This may suggest that the event itself is multiply attested and thus stands independently corroborated.

We already noted above that the connection between Jesus' example and the Sabbath controversy is not strained. It compares a violation involving food with violation of the Sabbath. The illustration focuses on the Law not being followed—not *when* it was followed—thus opening up the discussion about the Sabbath.

That Jesus and his disciples acted in a manner distinct from the Sabbath practices of some more pious Jews is likely. It explains the depth of distinct traditional stories we have about this dispute. It is hard to believe that Jesus would have engaged in such acts and not thought about a justification to be distinct from the pious around him. To act distinctly and know why is very Jewish.

Objection: The Directness of Jesus' Final Claim

Part of what troubles some about this scene is the directness of Jesus' final claim. In examining the literary form of the story, scholars call this final remark a "pronouncement" in what is called a "controversy pronouncement story." Jesus has been challenged, so a controversy is present. His climactic pronouncement is his decisive response and the point of the story. These features explain the name of the form. When the event portrays Jesus as proclaiming that the Son of Man is Lord of the Sabbath (Mark 2:28), this is a claim to have authority over a sacred day that God commanded.

The remark includes Jesus' preferred way to refer to himself, using the title the Son of Man. This expression refers to a human figure, just as a reference to a son of Stephen refers to his son. So a son of a human being (= Son of Man) refers to a human descendant. However, the addition of "the" to the expression specifies that not just any human being is meant. The New Testament Greek always presents the expression in such contexts as "the

Son of the Man." So we are looking at a particular human figure who is wielding a wide array of authority. We might even speak of the "unique Man." This consistent emphasis becomes clear as Jesus continued to use the term. Many of our twelve key events use the term, and we shall trace some of its key uses and develop our understanding of how Jesus uses it through the other events tied to it.[12] But even if a person knew nothing about the term, he could sense in the context of this Mark 2 saying that it involves a claim of high authority. To be over the Sabbath is to be over the sacred calendar and one of the Ten Commandments.

Some wish to tie the term to Daniel 7:13–14, where this human also receives divine honor and rides the clouds as only transcendent beings do; but the association with this passage from Daniel does not surface until the end of Jesus' ministry. At this early point, the use of the expression is more ambiguous— which reminds us of the rule of inherent ambiguity. It is not yet entirely clear how one should understand the Son of Man. Jesus is revealing himself gradually. What is clear is that this figure has authority that extends over significant sacred matters of Jewish religious life.

Here we are at a key point in our survey. The issue is very much whether Jesus had such an authoritative self-understanding. For now, I wish to leave this question open rather than making the case that he did have such a self-understanding on the basis of arguing for or from this one scene. It is better to look at a larger portion of the tradition and additional events before addressing the issue fully. We will come back to this again and again—either this emphasis goes back to Jesus, or the early church has thoroughly imprinted this understanding across the tradition in a series of distinct, created events. Many scholars opt for the work of the early church here; the theology is said to be too advanced for Jesus or too arrogant a self-claim. But for now, all I want to note is the extent of the claim and what the story sets forth as a crucial point about his authority.[13]

Stories of Sabbath Healing

Plucking grain on the Sabbath is not our only key Sabbath controversy event. We now turn our attention to other stories involving Sabbath healing. In the Sabbath healings, we again run into the worldview issue of whether miracles take place. Here our historical tradition throws us a real curveball. Amazingly, this emphasis on Jesus' work is multiply attested *in non-Christian sources*. Josephus tells us that Jesus did "unusual" work, an allusion to his reputation as a miracle worker (*Antiquities* 18:63–64). The Greek here speaks of *paradoxōn*, which refers to things out of the ordinary. The second and third strands of non-Christian testimony come from later Jewish tradition about Jesus, as well as Jewish debate with Jesus in the gospels.

An Ancient Objection with a Twist: Jesus' Miracles Were Demonic or Sorcery

The sources above indicate that the Jews who rejected Jesus accused him of either acting under demonic power or doing his work with the authority of a sorcerer.

In the gospels, the charge was that Jesus cast out demons and acted with the power of Beelzebul (Mark 3:22 = Matthew 12:24 = Luke 11:15; M: Matthew 9:34, multiply attested; Beelzebul is another name for Satan). In Trypho the Jew's mid-second-century CE debate with the Christian Justin Martyr, the claim is that Jesus was a magician (reported by Justin Martyr, *Dialogue with Trypho* 69.7, 108). The skeptic Celsus repeats this same charge to Origen a century later (reported by Origen in *Contra Celsus* 1.28, 1.68). Finally, the *Talmud* also repeats the charge, even a few more centuries down the road (*b. Sanhedrin* 43a).[14] This obviously is not a compliment, but the twist is that it concedes that Jesus worked with unusual power. The ancients did not deny he did unusual things; they debated where the power came from!

So the idea of Jesus doing miracles and other acts of power is not unattested in outside sources. In fact, Dunn argues that Jesus' role as an exorcist healer "is one of the most widely attested and firmly established of the historical facts with which we have to deal."[15] What was debated among the ancients was where the power came from.

An Objection Not Present among the Ancients: Jesus' Miracles Were Fabricated

The one option *not* on the table among the ancients is an option popular today—that nothing took place; it is all made up in order to validate Jesus' status. But if it was necessary to attach the miraculous to a major religious figure, then why did Jews not do it for John the Baptist or the Teacher of Righteousness who led the Qumran community?[16] Despite the tendency of rationalists to appeal to myth and legend, the fact that the ancients do not deny such events allows us to speculate on the origin and meaning of these actions. Since sources that were positive toward Jesus *and* those that rejected him accept exceptional acts in Jesus' ministry, this tells us something unusual was taking place and that this was not merely made up.[17]

Objection: Other Ancient Figures Performed Miracles

In fact, attempts to explain these scenes in terms parallel to other ancient accounts or modernistic terms fail to deal with this testifying element in the sources opposed to Christianity. They also fail to note key differences about the claimed ancient parallels, even though it is often claimed by skeptics that Jesus' miracles merely mirror what some other great ancients are said to have done.

Let's look at these claims. Rooting their defense in naturalistic readings, some modern scholars argue that Jesus accomplished some type of psychosomatic result on a consistent basis, or ap-

peal to the ancient gullibility when it comes to miracles. Both
explanations ignore the fact that ancients were capable of being
skeptical about miracles and requires that the ancient opponents
did not have the intelligence to formulate other explanations that
challenged the reality of what Jesus did. They also have to deal
with the repetitive nature of the testimony about what Jesus did.
Naturalistic explanations have a hard time coping with the stub-
born acceptance in our non-Christian sources that something
surprising happened.

So an alternative is to appeal to the fact that other ancient
figures are said to have performed miracles in the Greco-Roman
world. This is true. Those texts exist. So this is a perfectly appropriate issue to raise. However, the parallels here are not quite in
the same league. In most cases these miracles involve one or two
authenticating miracles for an individual such as an emperor, not
the host of miracles Jesus is said to have performed.[18]

The three ancient figures most mentioned as parallel are two
Jewish healers and one Greco-Roman figure. They are involved in
a series of healings or nature miracles.[19] Honi the Circle Drawer
and Hanina ben Dosa, the two Jewish healers, do not seem to be
miracle workers. They pray to God, and the work is seen clearly as
God's. Vermes's treatment works through the texts, but *m. Ta'anit*
3:8 is the example where Honi got his name. Here he prayed for
rain after drawing a circle around himself, saying he would not
emerge until rain came from God. So, as this text shows, Honi's
reputation is really that of a prayer warrior. In contrast, Jesus acts
directly as one who has this power inherently.

Apollonius of Tyana is the key Greco-Roman example. What
we know of him comes from a third-century CE work that many
take to have been created in imitation of what Christians were
saying about Jesus as these Christians were becoming more numerous in the Roman Empire of the time.[20] This origin raises serious questions about the parallel, especially when it is clear that
the story of Apollonius is not as historical in genre as the gospels.

Objection: Rabbinical Tradition Had Not Yet Ruled against Sabbath Healing

Nonetheless, in the Sabbath healing scenes, two more inter-twined objections dominate. (1) There is no indication that heal-ing was prohibited on the Sabbath in Jewish materials we have up to this date. So the reaction to the story does not culturally fit and is overdrawn in order to create (2) the conspiracy to kill Jesus noted in Mark 3:6. In other words, the scene is a fabrication of apologetics, not history.

Here the question is whether the possibility of public healing on the Sabbath, especially in a miraculous way, was sufficiently widespread to have required the oral tradition in Judaism to issue a ruling. With regard to the lack of notice about healing on the Sabbath one can argue one of two ways. *First*, we noted that the healers Judaism had were few and far between. We just noted the two most famous examples, Honi the Circle Drawer and Hanina ben Dosa. They cover a century-long period. This is one of those cases where the dynamic process of dealing with a fresh situation may have produced the reaction that Jesus had gone too far. As one text puts it in so many words: Okay, Jesus, heal—but not on the Sabbath; that is labor dishonoring to God (Luke 13:14).

On the other hand, one could argue we have circumstantial evidence that such an act was prohibited. The Jewish materials do have to state a ruling about saving someone's life on the Sab-bath (*m. Yoma* 8.6), suggesting that this topic was debated. If it requires a ruling to defend an effort to save a life, then simply healing also may well have been understood to need to wait until after the day.

The silence Meier leans so heavily on to say there was no rule may actually be evidence. It may show that a prohibition to heal on the Sabbath may have been a given, if acting for a life was debated. Even more, why would the church create a story stating a rule as its basis, if there was not such a rule? That very move would undercut the story's credibility. One can argue then that the rule in Luke 13:14 is evidence of Jewish expectation at least in one setting, if not functioning as a general rule.

A reason one cannot be sure which way to argue is that our historical access to the period and its practice is limited. We do not have all the sources about life and practice that the period generated. Only a portion of that material has survived and made its way to us. This is a limitation with which historical work always has to deal in assessing events. Generally, the older the event is, the less extensive are the sources.

As to the issue of the plot, or the second part of this complex objection, Mark 3:6 comes at the end of a series of five controversies. Mark has probably gathered these together in one sequence to show how Jesus came to be opposed (Mark 2:1–3:6). Thus, the plot is not a result of this one scene. Rather the plot is a reaction to several challenges Jesus made that countered official authority. That several events triggered a reaction is very credible.

All of this is important because of another expectation—that God would not honor a sinner or lawbreaker on the Sabbath. So if a healing did take place, it would immediately have engendered the question of where the power to do so came from. We already know the answer to this question: those who followed Jesus saw it as an expression of his authority and God's power; those who rejected him saw it as either demonic or magical. The entire event, if authentic, then has in it an implicit challenge about who Jesus is and who stands behind him.

We believe a strong case for the historicity of this kind of event can be made. Its authenticity isn't as corroborated as other events when we play by the rules, but we find the case to deny its authenticity is even less compelling. As Hagner concluded when he assessed the historicity of this theme, "As with all historical argument, we necessarily deal with degrees of probability rather than absolute certitude. But the evidence warrants acceptance of these accounts as highly probable, trustworthy history." [21]

MEANING OF JESUS' SABBATH CONTROVERSIES

The Grain-Plucking Event

The key to the grain-plucking event is not only tied to the importance of the Sabbath in the Jewish religious context; it is also related to how Jesus makes his case. His argument operates on two levels.

First, the David example shows there are exceptions to the Law, although Jesus never explicitly says on what basis. The remark about the Sabbath being made for man, not man for the Sabbath, suggests that the Sabbath was never intended to be so restrictive that basic life activity, such as eating, would be prevented by being called labor. The only thing the additional examples in Matthew do is add to the list of exceptions, with a note of explanation that God desires mercy over sacrifice. Ritual is less important than relationships. These are straightforward biblical arguments, what Jews called legal rulings or *halakah*. Had Jesus stopped here, everything about his response would have been completely Jewish, rooted in legal reflection. Had Jesus stopped here, he would have looked and acted merely as a prophet.

The *second* level of argument strictly centers on personal authority. Central here is the already noted claim that the Son of Man is Lord of the Sabbath. This remark ups the ante. This is not a legal argument, but an eschatological claim about the authority of the one rendering the judgment. It says, in effect, regardless of the legal and biblical examples I just gave you, I have the right to make this call and determine what is right. Again Hagner says it well: "This is no ordinary teacher or healer who has the temerity to violate accepted norms of Sabbath activity. He strides through the Synoptic tradition as one who has no parallel and whose unique authority is not a derived authority. . . . The sovereign freedom with which Jesus interprets Sabbath law is inseparable from his unique identity as the agent of God's redemptive rule. As Son of Man, he is Lord of the Sabbath."[22]

The Sabbath Healings

The Healings Point to Divine Connection

The Sabbath healing accounts add another dimension to the argument about the origin of this authority. If Jesus violates the Sabbath and God punishes sinners who violate the divine Law, then how do the people get healed? What power is at work that is able to accomplish this? It does not make sense to see Jesus violate the Sabbath and see people restored by him. Thus, these acts substantiate claims that Jesus is closely associated to God, since God is a healer and restorer. This is why miracles were called "powers" or "signs" in some texts. They were audiovisuals, Powerpoints, if you will, that stood behind claims of what was said. These events spoke on their own terms on behalf of Jesus. God is powerfully at work, they say. Claims that we cannot see or prove in terms of God acting are authenticated by acts that point to divine connection and vindication.

The Healings Show God's Care

There also was an ethic to these works of healing. They showed God's care for those who needed help. Human need was a priority to Jesus—thus, the Sabbath was made to benefit man, not man made to benefit the Sabbath. As one text says it, there was no better day to heal and honor God than the Sabbath (Luke 13:16). The kingdom represented the coming of God to reverse the presence of evil and suffering. In a sense they were preached events, not of words but of actions. And with these actions was the message that God is reaching out in restoration. As Jesus argued in the Mark 3 healing, one is to do good on the Sabbath (v. 4). Matthew's addition to the grain-plucking scene speaks of acts of mercy being what God desires. The remark is a citation of the Hebrew prophet Hosea (Hosea 6:6). Jesus' complaint was not against the Sabbath; what he challenged was an overextension of restrictions tied to it that prevented people from caring for their neighbors.

The Healings Have Cosmic Implications

In the work of service and restoration, there is another dimension introduced into Jesus' rationale for acting—the cosmic implications of what was taking place. In Luke 13:16, Jesus describes the woman he has healed as having been "bound" by Satan. To heal the woman is to free her from the grip of one who seeks to limit the potential God created in humanity. Jesus spoke far more of this cosmic opponent as his concern than he did any political entity, such as Rome. This is thoroughly eschatological thinking, reflecting a worldview where forces opposed to God are at work to disrupt creation. Liberation here involves freeing up what God had created to be fully human in ways God had intended. God is victorious over evil forces through Jesus.

So as with John the Baptist, the choosing of the Twelve, and, to a degree, the picture of table fellowship, Jesus' story is about eschatology and the promise of God. Jesus' activity represents a fresh move to restore hope and bring deliverance. Turning people back to God and participation in his promise sits at the center of Jesus' activity. It is this hope of deliverance and the picture of power and authority to bring it that the healings picture. Here on a day to honor God and contemplate the divine goodness in the creation, people are restored and delivered. Eschatology and hope are enshrined in these healings. They point to a better time and day. They also underwrite the one who does the healing as one with authority to act. They point to God's rule, his victory, and even the arrival of his kingdom through Jesus.

The Sabbath was made for man, but it also was made for the Son of Man. It stood in submission to him. In later Jewish tradition, the Sabbath also was seen as a symbol of the era to come.

The very late thirteenth-century Jewish text *Zohar*, discussing Genesis 48a, taught that the Sabbath was a mirror on the world to come—on that day each week one drew near to God in a special way different from other days. One day, those who are with God will be drawn near to him when God finishes what he has started. As the Sabbath pointed to a focus on God and even on the era to come, Jesus' healings on the sacred Sabbath said that this new era and its deliverance were dawning. It comes with, in, and through him. That is why the Son of Man was Lord even of the Sabbath.

This is also why Jesus' actions provoked a reaction by the leadership. As theologians, they understood and appreciated the scope of the claim. The example appealing to David might be what a prophet would do and say. That example pointed out how the Law of God was not being violated. But to claim to be Lord of the Sabbath was not the utterance of a prophet, it was a claim to be at the hub of divine authority and promise. Jesus' work on the Sabbath was not the violation of a commandment; instead, it affirmed the divine mercy God had intended the Sabbath to exalt all along. These were the new things God was now doing—and he was doing them through one who was far more than a prophet.

6

Jesus and Exorcism:

Authority, the Kingdom of God, and Cosmic Forces

T HIS CHAPTER treats a key theme that has two parts: kingdom proclamation and *Jesus' exorcisms*.[1] In the midst of discussing Sabbath controversies, we raised the issue of Jesus' healings. Here we look at a particular set of healings and what they show about Jesus' ministry and the core of his teaching. Jesus' major teaching theme was the kingdom of God. As the last chapter suggested, some things done within Jesus' ministry did not need words to communicate a message to his first-century audience. This is especially true of the exorcism events. We turn first to the case for historicity before looking at what these actions show.

RULES THAT APPLY TO JESUS' EXORCISMS AND KINGDOM PROCLAMATION

Attestation to Kingdom Proclamation

Jesus' preaching about the kingdom of God is one of the most widely accepted facts about his ministry. In support of Jesus' preaching of the kingdom, we have the summary in Mark 1:14–15 that says he proclaimed the nearness of the kingdom and called people to repent (= Matt 4:17). This mirrors the message of John who makes the same call according to Matthew 3:2. So we see that the kingdom theme is in the Markan sources. In a change of form, parables about this kingdom abound in the gospels. There are topical collections of such parables in Mark 4 and Matthew 13, and a smaller sample in Luke 8:4–17 and 13:18–19. These parables come through the tradition Mark uses, while others are unique to Matthew. So parables within this kingdom theme are *multiply attested*. John has the theme in John 3:3–5 and 18:36. L material includes a summary at Luke 4:43. Q has a major passage at Matthew 11:2–19 = Luke 7:18–35. This passage discusses Jesus, John, and the kingdom (esp. Matthew 11:11 = Luke 7:28). Such texts are so numerous that there is no doubt that his central topic was the kingdom (or rule) of God. This theme is multiply attested both in terms of *sources* and *forms*.

Attestations to Exorcisms

What about the attestation for exorcisms? Exorcisms and the battle with cosmic forces are part of a worldview associated with Jewish eschatological and apocalyptic hope. Central to this way of seeing the world is a belief in the struggle between spiritual forces of good and evil, not just social and political concerns. Among the Jews, Sadducees did not hold to this way of seeing the world, but many of those in other groups did, especially among the Essenes and Pharisees. Some Jews held a special hope in the figure of Enoch.[2] Hope for the kingdom remained strong among many Jews until the failure of messianic movements like the Bar Kochba rebellion in 132–35 CE. This rebellion produced a strong Roman reaction that crushed Israel politically and quashed such hope.

Attestation of exorcisms begins with the Q account of the

temptations, where Jesus faces off with Satan (Matthew 4:1–11 = Luke 4:1–13), which is itself an expansion of a shorter report in Mark 1:12–13. Q also has a summary about Jesus' exorcism activity in the report to be given to John the Baptist in Matthew 11:2–6 = Luke 7:18–23. Another passage from Q is part of the instruction for the mission of the disciples in Matthew 10:7–8 = Luke 9:1–2, where Jesus gives this authority to the disciples. This text also has a variation of a summary in Mark 6:7–13.

There are numerous texts in sources tied to Mark. A narrative summary on exorcism appears in Mark 1:27 = Luke 4:36, while an exorcism involving a Syro-Phoenician woman occurs in Mark 7:24–30 = Matthew 15:21–28. There is an exorcism in a Capernaum synagogue in Mark 1:23–28 = Luke 4:33–37. An exorcism of a person possessed by multiple demons appears in Mark 5:1–20 = Matthew 8:28–34 = Luke 8:26–39. An exorcism is performed on a boy in Mark 9:14–29 = Matthew 17:14–20 = Luke 9:37–43a. Disputes over an exorcism Jesus performed appear in Mark 3:22–27 = Matthew 12:22–37 = Luke 11:14–23. Some key material in this scene is unique to Matthew and Luke, suggesting Q also had a version of this dispute (Luke 11:20 = Matthew 12:28). In fact, as you can see, there is a lot of Mark and Q overlap on this theme, but in independent directions, as Luke 11:20 speaks of casting out demons by the "finger of God" and Matthew 12:28 speaks of casting out demons "by the Holy Spirit."

L has a saying of Jesus where he declares seeing Satan fall like lightning (Luke 10:17–19), as well as an exorcism involving an elderly woman (Luke 13:10–17). There is a unique note in Luke 8:2 about Mary Magdalene being the beneficiary of an exorcism. Passages in Acts also discuss the element in Jesus' ministry (Acts 10:38).

Sources unique to Matthew (M) have only one short exorcism (Matthew 9:32–33).

So *multiple attestation* of exorcism also occurs in terms of *sources* and *forms*. In form, we have narrative, summaries, controversy accounts and sayings. It is interesting that no unique exorcism material appears in John. In fact, there are no exorcisms at all in John. It is not clear why. Did he think it already well covered in the tradition? We do not know why there is this omission.

In sum, multiple attestation in its two forms points to the authenticity of both parts of this material.

OBJECTIONS

Objections to Existence of Spiritual Beings

As with Sabbath healing, one of the objections to these scenes involves the worldview issue of whether such spiritual beings exist and doubt about miracles in general. We already covered this question from an ancient source perspective in the previous chapter when we noted that even among Jewish sources there are notes that point to Jesus performing unusual works. Most other objections to the idea of exorcism relate to particular details in each account. These objections result in a claim that the events are implausible in their detail, even if one is open to exorcistic activity in the period.

Defeat of Satan in Jewish Texts

It is important to note that the idea of the defeat of Satan in the period of the kingdom in the age to come is a theme in many Jewish texts. The activity has cultural plausibility in terms of how such acts of exorcism, if they took place, would be understood.

The most explicit of these texts comes from the *Testament of Moses* (also known as *Assumption of Moses*). It is an old Jewish text, composed c. 300 BCE. In 10:1, the text reads, "And then his kingdom will appear in his whole creation, and then the devil will have an end, and sorrow will be led away with him."

This theme is so deep in Second Temple Judaism that it is

worth tracing to show that it came with the territory of kingdom hope for many Jews. It can be said confidently that the kingdom's arrival meant the defeat of Satan as a matter of course for Jews.

Another old Jewish Second Temple text comes from *Jubilees*, a work from the mid–second century BCE. We have manuscripts from this work from Qumran that date to c. 100 BCE. Chapter 23 expresses the hope of deliverance and restoration for Israel. Verses 29–30 read, "all of their days they will be complete and live in peace and rejoicing there will be no Satan and no evil [one] who will destroy, because all of their days will be days of blessing and healing. And then the Lord will heal his servants, and they will rise up and see great peace." The hope is rooted in Isaiah 65–66. Also chapter 50, verse 5, reads in a similar way, "And jubilees will pass until Israel is purified from all the sin of fornication, and defilement, and uncleanness, and sin and error. And they will dwell in confidence in all the land. And then it will not have any Satan nor any evil [one]. And the land will be purified from that time and forever." *Jubilees* is associated with Jewish groups whose descendants were Pharisees in the time of Jesus. Satan's defeat is a key part of what was hoped for in deliverance.

Yet another work dating a few centuries before the time of Jesus is the first portion of what today is called *1 Enoch*. Its roots are debated. Was there a distinct Jewish school of people who drew heavily on developed stories about Enoch as deliverer in the end? Or was there merely a group of Jews who had an intense hope in deliverance and saw Enoch as one figure in the drama? Either way, their hope is powerfully expressed in 10:4–6. The one thing we need to know before citing this text is that the lead evil demon had different names in Second Temple Judaism. The one we call Satan is named Aza'el in these verses. It reads, "And to Rafael he said: Bind Aza'el hand and foot, and cast him into darkness, and open the wilderness which is in Dadou'el and there cast him. And put him beneath jagged and sharp stones and hide him in darkness. And let him dwell there forever, and cover his face and let him not see light, and in the day of judgment he shall be led away to the furnace."

Other texts in this work make the same point. Another later segment of *1 Enoch* is in the Parables section of the book.[3] It was written a century or two after the earlier passage in *1 Enoch,* yet it also has this idea. In 55:4, the Elect One, who in other texts is called the Son of Man, judges Azaz'el (alternate spelling of Aza'el) and all his company.

A text at Qumran tells us that Azaz'el was head of the fallen angels (4Q180 1:7). This is how we know the figure is the equivalent of the figure of Satan in the Jesus tradition.

The *Apocalypse of Abraham* 23:6–8 has this leading evil figure as the one who tempts Adam and Eve. So his résumé parallels the figure we know as Satan. Yet a third set of texts comes from the *Testament of the Twelve Patriarchs*. Here the chief enemy is named Beliar. The variety of sources cited for this figure shows how widespread such thinking was in the period.

The *Testament of Levi* 18:11b–12 reads, "The spirit of holiness shall be upon them. And Beliar shall be bound by him, and he shall grant great authority to his children to trample over wicked spirits." The idea of binding the evil one shows up in various gospel texts in contexts where the battle with evil is present (Mark: Mark 3:27; Mark 5:3; L: Luke 13:16). Now some suggest this text from the *Testament of Levi* is a Christian addition to the Jewish text, in part, because remarks in verses 6–7 show traces of Christian influence that many do acknowledge. However, the text at this later point lacks any explicit Christian coloring. Rather, the text shows association with ideas from the Hebrew Scripture in Isaiah 24:22–23 with its theme of binding, Genesis 3:15 with the idea of trampling, and Psalm 91:3 with the thought of trampling the serpent.

Testament of Naphtali 8:4 goes in a similar direction: "If you achieve the good, my children, humans and angels will bless you, and God will be glorified through you among the gentiles. The devil will flee from you; wild animals will be afraid of you; and the Lord will love you; and the angels will stand by you."

Testament of Judah 25:3b expresses the hope this way: "There shall no more be Beliar's spirit of error, because he will be thrown into the eternal fire."

Testament of Zebulun 9:8 speaks of the end ransoming "every captive of the sons of men from Beliar." Other parts of this passage from Zebulun are seen as possessing Christian elements, since later there is a reference to God in human form standing in the temple. So this particular portion of the passage on Beliar is debated as to whether it expresses a Christian or Jewish hope. The theme fits other texts where there is less debate, so it may be another witness to this theme as Jewish. If the text is not Jewish, then several other Jewish texts make the point as we have just seen.

Last of all is the *Testament of Dan* 5:10–11. It reads, "And there shall arise from you from the tribe of Judah and [the tribe of] Levi the Lord's salvation. He will make war against Beliar; he will grant the vengeance of victory as our goal. And he shall take from Beliar the captives, the souls of the saints. And he shall turn the hearts of the disobedient ones to the Lord." This text looks Jewish, since God makes war with Beliar, not a messianic delivering figure as one would expect if the text were Christian. Later in this chapter in *Dan*, the righteous refresh themselves in Eden and rejoice in the New Jerusalem (5:12–13).

This row of texts, from a variety of Second Temple sources, shows a widespread Jewish expectation that the kingdom involved Satan's defeat. The kingdom of God these Jews preached was not merely about God's sovereign right to rule because he was the Creator. So "kingdom of God" is not a reference to God's generic right to rule because he made humanity; it is about God bringing something fresh. This is preaching about something else, something new. God was reclaiming something that had gone adrift and was held in the clutches of opposing forces. To believe that this battle would one day be won was to hope for something that did not yet exist and that needed to be gained. To hope in the kingdom was to look forward to the removal of a deconstructive power in the world.

So when John the Baptist and Jesus preached the arrival of the kingdom, it was this deliverance and victory that was anticipated. When Jesus acted against the forces of evil in exorcism, he evoked this hope. It was a part of the kingdom package. This theme is widely attested in independent sources that speak of Jesus acting. It also clearly fits a long-held cultural expectation that it is unlikely to be a later church creation. It is much more likely to be rooted in the experience tied to Jesus, where he proclaimed he was bringing something long promised and expected. To claim Jesus performed exorcisms in settings that knew his ministry, if he did not do such things, would be to expose the tradition to criticism. As we saw in the last chapter, we know the ancient debate was about the *source* of Jesus' act, not that it did not happen (see also the discussion to follow).

MEANING OF EXORCISMS AND KINGDOM PREACHING

The Authority of the Final Deliverer

The source of Jesus' authority becomes clear when he performs exorcism. Such action reveals Jesus to have authority over cosmic forces. He also proclaimed that the kingdom of God was dawning and the defeat of evil was beginning. The prophet Daniel expressed this hope, speaking of an everlasting kingdom cut from the stone of a mountain, not made of human hands (Daniel 2:44–45). Part of the vindication tied to the deliverance of God's people is the Ancient of Days giving judgment authority to one "like a Son of Man," a figure who represents God's people (Daniel 7:9–27, esp. vv. 13–14). It is a kingdom of power, might, and glory (Daniel 2:37, 5:18).

A look at what is said in the New Testament passages fills out the meaning of this picture. However, the host of Jewish texts already cited shows the cultural expectations and suppositions that would have come with such acts and kingdom claims. As N. T. Wright asks, "What did people see when they saw Jesus at work" in this way?[4] These ideas did not emerge after Jesus' ministry as products of early church teaching; they had long been present in the thinking of those for whom Jesus acted. As Wright goes on to say about the exorcisms, they were "not simply the release from strange bondage of a few poor benighted souls. [Nor are they all to be explained away by rationalistic reductionism.] For Jesus and the evangelists they signaled something far deeper that was going on, namely, the real battle of the ministry, which was not a round of fierce debates with the keepers of orthodoxy, but head-on war with the satan."[5]

In the same discussion Wright also observes how dissimilar all of this is with Second Temple Judaism and, to a degree, the early church. Neither group gave as much explicit and major emphasis to the final deliverer performing exorcism in the end as these acts by Jesus do. There are claims of such acts in the early church, as Acts 10:38 attests, but the point is that such claims and acts were not central to the acts or the message of the post-resurrection disciples. What Judaism argued for was God's defeat of Satan. Dunn notes how there is "surprisingly little indication that either royal or the priestly Messiah was expected to work deeds of power."[6] This is so, despite the fact that David and Solomon had well-circulated reputations in the period as exorcists.[7] When the idea of exorcism appears, it comes from the end-time prophet who announces the end in an Elijah-like manner. So the theme fits another criterion: *double similarity/dissimilarity*.

Defeat of Satan Suggests Arrival of the Kingdom

Our argument depends not so much on the details in these gospel exorcism texts as the fact that they repeatedly took place. Nonetheless, it is helpful to look at a few key texts and make the specific case for the individual events, as opposed to our general look at the topic that was considered above. This adds to the case for the topic as a whole.

In line with this Second Temple Jewish background comes Jesus' remark in the midst of a dispute about his ability to heal (Luke 11:14–23 = Matthew 12:22–32). In this setting the debate is whether Jesus casts out demons by the power of Beelzebul or not. Jesus answers the challenge in two ways. First, he argues that if Satan helps him to cast out demons, then Satan works against himself and his house is divided. Jesus suggests that this is neither consistent nor a credible explanation for what is happening. Rather, "If I cast out demons by the Spirit [Matthew]/ finger of God [Luke], then the kingdom of God has come upon you."[8] In other words, the defeat of Satan suggests the arrival of the kingdom.

Can one corroborate whether this saying goes back to Jesus? The tie of Beelzebul to the head of evil demons appears in *Testament of Solomon* 3:6, where he is named "ruler of demons."[9]

The saying assumes two kingdoms at war. John the Baptist had called Jesus the "stronger one" in Mark 1:7. In the Beelzebul passage, Jesus is shown as a strong one who plunders Satan's house and overtakes him (Q: Luke 11:21–23 = Matthew 12:29). We have two independently attested versions of the charge that Jesus casts out demons by the power of Beelzebul. Mark 3:22 appears in a distinct setting. It reads, "He is possessed by Beelzebul, and by the prince of the demons he casts out demons." These exorcisms serve as context for the crucial claim that if Jesus casts out demons with the help of God, then the kingdom has arrived.

The "Finger of God" vs. the "Spirit of God"

The saying itself is from Q. The only difference in wording is that Matthew refers to the "Spirit of God," while Luke speaks of the "finger of God." It is interesting that Luke is the gospel writer who speaks most explicitly about the Holy Spirit, yet in this saying he lacks the reference. This leads many to suspect that the original wording of the saying had "finger of God," which is an allusion to the power of God in saving.

Exodus 8:15 (8:19 in the English version; versification differs from the Hebrew) has this exact expression—"the finger of God"—and is the passage that shows this allusion to power. Luke retains the allusion, while Matthew appears to have explained and simplified the reference by referring directly to God. It is easier to see the passing on of the saying move in the direction of Matthew changing "finger" to "Spirit" versus Luke making a change in the other direction, although the direction of the change is debatable. Luke makes the figure of God's finger more concrete and explicit by indicating who is at work.

Matthew is the more Jewish of the gospels, and often Jews removed expressions about God that compared him with human activity or human forms. Such literary expressions are called anthropomorphisms. Luke does give evidence, however, of using such language, so he could have made the change ("hand of God"—Luke 1:66, Acts 4:30; "God's arm"—Luke 1:51). On the other hand, these other Lucan references take place in hymns and prayer contexts that may reflect the sources themselves rather than Luke. Alternatively, Matthew 7:11 has God giving "good things" to us when we pray, while the parallel in Luke 11:13 has God giving the "Holy Spirit." Luke also adds the description "Holy" to Markan references only to "the Spirit" (Luke 4:1 versus Mark 1:12 and Luke 3:22 in comparison to Mark 1:10). Thus we'd expect the retention of a reference to the "Holy Spirit" in Luke 11:20 had it been there originally. Regardless of which gospel writer made the change between "Spirit" and "finger of God," the two versions say the same thing. God's saving power is behind Jesus' ability to heal and exorcize.

The Value of Discussing the Details

The discussion of the difference in wording in this verse is important in order to show how scholars in historical Jesus discussion look at everything in detail. It also shows how historical judgments are in play throughout the entire conversation about what is going on. These discussions often have two levels. On the one hand, a baseline of what is taking place is clear, but the underlying direction for how we got there is more debated. So this set of texts is clear in claiming God was behind what Jesus was doing. However, the exact route taken to give us the distinct wording of these texts is less clear.

As well, there are radical historical critics who have accepted the genuineness of this saying.[10] The Jesus Seminar, which is normally quite skeptical about Jesus' sayings, also rates this saying pink, which means Jesus said it or something very much like it, even if the exact wording is not certain.[11] In commenting on texts like this, Rudolph Bultmann, who was often quite skeptical of the historical character in the gospels, said, "But there can be no doubt that Jesus did the kind of deeds which were miracles to his mind and to the minds of his contemporaries, that is, deeds which were attributed to a supernatural, divine cause; undoubtedly he healed the sick and cast out demons . . . he obviously himself understood his miracles as a sign of the imminence of the Kingdom of God."[12] I often tell my classes that when liberal and conservative critics on Jesus agree, which is rare, then we can be very confident we are on solid ground.

The allusion to Exodus 8 is interesting in light of later Jewish tradition. Whereas Exodus says nothing about how the Egyptian magicians explained what Moses did, the later *Exodus Rabbah*, a commentary on Exodus from a few centuries after the time of Jesus, says, "As soon as the magicians realized they were unable to produce gnats, they recognized the deeds were those of God and not demons. They no longer claimed to compare themselves with Moses in producing the plagues" (*Exodus Rabbah* 10.7 [on Exodus 8:15]). In other words, for Jews, the kind of evidence Moses gave showed he was working with God's enablement. Moses had access to the "finger of God." Jesus makes a similar claim in his time. All should see and understand this connection, as well as what it meant about the kingdom. Given a choice between positive and negative powers, Jesus' works give evidence of being rooted in positive forces. As Pharoah was defeated by the divine signs of Moses, so Satan stands defeated by Jesus as the kingdom comes. This saying has good reason to be seen as authentic. It also serves as the most significant explanation of what Jesus' healing activity means to those who heard and embraced his message. That perception of Jesus was rooted in the things Jesus did and taught, as even the rules of corroboration show.

Conclusion

In the previous discussion on the Sabbath we spoke of Jesus' authority over sacred days and commandments. In this theme, we encounter a display of another level of authority: Jesus' ability to oppose and defeat negative cosmic forces. In the battle between God and Satan, we see a confrontation in the pursuit of human souls. Jesus intervenes. He heals, casts out demons, and restores oppressed people to wholeness. He is a roadblock to all Satan seeks to accomplish. Jesus' actions announce God's initiative to deliver humans, who are in dire need of a powerful deliverer, from the grip of evil. By defeating the forces of evil, Jesus' actions show the arrival of the delivering rule of God with a power that transforms the landscape of life at a profound level. Jesus deals with spiritual forces we otherwise cannot see. Claims with words are often cheap and empty, but actions can raise questions and show things words can only attempt to describe. So Jesus does not appeal primarily or merely with words; rather, he acts and explains. In this way, those around him can see he has acted with unusual force and authority.

Jesus argued that his coming represented the coming of a new time and day. How can we know? Look and see what kind of delivering power this is. The finger of God is at work. Demons flee. The grip is lifted. His house is plundered. His kingdom is being dismantled. At the center of it all stands Jesus. In a sense, the exorcisms were an invitation, calling people to join in the liberation of the soul that the removal of evil made possible.

7

Peter's Declaration at Caesarea Philippi:

A Cautious Word about Messianic Hope

Our focus turns back to specific events.[1] Virtually all scholars recognize Peter's declaration at Caesarea Philippi about Jesus being the Messiah as a key turning point in the Jesus story of Matthew, Mark, and Luke. Yet as clear as Peter is, Jesus initially advises that this recognition be handled with care, even silence. In scholarly circles, this hesitation is called "the Messianic Secret," an idea that has engendered no lack of debate in historical Jesus discussion. Why the word to be silent after the declaration? Why keep the understanding in-house? This event is so crucial that much time shall be spent interacting with objections to it. Only a careful look at the first-century perspective on the Messiah and Jesus' handling of it can help us to understand the caution Jesus initially had about being publicly labeled the Messiah during his ministry.

RULES THAT APPLY TO PETER'S
DECLARATION ABOUT JESUS

The central passage is Mark 8:27–30 = Matt 16:13–20 = Luke 9:18–21. Though presented with some variation, Peter says Jesus is the Christ in every rendering in these gospels. Mark has "the Christ." Matthew has "the Christ, the Son of the living God." Luke has "the Christ of God." John (6:66–69)[2] has "the Holy One of God." All the versions see Jesus occupying a unique place in God's program as either the anointed one (Messiah) or as one set apart by God (Holy One). This is the gist of the event we examine. *Messiah* means "anointed" in Hebrew. The Greek term is *Christ*. However, all kinds of figures can be anointed in the Jewish context: especially kings, prophets, and priests. When Peter uses the term, the remark is placed in a final-deliverance context. The Messiah is to be distinguished from a solely prophetic understanding of Jesus—the passage contrasts Christ with the crowds' view that Jesus is some kind of a prophet.[3]

The important authenticating criteria we will look at are Palestinian environment, embarrassment, and coherence. First, we will look at the environment.

Palestinian Environment

Caesarea Philippi is not a natural locale for this event, although its place in first-century geography is well known. In fact, if one visits the Holy Land today, this is one of the popular tourist spots. It is located just outside ancient Galilee and features a sheer cliff running up several hundred feet. Carved into the rock at various spots are niches that once held idols. These sacred sites were located by streams that ran near the base of the cliff. Some of the niches were carved after Jesus' time, but the character of the location dates back to before his ministry. These niches tell us that this locale was home to many temples and the worship of many gods. The god Pan and the emperor Augustus are among the more prominent figures honored here—in fact, an alternate name of the location is Paneas (for Pan). In other words, this is one of the most prominent locales for worship of multiple gods in the region. It is about as un-Jewish a spot as one could have found in the ancient land.

Some wish to argue that this setting is a later creation because of its connection to Hellenistic religion and its implicit argument that Jesus is superior to their gods, including the emperor. However, the presence of this place's name appears in a manner uncommon for Mark's naming of locations. The locale is too specific for the kind of transition taking place here (compare Mark 1:21; 2:1; 3:1, 20; 5:1; 6:16; 7:24). Mark speaks of the "villages of Caesarea Philippi," so he does not evoke this specific temple locale but merely the regional association. This more implicit connection reads more ambiguously than an explicit location. It gives less of a sense of a created location. More than that, the expression is not like Mark, who tends to refer to a region or district in such descriptions (5:1—region of Geresenes; 17—their region; 7:24, 31—region of Tyre; 8:10—district of Dalmanutha). In other words, Mark did not create this note about the location. It is not the way he points to settings. At the least, Caesarea Philippi belongs to the tradition about this event.

In addition, the locale is out of character with much of Jesus' ministry, which focused on Jewish concerns and preaching to the nation. The events described and the moment of the great declaration are not associated with Jewish imagery and a setting like the edge of Jerusalem or the singular temple, but the most contrastive religious environment of polytheism. Yet this is evoked only indirectly by the use of a town's name.

In support of the scene's authenticity are indications of a distinctive memory.[4] When Jesus is in these regions, he is not described as going into the cities, but as staying on the outskirts or in villages. That part of the story fits Jesus' ministry practice elsewhere. A made-up story may have made more explicit some of the associations of the location and made the challenge to polytheism more explicit. Even more, a story created in line with the rest of the gospel story would have had a more Jewish focus than this locale does. Why not place this central declaration in a more Jewish locale, since one can place it anywhere if the story is made up? Why not tell it as Jesus draws near to Jerusalem or in the context of his ministry near his home and the Sea of Galilee?

Yet another detail here is that the placement of this event comes at a time just after John the Baptist has been beheaded. This may explain a sojourn north of the jurisdiction where John met his fate. Jesus moves away from danger for a time. Antipas is alluded to as knowing about Jesus in Mark 6:14, and Jesus is next described in places as diverse as Tyre and Sidon, the Decapolis, and Bethsaida, as well as in Caesarea. All these locations are outside the jurisdiction of Antipas.

All of this Palestinian background points to a real event.

Embarrassment

A second rule that applies to the scene is the criterion of embarrassment. Peter challenges Jesus when Jesus mentions his approaching suffering right after this declaration. Jesus replies to Peter, telling him, "Get behind me, Satan!" (Mark 8:33 = Matthew 16:23). The detail is shocking enough that Luke omits it. This strong rebuke is not likely to be part of a story the church creates to present itself. It ends up having one of its key leaders severely rebuked, not exactly the way to commend your leadership to a public already raising questions about what you believe. In other words, this is a classic example of the criterion of embarrassment. Why create a story that embarrasses one of its leaders like this? The embarrassing detail is in the story because it is authentic. It strains credulity to see this story created with this unflattering picture of Peter and retained in the church's tradition about him, when those who kept this tradition had a high regard for Peter.[5] The reason such a detail would be retained was because the event, with its note of confrontation, made a lasting impression on community memory.

Coherence

The final criterion to consider is coherence. Now it must be acknowledged that this criterion is one of the most subjective in the list. Coherence can be in the eye of the beholder. Working backward from Jesus' execution ordered by Rome, we know that Jesus has to be seen as some type of insurrectionist in their eyes, because sedition was the only kind of charge that led to public execution.[6] A claim to be the Messiah, a leader of the people in deliverance, fits this category better than being a nonviolent prophet.

Working forward from John the Baptist, one recalls that his ministry evoked the eschatological hope of deliverance for the nation. We see the Twelve being selected, symbolizing a reconstituted people of God with Jesus at its head. The kind of activity Jesus engages in reads like the hope expressed in a text from Qumran (4Q521). Here God will perform marvelous acts in the decisive deliverance: "for he will heal the badly wounded and will make the dead live, he will proclaim good news to the meek, give lavishly [to the needy], lead the exiled and enrich the hungry."[7] Earlier in the text in line 1, there is mention of at least one messianic figure, so it is not hard to think that the Messiah could be the one through whom God works these acts. At the least, the text shows that God's activity is tied to the eschatological period that includes the Messiah or some prophet-like, end-time figure.[8] The expectation for those who held to such a hope is that God would act and do so through some commissioned figure. All of this coheres with the story line we have developed in the events and themes we have argued for as authentic.

Jesus' actions and words spoke of his messianic identification. This is clearly the case in the new community that preached Jesus after his death—they preached him as the Messiah, even calling him Jesus Christ, where the second name is not a last name but serves as a central title to identify him. In texts from L in Luke 19:11 and 24:21, the disciples express the hope that either the kingdom is arriving, or that Jesus was the Messiah. If Jesus had not presented himself in such a light to some degree (and, in fact, had refused to accept such a title, as some scholars claim), then it is very unlikely his later followers would have placed him in such a category as a central way to see him. Why claim this if trouble and persecution come with it? If Jesus evoked such hope generally, then he almost certainly did so among his own disciples. The fact we know they believed this and died for that belief adds to the likelihood that such an understanding was rooted in things Jesus did and said. Dunn argues that Peter's being the one to "blurt out their common hope" fits with the character we have of Peter elsewhere.[9] In Jesus, we are dealing either with a figure who presented himself as an eschatological prophet or one who acted as the end-time deliverer, that is, the Messiah. The claims of authority already traced in the meals, Sabbath, and exorcisms cohere with a figure who is more than just a prophet.

OBJECTIONS

So Palestinian environment, embarrassment, and coherence speak for this event. If so, however, there is a surprising element in this authenticated event that also needs attention. It is Jesus' command of silence that follows Peter's declaration. Here some raise an objection, arguing as did William Wrede in 1901, that this "secrecy" was actually substantially a product of Mark's creative presentation of Jesus to cover up what had been a nonmessianic ministry of Jesus and give it the appearance of credibility.[10]

Those after Wrede took his theory and turned it into a full denial of such an understanding for Jesus. This idea has become exceedingly popular in New Testament studies. If it is true, then the scene involving Peter is a construction of the early church and not a historical clue about Jesus.

Objection: Jesus' Call for "Secrecy" Casts Doubt on His Messiahship

Here we run into one of the major objections to this scene, if not to the entire gospel portrait of Jesus' ministry. The tension within the event is summarized in this question: Why would Jesus elicit a declaration of who he is only to silence that recognition? In other words, is this event a piece of early church apologetic projected back on Jesus to make his ministry *appear* messianic when it was not? Is Jesus' hesitation about the title actually a reflection of his having rejected the title? To get at this objection we have to discuss the varieties of Jewish messianic hope that existed in the period. We also have to examine what a person would evoke in appealing to this title, suggesting why it would need to be done with care. Finally, we need to consider the idea of a later messianic secret.

The most outstanding historical reasons to reject the idea that Jesus' messianic identification is a later construction of the church involve three arguments.

Wrede Eventually Doubted His Own Theory

Wrede, on reflection, came to see that his proposed theory was probably flawed.[11] This is important because it shows he came to doubt, on historical grounds, that the scene was created, and he was the one who generated that view!

The Resurrection Is Not an Assumed Messianic Act

In Judaism the resurrection was not assumed to be an act that the Messiah would experience. Wrede's original explanation of the secret requires that a belief in Jesus' resurrection would lead the community to begin to teach Jesus as the Messiah after he had failed to make such claims during his ministry. However, there was no precedent for teaching that the Messiah would be resurrected from the dead in Judaism. So if the church came to believe Jesus was raised (whether for historical reasons or not), that belief would not lead them to take a nonmessianic Jesus and make him messianic. There was no Jewish need or precedent for this, and we know that the belief in Jesus' messianism appeared in the earliest phase of the life of the new community. So the messianic view of Jesus must have preceded his death and resurrection, since the resurrection would not have generated it.

There is another example that shows this lack of linkage. When Jesus' ministry surfaced, some pondered whether John the Baptist had been raised—without making John the Messiah, but rather merely a miracle worker (Mark 6:14). Other Jewish figures exalted to heaven get there without a messianic tag being attached to them (Moses, Elijah, Isaiah). Dunn says it this way: "The messiahship of the crucified Jesus is the *presupposition* of the scriptural apologetic mounted by the first Christians, not its achievement; the title 'Messiah' was inseparably connected with the name of Jesus because Jesus was condemned and crucified as a messianic pretender." [12]

The Ambiguity of the Title Argues for Authenticity

There is another problem with arguing Mark created this scene. It is not clear why Mark would focus the confession on Jesus being the Messiah, when "Son of God" and "Lord" were more important and central titles for the early church, and "Son of Man" was more central for Jesus. The ambiguity with which this title is placed on the table for consideration makes it more likely that this is a text rooted in Jesus than from the early church. [13]

Dealing with the Objection: An Explanation for Jesus' Call to Be Silent

Jesus Qualifies His Messianic Role as "Son of Man"

So if later additions by the early church cannot explain Jesus' call to silence, then what can?[14] Would Jesus really tell them to say nothing? Why would he do this? The key to unraveling this scene is the relationship between the Messiah in this text and the Son of Man in the prediction about suffering that follows. In terms of the use of titles, the same type of exchange as here happens at the Jewish examination by Jesus. Someone says Messiah or Christ, while Jesus responds discussing Son of Man. The title Son of Man is multiply attested and is a title only Jesus uses, never appearing as a title independently of Jesus in any epistle in the New Testament.[15] This lack of usage in the letters shows Son of Man was not a confessional title for the early church. Unlike Messiah, Son of Man is an empty term, in that it is an idiom for a human in normal Semitic usage. It also is a picture of an authoritative figure in Daniel 7:13–14, who rides the clouds like transcendent beings do. Up to Jesus' time, it was not a technical term of any kind, unless one includes the use of the title in a work like *1 Enoch*.[16] As we have seen, Jesus uses this term in contexts pointing to his authority. Son of Man is Lord of the Sabbath. It is his preferred title. He also uses it in this declaration scene to announce his coming suffering. This is a new take on the Messiah that Peter just confessed. This prediction of suffering Peter initially cannot accept because for him the Messiah is a figure of power not humility.

Here is a major clue that Jesus accepts but qualifies this messianic understanding of Peter. The disciples do not yet understand all that Jesus sees in himself as God's sent deliverer. They still have some things to learn, especially about his coming suffering. The same would be true of the crowds, if Jesus were

openly proclaimed to be the Messiah. So the disciples are to wait
on making this proclamation until they understand all that it
truly means.

Publicly Marking Jesus as "Messiah" Would Place Him at Risk

Yet another factor in Jesus' care about using the term *Messiah*
is that if Jesus were publicly proclaimed the Messiah (or King,
as John 6 says it), this would place him at immediate risk before
Rome. The rulers of Rome preferred to appoint and recognize
who was king! Rome would have seen this outright claim as a
direct challenge. But as we saw with the discussion on kingdom
and exorcism, Jesus' understanding of his battle was not primarily
with Rome, but with more profound spiritual realities.

A look at the variety of Jewish expectations on the Messiah
shows what would have been expected had Jesus gone public with
this title.[17] There was no single understanding of this figure, but
all the options had a powerful figure who did not suffer. *Psalms
of Solomon* 17–18, written in the century before Christ, probably
after Pompey took Rome in 63 BCE, has a political and militaristic Messiah who conquers the nations. The parables of *1 Enoch*
(37–71) have a long discussion of a more transcendent delivering figure. As just noted, this work likely also was written in the
later part of the century before Christ or early in the first century
of his birth. This messianic figure judges with God from heaven
and exercises power from God's side. The messianic expectation
at Qumran was of two messianic figures, a political deliverer and
a priestly Messiah, with the priestly figure having the prominent
role (1QS [Rule of the Community] 9:11). So to utter *Messiah* to
a Jewish public in the first century would generate one of these
powerful images and potentially incite a Roman response. Given
the variety of messianic conceptions, the exclusive emphasis on
power, and the height of political expectation coming with the

title Messiah, Jesus preferred to speak of the Son of Man and teach his disciples about the prospect of suffering, which they had not anticipated.

So we are arguing that Jesus accepted this title in a qualified way. In it, Jesus accepted the idea that he was more than a prophet. This is the only way to make sense of Peter's declaration that Jesus is Christ in contrast with the public's view that he is some kind of a prophet. In saying this, Peter saw Jesus standing in the center of God's deliverance program. Jesus was not ready yet to make a full public disclosure, so he waited to use it or associations with it until the end of his public ministry. He also waited to use the title extensively in public until the disciples were in a better position to begin to appreciate the suffering that would come with Jesus' activity.

Jesus' Acceptance of the Title in Matthew

The important difference in Matthew's presentation fits in here. Matthew's account is less ambiguous about the title and is clear that Jesus embraced it. Matthew has additional remarks from Jesus to Peter stating that Peter has received a revelation from God. This full embrace of the title is the result of where one ends up when one looks at the career of Jesus as a whole. Jesus affirmed this title, provided it is understood in the sense of Jesus being Messiah, sufferer, and even Son of God. If Mark had intended a denial of the title, it is hard to see how Matthew, not to mention the early Christian community that confessed Jesus as the Messiah, could end up confessing Jesus as Christ so emphatically and accept both the Matthean and Marcan versions of the event.

This is the last event outside of the climactic events in Jerusalem we shall examine. In the final stage of his ministry and in the capital city that was the center of the Jewish world, Jesus will become more forthcoming on his claims.

MEANING OF PETER'S DECLARATION
AND JESUS' REACTION TO IT

At Caesarea Philippi, Peter declared that Jesus was the agent of final deliverance, the "anointed" one who brings the eschaton. This stood in stark contrast to the popular perception of Jesus as some kind of prophet. Instead, what prophets foretold, Jesus embodied. That higher hope was why the disciples gathered around Jesus. They were hoping for a powerful ministry of deliverance. Jesus claimed to bring this in announcing the kingdom, but not in the way they expected. So Jesus accepted Peter's declaration, called for silence, and began to teach them what they did not yet understand, that the Messiah would also suffer.

Jesus' Actions Proclaimed Him Messiah

The attestation to Jesus as Messiah was not made so much by Jesus' claims and words as by his actions. The activity pointed to the nature of the time as one of final deliverance, and thus to Jesus' nature as the one at the center of God's saving program. In this case, actions spoke as loud as any words. The activity of deliverance and the claims of authority over things like the sacred day and evil spiritual forces led the disciples, as represented by Peter, to this affirmation.

As Wilkins says in his essay, "In his relationship to the eschatological prophet John the Baptist, Jesus is also explicitly regarded as a prophet (Mark 6:4, 15; John 6:14). But his authority in exercising the power of the kingdom leads to the understanding that his ministry included a royal dimension, and in that sense he was 'anointed' by God not only as a prophet but as a king."[18] By the time of this declaration, Jesus has come to be anointed by John, preached the kingdom, called the twelve disciples, associated in a fresh way with sinners and tax collectors, ruled about the Sabbath, and performed healings and exorcisms. Peter saw more than a prophet in all of this. *Messiah* was Peter's best choice for describing this activity.

All of these factors indicate that Jesus saw himself as a messianic figure as well. The subsequent naming of Jesus as the Christ in the early church indicates the likelihood that this was a description rooted in Jesus' activity. Jesus' appeal to the kingdom being present necessitates a delivering figure, even if that figure was defined in various ways by Jews of the time. In fact, this variation gave Jesus room to present his take on what this figure was going to do. This scene has the feel of a special moment in Jesus' ministry—he generates a disclosure from his disciples about how they see him, but immediately goes to work to shape that understanding in some fresh directions.

"Messiah" Reveals Jesus as More Than a Prophet

There is one other important implication here. Assessments of Jesus in our time want to make him a great prophet—which is seen as an act of respect for Jesus, for only a few achieve such universal global status. Yet this event in Scripture sees such a conclusion as far short of Jesus' true identity. The claims of those closest to him, those who knew him and his mission best, as well as Jesus' own acts, argue that Jesus presented himself as more than a prophet. In making this point, we are not engaging in psychoanalyzing Jesus by trying to get into his head for his self-understanding. This charge has often been raised in the last century since the work of Wrede. The claim is that historical analysis cannot sustain a claim to show how Jesus saw himself, since he left us nothing written from himself. This objection serves as a way to block access to considering how Jesus saw his mission and whether he presented himself as having a unique vocation. The claim is that we cannot get back into Jesus' mind, that our sources cannot take us there. Sources do have limits, especially when we do not have any sources directly written by the person in view. Yet access to a person's goals is not limited to access to his words.

In other words, a person's actions can tell you a lot about what they intend and how they see themselves.[19] Sources may not be able to penetrate the mind, but they can reveal the goal of one's actions. These sources are telling us that both the disciples and Jesus did not see him as one figure among many in the religious pantheon. Prophets were common in the religious world, but Jesus occupied a unique space in the promise and program of God. With him came a kingdom declaration the prophets had only anticipated. With him, something new had come. That Jesus set up this confession in a region associated not just with Israel but with the gods of Rome indicates an intention to impact how the world sees religious activity. Jesus' work is about more than Israel. Things were no longer the same in God's program. This is what the disciples claimed Jesus meant, and nothing Jesus said or did robbed them of this impression. Not even the prospect of death later in their lives would take this belief from them. What Jesus did and said had planted a conviction of Jesus' indispensable role in salvation deep within their souls. To them, Jesus was unique. The final events in Jesus' public ministry laminated this faith into them. We turn to those key events next.

8

Jesus' Atriumphal Entry:

A Different Kind of King

JESUS' ENTRY into Jerusalem at the end of his ministry is normally called the "triumphal" entry.[1] However, Jesus' entry was anything but triumphal by ancient standards. But it *was* an entry, staged to make a claim, to symbolize something, to provoke and force a decision. From that standpoint, it was a success, because the events that take place here set into motion Jesus' purpose in coming to Jerusalem. What does the way Jesus entered into the nation of Israel's capital tell us about his mission?

RULES THAT APPLY TO THE ENTRY

This event is one of the most familiar in Jesus' ministry. It has made a great impact on popular culture thanks in part to the numerous movies made in the 1950s and '60s about Jesus' life. In those movies, this event kicks off what is called "Easter week" with a bang. The movies give the impression that all of Jerusalem swarmed to meet and greet Jesus. But from there, everything turned south for Jesus. A city that greeted him with open arms turned on him by the end of the week. But was it so, and did it start the way we often have filmed it?

This event is very special. It is one of the few that appear in all four gospels (Matthew 21:1–11; Mark 11:1–10; Luke 19:28–40; John 12:12–15). It also was an intentional act by Jesus. The accounts show his entry was arranged. So what does it show? How did it fit with other entries of other ancient VIPs? Asking this question will help us sense the event's significance.

The case for the event involves three of our rules: the criteria of *multiple attestation, embarrassment,* and *effect.* This final rule will become more important in the series of events that make up the last week of Jesus' ministry. The closer we get to his execution, the more important it becomes to understand how Jesus came to his demise. The fact that these remaining events are close together means that each event serves as a kind of context for the others. It is important to keep the sequence of events in mind, because sometimes scholarly treatments take these events as singular units. By detaching them, some keys to understanding them are lost. Like pulling a loose thread, trying to separate the connections between these events unravels an accurate understanding of them.

Multiple Attestation

It may seem odd to appeal to multiple attestation, when the account is in all four gospels and many of the details match. Thus, sources reflected in Mark could be seen as the only point of reference for this event. However, John's gospel differs just enough to make it likely that a second source was involved. *First,* John lacks any discussion of the event being arranged as Matthew, Mark, and Luke tell us. *Second,* although all the gospels treat Bethany as the backdrop to the event's origin, John has a different focal point; where the first three gospels have a healing of a blind man, John tells the story of the raising of Lazarus. *Third,* the description of the crowd size differs. Mark tells a story of disciples leading Jesus in with little sense of a larger crowd until Jesus is close to the city. John notes crowds throughout. Whatever is to be made of these differences (and we shall treat them below), they suggest the input of other sources for John. So these differences point to likely possibility of multiple attestation.

Embarrassment

The criterion of embarrassment argues that the church would not create a story that embarrasses figures in the church or creates problems for them that otherwise they would not need to face. Here we encounter two points that converge: (1) a conspicuous entry is a political act and (2) the church was normally very careful about actions that could be read as seditious against Rome. The early post-Easter community was especially careful about sending explicit signals that could be read as challenging Rome. One need only think of how Paul is portrayed in his trials of defense. He goes out of his way to say he was doing nothing to disturb the peace or be a problem to Rome (Acts 24:12, 25:8). So Jesus' entry into Jerusalem with a public regal emphasis does not seem like something the early church would invent.

The community was, in fact, already under much suspicion for its activity. The early church functioned separate from Roman culture. A Roman governor had executed its leader for sedition. Its focus on one God meant that all the gods Rome honored were set aside—this led to Christians being called "atheists" by the Romans because they denied any connection to the many gods of the world power. The ancient Dio Cassius vividly describes such religious withdrawal to Augustus, who was the Roman emperor at Jesus' birth, saying, "Those who attempt to distort our religion with strange rites you should abhor and punish, not merely for the sake of the gods . . . but because such men, by bringing in new divinities in place of the old, persuade many to adopt foreign practices, from which spring conspiracies, factions, and cabals" (Dio Cassius 52.36.2). New religion was seen as suspect, especially when it did not add to the collection of gods, but turned its back on them. For most Romans, the more gods, the better. One should barter for favor with each god and the distinct area each god managed. It was a way to make sure every area in life was covered.

Jesus' act also had its roots in the *parousia,* that is, the coming of a dignitary. A city would spread the red carpet and show its respect to a dignitary who had honored them with his presence— typically a ruler who held power or a general who had brought victory. These celebratory welcomes are well documented in ancient Roman sources, such as Dio Cassius 51.20–24; Suetonius, *Augustus* 53.1; *Caligula* 4.1; *Nero* 25.1–3; and Pliny the Younger, *Pan* 22.1–5; they took place all across the empire and were well known as the way to respond to a dignitary.[2]

It was this cultural convention Jesus' act evokes (with some important differences). In mimicking such entries, Jesus was making a social and political statement that was a direct public political challenge to authorities, much more than most of his ministry had been. It left Jesus open to the charge of claiming to be king (John 12:13). Such a claim had consequences from a Rome that had not given him this role. Rome believed only she should determine who would rule, so this claim came with a danger of being charged with sedition. Mark 15:2, 9, and Luke 23:2 show how this claim is important in Jesus' later appearance before Pilate. Even later, in Acts 17:7, disciples are having to fend off such a charge against the movement. So the criterion of embarrassment fits: Why would the community create an event that leads into all of this trouble unnecessarily if the early church believed or could believe *less* about Jesus than the story suggests? Why invite such trouble? The criterion of embarrassment says that the emphasis on Jesus' royalty is in the story because it was an authentic part of the event.

Effects

This background leads directly into the criterion of effects. Jesus' actions had to have had enough of a cultural and political edge to lead to his death for sedition by Rome. The *titulus* on the cross tells us Rome sent Jesus to his death for regal claims—it detailed the charge that Jesus was dying as King of the Jews.[3] This entry into Jerusalem is the only event in the gospels where Jesus and kingship are directly linked in open public by Jesus' initiative. Three earlier figures had made such claims in Israel during the time of Roman rule. In each case, Rome moved to crush them. The first-century Jewish historian Josephus tells the story of all three (*Antiquities* 17.271–72—of Judas, son of Ezekias; 17.273–77—of Simon, slave of Herod; 17.278–81—of Athronges). Rome believed in law and order. The policy was "You keep our law or we will impose the order!"

So three criteria apply to the event, at least initially. They point to its likelihood, but the cultural implications of the event lead into a natural question, one that serves as one of the objections to the event. If such an act was seen as so subversive, then why did Rome not challenge and arrest Jesus immediately?

OBJECTIONS

Objection: Why Did Rome Not Arrest Jesus Immediately?

The question of why Jesus was not arrested immediately can be described as an objection based on a *historical anomaly*. The claim is that the event does not fit the reaction it would have engendered.[4]

The objection is that had Jesus made such a public declaration, the Roman response would have been immediate.

Response: Geography, Crowd Size, and Timing Are Crucial

Here knowledge of the geography and festival timing of the scene is crucial. Jesus is approaching Jerusalem from Bethany, coming down the Mount of Olives from the east. He is still quite a distance away from the location of the Roman troops at the fortress of Antonia, located just outside the northwest corner of the temple. The entire temple mount is a huge area of thirty-five acres, and the Romans are on the opposite end of that complex from Jesus. Josephus tells us these Roman soldiers clustered around Antonia and the temple precincts during such celebrations (*Jewish War* 5.243–45). Meaning they are a few football fields away, and this is in an era before binoculars! There are no General Pattons in charge with long-distance access to a closer view. Unless there was some kind of violent chaos or disturbance, nothing would draw attention to Jesus so distant from the locale the Romans occupied.

More than that, this was a festival time. People were pouring into Jerusalem from across the countryside to celebrate Passover, one of three festivals annually where people traveled to Jerusalem from across the nation. This national celebration's popularity meant that the number of people in Jerusalem was said to triple during these times. Estimates of the population of Jerusalem in the first century run from about 25,000 to 50,000, so the city would swell to somewhere between 75,000 and 150,000.[5] Entrances to the city, like the one Jesus was approaching, would have been as crowded as a stadium entrance just before a sporting event. Streams of people were entering the city at once. These people were coming to celebrate. They would be singing and rejoicing as they approached. From a distance, nothing too unusual would appear to be going on as long as nothing violent was taking place. Amid the commotion of the crowds entering Jerusalem, there was no guarantee at all that anything could be heard by the bulk of the soldiers hundreds of yards away.

With no threatening precipitating act to provoke a police response, a lack of Roman reaction is not surprising.

But what of the size of the event as it is popularly conceived? If whole crowds were responding, would that not gain attention? This is where it is important to carefully read the accounts. The initial action seems to have been much smaller and more confined than is normally associated with the event. In Mark 11:8–10 we are told that the disciples spread the garments on the animal and spread the branches. By itself, without a context, this would indicate only the arrival of an important person. Only those who heard what the disciples said would have more insight into what was intended. This group of disciples is likely not very large, since in Acts 1:15 we are told 120 disciples were gathered in the city after Jesus' death. Matthew 21:8 refers to "most of the crowd." Yet two verses earlier, this group is said to be mostly disciples (v. 6). There is no number here. The group may not be large compared with the thousands arriving. In Mark 11:9–10, those who go before and behind cry out, as also in Matthew. Luke 19:37–38 speaks of a whole multitude of disciples. This is not the entire crowd either, but a subset.

Kinman concludes, "To revisit Sanders's earlier objection, one need not imagine that the crowd accompanying Jesus outside Jerusalem was so large to have commanded the attention of the soldiers, who were primarily concerned with events inside the city and temple. In fact, one valid way of reading the texts is that the lack of military intervention suggests a smaller group accompanied Jesus than is often envisioned."[6] Only John's gospel looks like it has a "large" crowd (John 12:12). However, this "crowd" is linked in the narrative to those who were friends of Lazarus or were curious about his healing (12:9), which also points to a relatively smaller group. This conclusion is likely, since they are renamed in 12:17 and said to be a group that could be housed within a home in 11:31. So two factors make a Roman reaction to the scene unlikely: (1) a modest crowd of participating disciples and (2) the factor of distance in the midst of an arriving throng. This very culturally probable scenario makes it unlikely that the Roman soldiers were even aware of what was taking place.

Objection: The Event Is Out of Character for Jesus

The second key objection is that this event is out of character for Jesus. The gospels show him avoiding direct public messianic claims. We already saw this in a previous chapter about Peter's confessing Jesus to be the Messiah. In fact, this statement about Jesus' hesitancy well summarizes the course of the bulk of Jesus' ministry. So this event is a *theological anomaly* out of character with Jesus' ministry.[7] Rudolph Bultmann stated this objection most forcibly in his work on the synoptic tradition in 1931. The citation translated reads, "The presuppositions, which one must make in order to view the report as historical—that Jesus wanted to produce the fulfillment of Zech. 9:9, and that the masses immediately recognized the donkey as a messianic mount—are absurd." Zechariah 9:9 reads, "Rejoice greatly, daughter of Zion! Shout, daughter of Jerusalem! Look! Your king is coming to you: he is legitimate and victorious, humble and riding on a donkey— on a young donkey, the foal of a female donkey." However, contrary to Bultmann's claim, what is more at stake in the tie to Zechariah is the recognition that what Jesus was doing fit God's plan as prophesied in Scripture, not the political significance of the act. A closer look at the event will reveal if Bultmann's skeptical description of the depiction of the event is accurate.

Response: The Disciples Did Not Immediately View the Event as Messianic

Let's look at the objections in reverse. Bultmann's portrayal of the event seems to be a caricature. John's gospel makes it clear that the association with Zechariah 9:9 was not something those present grasped at the event but only discovered in later reflection on it. John 12:16 says, "His disciples did not understand these things when they first happened, but when Jesus was glorified, then they remembered that these things were written about him and that these things had happened to him." What eventually dawned on Jesus' followers was that Jesus' activity was part of a prophetic divine plan that Scripture had recorded. However, the treatment of Jesus as a dignitary, which is what we are examining, was evidenced by the setting down of the palm leaves in front of Jesus—not knowing the scriptural connection with Zechariah. The central association with kingship was something the disciples introduced as Jesus entered the city. Their understanding of who he was framed Jesus' action. The laying down of the palm leaves revealed the hope these followers had as they entered the city. They realized the connection to Zechariah sometime later.

Response: Disciples Saw Jesus as Delivering Figure

The precedent for the laying down of leaves, a kind of ancient red carpet, is the entry of King Jehu in the Hebrew Scriptures in 2 Kings 9:13. Also worth noting is that Solomon rode a mule into the city when David selected him as heir to the throne (1 Kings 1:33–40). The choice of a mule over the powerful horse a Roman ruler would ride is important. The Solomon story is the background to the text of Zechariah 9:9, which the disciples later came to see as a parallel to this event. It is one of the important differences between Jesus' act and the entries of Roman dignitaries.

But what exactly are the disciples doing as they enter Jerusalem? Mark 11:9–10 references declarations about the coming of one in the name of the Lord, an allusion to Psalm 118:26. Originally written long before the time of Jesus, this psalm points to a figure, likely a king, welcomed in the temple as one blessed by God. The disciples show their welcome of Jesus in a similar way and call on others to join them by using the language of the psalm. Jesus' disciples also cry out about the arrival of the kingdom of David, an indirect reference to Jesus with emphasis on his kingdom. This cry about David does not look like a created detail from the church, since it has an inherent ambiguity in pointing to Jesus one would associate more with an earlier declaration. This hoped-for kingdom accompanied by a delivering figure was the prominent theme of Jesus' preaching. It also belonged to a widespread but diversely expressed messianic hope in Judaism, as our discussion of the background to Peter's declaration showed. So, that his disciples would make this claim about Jesus fits with the multiply attested emphasis of the gospels and the cultural setting of Jesus' ministry. Nothing in this portrayal is too much for disciples to have said and seen.

Objection: Jesus Stressed Kingdom Hope, Not Messianic

A more recent variation on this objection comes from Paula Fredriksen.[8] Her objection is more nuanced. She argues that Jesus stressed kingdom hope, not himself as Messiah. She argues this by noting that Jesus never presented himself as Messiah anywhere else, not in Galilee, not on the way to Jerusalem, nor to his disciples. What she posits happened is that his followers got excited with this entry, possibly because he announced the kingdom would come after this visit to Jerusalem. So they greeted him as the one who announced this kingdom and "perhaps" even as king. The impetus for the event, Fredriksen claims, and its regal intention is the interpretation of his followers. The understanding does not come from Jesus nor does it reflect his intent.

Response: Peter Clearly Declared Jesus as Messiah

To do this, Fredriksen has largely ignored the import of the Caesarea Philippi event, which she regards as told so differently in Matthew, Mark, and Luke that we cannot make anything substantive of it in terms of the historical Jesus. Much of what we get in Mark about that event tells us about theology, not Jesus.[9] Here we see how appealing to the messianic secret not only impacts how we read Peter's proclamation but also subsequent potentially significant events. If Peter's proclamation is authentic, as we have tried to show, then this objection to the entry falls away as well.

Albert Schweitzer (on the right) had a reputation as a great organist as well as a theologian. Here he is portrayed seated, with Amadeus Mozart on the left, next to an organ they both played, in a church in Strasbourg, France.

Gotthold Ephraim Lessing (1729–1791) was the author of the concept of Lessing's ditch about the difficulty of getting back to the historical Jesus from the Christ of faith in the gospels. This sculpture of him is from the Deutsches Museum in Berlin, Germany.

This picture is from a tour I was a part of in Israel. This is a traditional site on the southern Jordan River where John performed his baptisms somewhere along this river. Jesus was baptized in a locale much like this.

When we met in Israel in 2008, we filmed a documentary on our work for Day of Discovery. Many of our writers participated. Here we are seated in the synagogue in Capernaum by the Sea of Galilee. Left to right on the bottom row we have Michael Burer, Grant Osborne, and Michael Wilkins. On the top row we have Klyne Snodgrass, Robert Webb, Brent Kinman, Craig Evans, and the Day of Discovery host, Mart De Hann. I am standing preparing to lead the interview we had here about Jesus' Galilean ministry.

The IBR Group meeting in Tübingen. From left to right: Michael Burer, Michael Wilkins, Robert Webb, Klyne Snodgrass, Don Hagner, and myself. (Note the M&M's in the middle of the table.)

Here we are filming at Caesarea Philippi. You can see the niches for idols in the cliff behind us. Being interviewed (working left to right: myself, Michael Wilkins, Michael Burer.)

Here is a look at the full face of the site at Caesarea Philippi. The cliff with the niches would have been one wall for the temples built in front of them.

This is a model of first-century Jerusalem at the Shrine of the Book in Jerusalem. In this picture you can see some key locales for Jesus' entry and the temple action. To the left are the Southern Steps, by which Jesus would have entered the temple before he cleansed it. The portico to the left above the steps is a likely location for the money changers. On the upper right-hand corner is the location of the Roman fortress Antonia. Here the soldiers could keep watch on temple activity without being on the grounds and rendering the sacred grounds unclean. This entire area was several acres in size. Also from Antonia they would have looked out to the Mount of Olives to watch pilgrims enter the city for Passover. The photo is taken from an angle that sees the temple from the Mount of Olives.

This is a closer look at the model of the Southern Steps and the portico area of the temple where Jesus' temple act took place. The model was done before the Southern Steps were archaeologically investigated. When they dug up the actual site, several *mikvaot* (or baths for ritual cleansing) were discovered. So the model of the steps is not completely accurate.

Here we are reclining in ancient style as would have been done at the Last Supper. This is not quite as Leonardo da Vinci pictured it! We did the entire interview on the supper in this position. It is not comfortable at all. Pictured from left to right: Robert Webb, Mart De Hann, myself, and Michael Wilkins.

In Jerusalem near the King David Hotel are tombs from the family of Herod. Here is a picture of the kind of large stone that covered such tombs.

We are preparing to be interviewed about the empty tomb and resurrection. Left to right: myself, Grant Osborne, Mart De Hann, and Craig Evans.

Beyond this, the Markan framing of this event involves the healing of blind Bartimaeus, who cries out to the Son of David to heal (Mark 10:46–52). This is a cry by a "blind man" who sees who Jesus really is. It gives a messianic tinge to that healing and sets the stage for this entry into Jerusalem. If the healing is historical, and a case can be made for it, then it shows Jesus opening up to public disclosure of who he is as he draws near to Jerusalem.[10]

Objection: Jesus Did Not Customarily Proclaim Himself Messiah

The only remaining question is whether Jesus would have chosen to engage in such a potentially provocative act. We have already argued that up to this point he did not customarily go around making a public point of who he was in terms of messianic categories. He let his actions speak for him and highlighted the time that he was bringing. So how does that fit with the more personal public focus we see here?

Response: Jesus' Strategy Has Now Changed

The last week of Jesus' life is full of provocative acts and sayings. It feels as if Jesus comes to Jerusalem with a new intensity to his mission. He will challenge the religious leaders with his acts in the temple. He tells a parable of Israel's history that would certainly provoke his hearers, a prophet's rebuke to the nation—and in addition Jesus speaks of a son being slain within the parable.[11] Also quite full and direct are Jesus' remarks to the Jewish leadership at their examination of him. He claims that God will give him a seat at the deity's side, which leads to controversy about Jesus' claims and the charge of blasphemy. Matthew, Mark, and Luke present numerous other controversies in this last week that only add to this picture.

So Jesus' strategy appears to have changed as he comes into Jerusalem at this time. Now he will proclaim who he is and directly challenge the Jewish leadership. This new tactic forces a confrontation, and this event is but the first act.

The event has internal cultural coherence and fits well with what we have already seen in previous events in terms of Jesus' claims about authority. Even though it represents a change in Jesus' public strategy about permitting a public messianic claim from others, it meets the criterion of coherence in terms of how it connects to other events in Jesus' career.[12] The question of what Jesus intended concludes our look at this event. Our consideration of the event's meaning will include examination of its intent.

Meaning of Jesus' Atriumphal Entry

Jesus' Entry Was a Sharp Contrast to Pilate's

To fully appreciate this event, we need to describe what Pilate's entry into the city would have looked like. The *parousia* (or coming) ceremony was an elaborate greeting custom for a major dignitary, and it had one of two goals: to gain favor or temper wrath from the one being honored. Such a greeting for Pilate would have been likely, given his Roman prefect (governor) status and the fact his headquarters was located in Caesarea Maritima, some sixty miles to the west.[13] Such an elaborate entry would have just happened or would soon be happening on the week Jesus entered Jerusalem, depending on when the prefect made his appearance at the feast. Pilate's entry was a time to ingratiate oneself to the ruler—city leaders, merchants, and citizens did all they could to show honor and respect. Citizens would be urged to greet the ruler as he arrived. The Sadducees, the most powerful political Jewish sect at the time who cooperated with Rome, would have wanted to make sure Pilate felt welcome in what might be compared with either a state or royal procession today. If the greeting can be compared with one Cicero describes that took place for a ruler's entry made in Egypt in 51 BCE, then "extraordinary throngs of people have come to meet me from farms, villages, and every homestead" (*Ad Atticum* 5.16). Social, religious, and political leaders would have proceeded outside the city walls to greet the dignitary and escort his entourage into the city in a formal welcome.

Signs of Roman power would also be prominently displayed; this was designed to discourage anyone from even thinking about acting against the empire. Thus, Pilate would have entered the city with a fresh array of soldiers and horsemen, perhaps a thousand troops or so. Each soldier would have carried a large shield, breastplate, and headpiece, and either a sword, spear, axe, or pickaxe. Horsemen would have had breastplates, headpieces, sword, shield, and several spears. In short, it was a show for both sides. The ruler was making sure the city understood who was in control, while the city was acknowledging this reality, even if many did not like it. The entry was a claim to such rights.

All of this stands in contrast to Jesus' entry. No one from the city came out to greet him. Honor came from those streaming to the city, mostly from his disciples. No military authority came with Jesus, just ordinary celebrants entering the city to enjoy Passover. No powerful horse was his mount, just a simple donkey. The God he represented, however, was not the divine wisdom and power of Caesar, himself called a son of God, but the God of promise and the God of Israel. The disciples hoped, as did Jesus, that the people of Israel would see Jesus as closer to them than Rome was. So they cried out about the kingdom hope of this God and the one who offered it. The only thing that connected to a Roman entry was a claim about the right to rule.

The "welcome" Jesus received was less a welcome than a statement from his own supporters that here was the one who was blessed of God. They hoped that the people would see Jesus as bringing God's promise with him, one who acted in God's name and power. The modesty of the display belied, at one level, the depth of the claim. As the opposite of Pilate's kind of entry and reception, this is at best an atriumphal entry in terms of style.

Jesus Accepts Regal Acclaim

Nevertheless, there is much of significance in Jesus' act. Jesus accepts the claim of those around him to be tied to a kingdom Rome has no responsibility for bringing. The act itself, if it is understood against a biblical backdrop, points to a regal entry, a king coming to his capital. Jesus comes just as Solomon had. David's appointed successor rode on the mule David had him placed on; so David's son, Jesus, rode a mule to present himself as an appointed successor. Yet the modesty of the entry accomplished two things: it kept Rome from reacting, and it indicated that Jesus did not use or need the kind of power that Rome's representative utilized. Jesus bore a different kind of power. It did not require soldiers; it required hearts. The absence of any additional display beyond riding and the leaves placed before him made the event seem tame by Roman standards. Nonetheless, Jesus intended by the act to present himself to Jerusalem as Israel's king and as an eschatological figure of hope.

Four points about Jesus' ministry give the context for Jesus' action and support this intention.

First, Jesus preached the kingdom of God and presented his authority in that light as one who both announced and brought that kingdom. Earlier, as we saw, Jesus had said that if he cast out demons by the finger of God, then he brings the kingdom.

Second, the subsequent trial of Jesus before Pilate is about claims of kingship. Crucifixion was reserved for those who committed sedition against the Roman state. So Jesus' execution came for political reasons as far as Rome was concerned. The charge above Jesus' head at the cross pointed to this earlier regal claim.

Third, the early church spoke of Jesus' royal descent, as do the two genealogies in the gospels. One need only connect Jesus to David to make a point about his royalty (Romans 1:3; 2 Timothy 2:8; Revelation 5:5; Matthew 1:6; and Luke 3:31). A kingdom has a king, and although it is God's kingdom, the early church insisted that Jesus was its appointed leader, even by calling Jesus, Jesus Christ. For these believers who had walked with Jesus, he was the anointed one sent by God. If one asks anointed for what, then the answer is surely for the kingdom.

Fourth, any doubt as to this connection seems to dissolve when we recall that Jesus gathered a group of twelve around him to picture the restructuring of Israel he was bringing. Jesus was forming a new social structure around his call for Israel to be restored.[14]

SUMMARY

As we place the events we are considering next to one another, we can see a more coherent portrait. Jesus emerges as a central figure in God's promise—a function Jesus showed in his actions more than he claimed publicly by words. However, now in Jerusalem, Jesus shows his full hand. This act is out of character from Jesus' general method of public disclosure in the past, but now Jesus is at the capital. Now is the time to present himself to the nation. It is the moment to challenge the Jewish leadership to affirm, as Israel's religious representatives on her behalf, where they stand on him. This event is unique in the way Jesus makes an intended public claim of kingship. His subsequent actions in the city will only reinforce this claim. Jesus' entry was a call to decide who he was and to choose whom to follow. Was the kingdom coming? Was Jesus bringing it? The act Jesus undertook here was an invitation or a provocation depending on what one thought of the dignitary now arriving to make his claim. If Jesus was bringing the kingdom, the time had come to get on board. If not, the time had come to try to stop him. The rest of the week disclosed the leaders' answer.

9

Jesus' Temple Act:

Authority and Sacred Space

AFTER JESUS' atriumphal entry, he went to the temple.[1] Both events are out of character for Jesus—the entry into Jerusalem because he permitted his followers to publicly display who he was claiming to be. In the same way, Jesus' act in the temple was out of character—here, he displays anger and violence we do not see anywhere else in the Scriptures. Is this display credible? If it is, then what caused Jesus to react in a manner so atypical of his public ministry? And what does it mean for his mission and ministry? How could Jesus even consider such an act in the most sacred spot in the world for all Jews? If actions speak louder than words, what was Jesus doing and saying by overturning the tables of the money changers in the temple?

RULES THAT APPLY TO THE TEMPLE ACT

Almost all Jesus scholars agree that this event took place and was significant in determining Jesus' fate—scholars as diverse in perspective as E. P. Sanders, Tom Wright, John Dominic Crossan, and Marcus Borg all accept that this event took place.[2] The debate is found not in its authenticity but its interpretation. When Jesus went into the temple and overturned the tables of the money changers, was he declaring the end of the temple or merely engaging in a symbolic act to emphasize its need for cleansing? Good cases can be made for both options. But first, let's begin with why so many believe this event took place.

Multiple Attestation

Two rules are key in the corroboration of this event, although four rules can be applied to this event to indicate it took place. First, the scene is multiply attested in versions that involve sources rooted in Mark (Mark 11:15–18 = Matthew 21:12–16 = Luke 19:45–48) and in John (2:13–22). The account in John has a distinct placement early in his gospel versus the Synoptics' placement in the last week. Only John mentions a whip with cattle and sheep being driven away. John lacks the allusions to Isaiah 56:7 and Jeremiah 7:11 that are in the other gospels, opting for an allusion to Zechariah 14:21 instead.[3] In John, Jesus tells the sellers of the doves to go, while in Matthew and Mark their seats are overturned.

All the accounts note how Jesus was asked about his authority to perform such an act. John does it by asking Jesus to give a sign to support what he is doing, while the Synoptics ask about authority directly. Mark and Matthew have the cursing of the fig tree in proximity to this event, while Luke and John do not mention it. The number and nature of such distinct details are sufficient to be regarded as reflecting a distinct source for John. The presence of two sources yields a judgment in favor of multiple attestation.

Effect

The second key rule is the criterion of effect. It is easy to see how Jesus' challenge at the temple paved the road for his arrest and eventual death. The act was a direct challenge of the authority of Jewish leaders over the temple. This locale was the most sacred space in the world for all Jews. The protest was so public and the repudiation so obvious that leaders needed to act to stop Jesus. Their act would be an important public reassertion of the leaders' authority over the management of the faith. The fact that all versions of the account mention the leadership asking Jesus where he got the authority to do this shows how deep an impression this event made (Matthew 21:23 = Mark 11:28 = Luke 20:2; John 2:18). The leaders' question makes it clear they had not given him this authority, so in their view Jesus was acting in a dangerous, independent manner. This coheres with the later effect of their acting to stop his challenge of them.

Inherent Ambiguity

The ambiguity of the event at many levels supplies a third ground that supports its authenticity. *First* is the ambiguity in the account's exact meaning concerning how Jesus saw the future of the temple. A created event would be expected to have a clearer message. *Second*, the event serves no major, explicit christological purpose. Thus it lacks a key motive often attached to claims about an account being created by the church. *Third*, the issue of the role of the money changers in the temple is not such an early church concern that they would create a story in which Jesus acted against them. In fact, elsewhere Matthew shows Jesus urging payment of the temple tax, which required their presence (Matthew 17:24–27). So Jews who were in the church were told to continue to engage with the temple and the activity associated with it. The book of Acts shows the believers in Jerusalem continuing to participate in temple activity (Acts 2–5). So the real issue appears not to be the fact that there are money changers but something else. The ambiguity over exactly what that was indicates that the event was real.

Embarrassment

Fourth, there is the criterion of embarrassment. What did the church gain by creating such an event if it did not take place? It would simply serve as another challenge by Jesus, but the tradition about Jesus seems filled with such accounts. Yet this is such a frontal attack on the running of the temple by the leadership. Would the early church seek to fan the flames of tension with Judaism at a time when it was trying to win Jewish people to its views? More than that, the early church made the argument that it was not a seditious movement and was careful about leaving this impression. Creating an act that could be painted as sedition is less likely than recalling a challenge Jesus actually made. So it is historically more probable to see in this tension the memory of a real confrontation rather than a fabricated one.

A Complicating Factor: The Different Placement of the Event in the Synoptics and John

Another element in assessing the authenticity of the event is the difference in where the Synoptics and John place the event. This is sometimes seen as a problem for accepting this event, but most opt for a literary explanation for the difference. John has it early in Jesus' ministry, while the Synoptics have it in the last week. Some see the differences as so great but the symbolism as so similar that they posit two cleansing events. In this view, one cleansing comes at the start and the other at the end of Jesus' ministry. In this view, both placements are correct and there is no literary move.[4] However, most regard the idea of Jesus getting away with this twice as unlikely. So they opt for choosing between two possible literary placements of the one incident. Either the Synoptics moved an early event to the last week or John placed a late event earlier. Usually John is seen as moving the event forward from the end of Jesus' ministry where Matthew, Mark, and Luke have it. John does so to introduce Jesus' ministry as one where his own people did not receive him. So the John 2 event illustrates the remark about his own people not receiving Jesus in John 1:11.

Those who challenge seeing the Synoptics as giving us the proper chronology make three arguments for John's placement. *First*, John has chronological links with multiple trips to Jerusalem, while the other gospels have Jesus going to Jerusalem only once, so they have to place the event here. *Second*, the Jewish leaders' debate about the temple charge in Mark's version might make more sense if the event took place a few years earlier versus a few days back. *Finally*, the allusion to forty-six years of renovation work on the temple seems to point to an earlier date of 27–28 CE for this incident, if one assumes a starting point as 20–19 BCE for this work, one of the common dates proposed for when it began. That date total fits the early part of Jesus' ministry and John's placement better.

Nonetheless, the closer connection between the provocation and the arrest causes most to see the Synoptics as giving the better placement, with John relocating the event in a literary move to introduce Jesus' challenge early in his gospel. Discussion about when to count the start of Herod's work and whether years are counted inclusively or not means the chronology has a range of years that could include either placement. The point about John's multiple trips versus one trip to Jerusalem is correct but does not require the event be earlier.

Despite all of this discussion about where a real event might fit, a few scholars have challenged the authenticity of the entire event. What are their objections?

GENERAL OBJECTIONS TO THE EVENT AS A WHOLE

Objection: Event Is a Markan Creation

Some see the themes as part of a basic Markan development. The cleansing is a key created act of provocation mirroring challenges Jesus made elsewhere in Capernaum (Mark 1:21–28). So Mark creates a scene with the standard themes of provocation (driving out the money changers), scriptural teaching (allusions to Isaiah and Jeremiah), the chief priests' response, and the crowd's amazement. Once one removes these standard motifs, there is nothing left to the event.[5] However, the claim of parallels between Mark 1 and this scene is exaggerated. There is no provocation by Jesus in Mark 1, only an exorcism he chooses to perform. The view also argues that Mark is anti-temple, on the rationale that challenging the temple's existence is the point behind the church's creation of the event. However, Mark is not anti-temple here, since he has Jesus say that the temple will be a place for prayer for the nations. This seems to anticipate a future role for it.

Objection: Event Doesn't Fit the Portrait of Jesus

Others argue that the event does not fit with the portrait of Jesus elsewhere. His use of raw power and his seeming concern for the temple's sanctity and for Gentiles are out of line with what we normally see from Jesus.[6] *However,* Jesus is seen in the temple, teaching and participating in its rites, in all the gospels. He shows respect for temple rites. Two examples make the point about respect for temple practice. In Matthew 8:4 = Mark 1:44 = Luke 17:14, Jesus tells the leper to follow the law in announcing that one has been cleansed of leprosy. In Matthew 5:23–24, Jesus talks about the right attitude in bringing a sacrifice to the temple. *Sec-*

ond, the way Jesus expresses Gentile involvement here parallels what was already taught in the Hebrew Scripture (Isaiah 2:2–4; Micah 4:1–3; Zechariah 14:16; 1 Kings 8:41–43—at the temple's dedication by Solomon). Jesus was not advocating anything new here, but a return to what the temple was designed to be. Third, even the anger of Jesus is not without precedent (Mark 3:5) and yet no one is hurt. The protest simply represents a vivid, symbolic challenge to the activity, much like a prophet might have performed.

OBJECTIONS ABOUT THE SIZE AND NATURE OF THE TEMPLE ACT

The most compelling objection is the impression of the text that Jesus took over an area of more than thirty-five acres by himself. This issue is old, having been noted in the third century by Origen.[7] The argument is that the area was so protected, such an act to the extent described would surely have produced a reaction to bring things to order. This objection requires a close look at the event, its background, and how it is really told.

The issues of the act and the size of the temple area required for it have often led to the conclusion that either the incident was smaller than the gospels suggest or involved a gesture that has been symbolically worked up into something more.[8] Jesus is said to have done four things: drive out the sellers, overturn the tables of the money changers, overturn the dove sellers' seats, and not allow anyone into the temple. It is especially the last description that raises the issues, given the size of the temple. So a closer look is needed at all of this activity. Was there anything about the temple requirements that meant doves, animals, and money changers needed to be proximate to or in the temple area?

Sacrifices of various types were required at the temple, and what was offered had to be without blemish to reflect an offering appropriate for God. Sacrifices involving doves for those of modest means are noted in Leviticus 5:11 and 12:8. Economically, doves were slotted between animal sacrifices for the rich who could afford it and grain offerings for the poor. So pilgrims traveling to the temple had two choices. *Choice 1*: They could bring the sacrifices with them over the hundred or so miles they might have to travel, if they came from Galilee as Jesus and his followers did. This brought the risk of something happening that would prevent the sacrifice from being present or unblemished (as required) when they arrived. *Choice 2*: Or, they could pick up their unblemished offering at the temple's door without any worries about the condition of the offering. It is not hard to determine what often happened or why the doves and animals were supplied at the temple.

Money changers were present to help with the temple tax, which was required for men twenty and over. At the time, this was paid with a Tyrian shekel, because of the high quality of its silver, not because it lacked offensive images as some claim.[9] The coin had a portrait of the god of the city of Tyre, Melkert-Hercules, on one side, portrayed like Alexander the Great. On the other side was a Ptolemaic eagle, the bird of Zeus. These symbols were not neutral for Jews, but the tax had to be paid somehow. It was seen as the best coin available, given that Israel was not allowed to mint her own coins. So just as one needs currency exchange at an international airport, the temple had money changers to help worshipers have the correct currency to pay their temple tax. There may have been additional charges for the service, but whether this was the case we do not know.

Where were these temple conveniences located? The best we can tell from descriptions, they had been placed on the temple mount itself at the top end of what is called today the Southern Steps.[10] On this southern side at the top of the steps was a long portico. It was the first place one entered at the top tier of the ascent. Here one gained access to the temple's outer court, the court of women and the temple proper. In other words, we are not thinking of controlling the entire temple mount to get to the money changers. Rather we are speaking about an entrance into the temple area proper, a little bottleneck for traffic as it funneled people in. Turning over a few tables in this confined area would have brought things to a temporary halt.[11] Understanding this configuration means Jesus' act could have "stopped the show" for a time, much like a stalled car can cause a logjam on a freeway. This was quite a confined area. Whether animals were also in the area is disputed, since we have so little ancient evidence to work with on this specific point, but some have made the case for it.[12] This area also was not well fortified—the bulk of soldiers were at the Antonia fortress, located just outside the northwest corner of the temple. In other words, the soldiers were outside and on the opposite side of the complex.

The leadership confronted Jesus for his act by challenging him about the source of his authority. Matthew 21:15–16 makes this the most clear. Yet the leaders were careful because Jesus was popular, and doing something drastic to him may have made matters worse. This is why some texts mention the leaders' fear of Jesus because of his popularity (Mark 11:18, Luke 19:48). The leadership was nervous about losing so much control that the Romans would seek more control of the city and temple.[13]

Richard Horsley argues for the authenticity of this event, and cites two examples as support for the idea that reaction to such an incident might not be immediate. There was a precedent with Archelaus in 4 BCE and a later event involving Cumanus sometime after 48 CE. In both cases reactions to potential temple disturbances did not take place immediately. Josephus describes these events (*Jewish War* 2.10–13 = *Antiquities* 17.211–18 [Archelaus], *Jewish War* 2.223–27 = *Antiquities* 20.105–12 [Cumanus]).

The first incident involved people mourning some rabbis and taking vigil in the temple, while the second was in reaction to a Roman soldier who showed his backside to the crowd at the temple, inciting them to react. In each case, the leaders did not react until a great crowd gathered and became a potentially dangerous multitude. So although leaders watched over the temple, they used their power carefully there.

The Meaning of the Event

Jesus Protests Against the Injustice of the Priests in Terms of Monetary Gain

So what did Jesus' act mean? At the very least, it was a protest against the way things were being done at the temple. Some argue that it was not a protest about any type of corruption in the way the money and commerce were being handled.[14] This is in reaction to an older common view, triggered in part by Jesus' remark that the temple had become a "den of robbers." The major point made in excluding the commerce is that supplying sacrifices was a requirement of the Law, which is true, and that Jesus makes no direct remark against those handling the money. The question is not if commerce needed to be conducted, but how it was done and who controlled it, so when Jesus protests the turning of the temple into something it should not be, he is complaining against the priests who oversee it. Everyone knew who oversaw the temple, so Jesus did not need to be explicit. Yet only by denying that Jesus alluded to Jeremiah 7:11 and the den of robbers can one exclude some allusion to either corruption or commerce as part of the point.[15]

One should not reject Jesus' use of this theme. *First*, throughout his ministry Jesus argued that the leadership and Israel were in a low spiritual state, comparable with other spiritually dry times in her history. It is the premise of his call to repent, rooted in Markan sources (Mark 1:14–15), but appearing also in L material (Luke 13:1–5; 15:7). The comparison with the low spiritual time of Elijah and Elisha or with a line of prophets is multiply attested, so much so that some people thought of Elijah when they heard about Jesus (Mark: Parable of the Wicked Tenants; Mark 8:28 = Matthew 16:14 = Luke 9:19; L: Luke 4:24–30, 7:16, 13:33; John: John 4:19, 7:52). The time is like that of people without a shepherd, an allusion to Ezekiel 34 and exile (Mark 6:34 = Matthew 9:32). Jerusalem is on the edge of an exile-like judgment (Matthew 23 = Luke 11:37–54; the Olivet Discourse of all the Synoptics). So such a perspective runs deep in the teaching of Jesus, touching all its traditional strands.

Second, others shared in this charge against the leadership. The Qumran community argued that the "wicked priest" who served as an ancestor to the current priesthood amassed wealth at others' expense (1QpHab 8:7–13 commenting on Habakkuk 2:5–6). Other texts in Qumran's treatment of Habakkuk repeat the charge (1QpHab 9:2–16, 10:5–6, 11:2–25). Similar in force is 4QpNah fragment 3 and 4 1:10. It protests the gathering of wealth appealing to Nahum 2:14. Other texts from Qumran repeat the charge (CD A 6:14–17; 4Q Ps 37 2:14, 3:6, 12; 4QMMT 82–83). So this theme is even multiply attested as a charge at Qumran. Elsewhere in Second Temple Jewish texts the charge also appears (*1 Enoch* 89:32–33; *Testament of Levi* 14:1–15:1, 17:8–11; *Testament of Judah* 23:1–3; *Testament of Moses* 5:3–6:1). Josephus narrates stories about the corruption in the priesthood (*Antiquities* 20.179–81; 205–7). Later texts also make the point. A text in the *Mishnah* points out an excessive charge of a golden denar (an ancient coin) for a pair of doves (*m. Keritot* 1:7). So the charge about money and the temple is everywhere in Judaism across several generations. The text from the *Testament of Moses* is even about our period. So Jesus was complaining about how activity at the temple was taking place, probably by taking advantage of worshippers. But is that all that he is saying?

Was Jesus Predicting the Temple's Destruction or Cleansing It?

Some argue that to say Jesus challenged commerce in the temple says too little. This is probably correct. This activity is but a symptom of a deeper issue. But is Jesus calling for a cleansing of the temple or, more dramatically, is he predicting its destruction? Scholars are genuinely divided on this question, and a good case can be made for either option.

Two key elements favor the idea that Jesus is predicting the temple's destruction. *First*, the term for robbers is not the normal one for something like swindling, but rather it means to take something with violence, like a bandit. So the argument is that more than commerce is in view. *Second*, when viewed in light of Jesus' cursing of a fig tree and the later prediction of the destruction of the temple in the Olivet Discourse, then a good case can be made that Jesus' purposes were also prophetic in nature.[16] For some, this included the idea of the end of sacrifices.[17]

There also is a good case that can be made in support of the idea that Jesus sought only to cleanse the temple. Such support is found in Jesus' remark that the temple is designed to be a place of prayer for Gentiles, which does not look like a statement that is arguing for the end of the temple. The force of the remark is seen in a couple of ways, either of which could be in play here. In one variation of this view, Jesus' point is that the temple was not operating in the manner it should—it was too much like a civic center.[18] So just as the nation needed reform and cleansing, so did practice at the temple. Jesus was calling it to return to a more faithful level of worship. Another variation of this view sees the cleansing as preceding the eschatological arrival of a new era for the temple, so the act is part of the eschatology of Jesus and his preaching of a new era of hope.[19] A place for Gentiles is what the temple will be from now on.

In fact, Jesus could be making both points simultaneously.

What the temple will be is also what it should have been. Supporting this idea in either form is the fact that members of the community around Jesus continued their participation at the temple after his death. They did not sense that his remarks were about ceasing all activity at the temple.[20]

So Jesus' teaching as a whole appears to speak of cleansing here while predicting destruction elsewhere.[21] This combination points to the possible idea of future temple renewal associated with Jesus' work, since the temple is seen as a place for Jews and Gentiles. Whether one sees cleansing or destruction here, an eschatological promise and hope are in view. Either the temple is cleansed and will be renewed one day, or its destruction points to a new kind of sacred presence in the church.[22]

It seems likely that Jesus' protest was against the feel of the temple having become too much like a civic center. Herod the Great had extended the temple on a Roman model of the basilica. In Roman culture, the basilica was a site for commercial activity. This was part of the "robbery" Jesus complains about. The sacred site risked being trivialized and given the feel of a bazaar or mall instead of a place to concentrate on meeting God. The social-political-spiritual dimension of all of this led to Jesus' reference to a "den of robbers." Jesus' complaint was about more than money and commerce: Jesus was protesting that the temple was being trivialized and exploited in a variety of ways that impacted on its sacredness.

The Eschatological Dimension to Jesus' Protest

It is the complaint's scope that points us ultimately to seeing an eschatological dimension within his protest. Jesus has just entered the city, accepting acclamation as a central figure tied to kingdom hope. Associated with that hope is the idea that Jerusalem will be purged and cleansed. Some texts even discuss the purging accomplished by the ruling figure to come. *Psalms of Solomon* 17:21–30

[23–28] speak of this in some detail.[23] Verses 28–30 [26–27] read, "And he shall gather together a holy people, whom he shall lead in righteousness, and he shall judge the tribes of the people that have been sanctified by the Lord his God. And he shall not suffer unrighteousness to lodge any more in their midst, nor shall there dwell with them any man that knows wickedness, for he shall know them, that they are all sons of their God."

One advantage of seeing the full cleansing and renewal of the temple in view here is that it permits an association with both cleansing and the destruction of the temple. A fully reconstituted temple is part of the reform and restoration that comes with the new era. It also fits a host of Second Temple Jewish texts that look to a rebuilt temple in a new era of justice, as well as a few texts that follow the Second Temple period. Eight ancient Jewish texts teach this idea (4Q174; 11Q Temple 29:8–10; *1 Enoch* 90:28–29; Tobit 13:16–17; *Jubilees* 1:15–17; *Sibylline Oracles* 3:286–94; *2 Baruch* 68:5–6; Benediction 14 of the national prayer of blessing known as the *Shemoneh Esreh*). The benediction concludes, "Blessed are you Lord, God of David, builder of Jerusalem." This associates David, God, and the building of Jerusalem. Most of these texts predate Jesus. When Jesus acts and uses Isaiah 56, he appeals to a text calling for setting things right in the temple and gathering those previously excluded. This appeal shows that he intends to affirm an act of hope and restoration.

As if this were not enough, there is one other crucial point this event makes embedded in the question: "Who gave you the authority to do these things?" Jesus' answer—pointing to John the Baptist—is not likely to be a creation of the church because it compares Jesus with John, when the church elevated Jesus over John. The leaders ask this question because they thought of themselves as the representatives of God and as those who had authority over the temple. They had not given Jesus the right to act.

Jesus replies using John to argue that God is able to sanction the authority of figures the leadership did not appoint. Implied in the answer is that Jesus' authority is from God as John the Baptist's was. Even though Jesus does not answer the question explicitly, his question about John is the answer. Jesus is in the eschatological chain of authority that John has.

But there is even more still. Jesus is not at the Jordan River. He is exercising authority over the world's most sacred spot for a Jew. This act, even though it is prophetic, points to a figure larger than a prophet. It falls alongside Jesus' claim to be Lord of the Sabbath and his authority over transcendent forces. It followed his entry accepting a claim to be king. It points to him not only announcing the kingdom but showing authority as to its character in the most holy of locales. One need not be a student of ancient history to know that the Temple Mount is a sensitive location that causes passions to rise in the religious heart.

The Middle East today teaches this lesson on occasion when something significant or controversial happens there. Snodgrass says it this way: "However one sorts out the significance of the event, this symbolic act was designed to bring to mind the expectations of God's restored temple and to stop people in their tracks so that they had to reconsider what was going on in the temple, reconsider their own worship, and ascertain who Jesus really was. The question of authority naturally follows. In effect, the authorities asked, 'Just who do you think you are?'"[24] Jesus' act and answer came on the most holy of sites and said, "One uniquely sent by God to announce and bring the new era."

10

The Last Supper:

Sacred Liturgy and Authority

ONE OF the most famous events of Jesus' last week is the Last Supper.[1] Here it is said that Jesus took a final meal with his key followers and revealed what he was facing in Jerusalem. In the Synoptics, his meal took place during the period of Passover, a major feast for Israel, and Jesus used this backdrop to describe what was ahead for him, using bread and a cup of wine to explain what he was about to experience. So we turn to this crucial meal, taken as Jesus stands at the edge of the final events of his ministry. What case can be made for Jesus having held such a final meal? If the meal did take place, what does it—and its inherent symbolism—tell us about Jesus?

RULES THAT APPLY TO THE LAST SUPPER

This scene is so potentially important that it has been the topic of much discussion and debate. Thus the bulk of this chapter will deal with the objections made to the scene, especially as they relate to key details within it. We will apply some of the rules to the discussion when we cover those details.

Multiple Attestation

For the historicity of the core event, we can apply the criterion of multiple attestation. There appears to be two versions of the disclosure part of the event. If we take a close look at what was said over the bread and the cup, we see one version reflected in Mark 14:22–25 = Matthew 26:26–29, while the other appears in Paul's account in 1 Corinthians 11:23–25 and corresponds to Luke 22:14–20. Paul attributes the saying to tradition, noting he passed on what he also received. The wording found in the version in Mark/Matthew is virtually identical, as is the distinct wording found in the second version in Paul/Luke. While the two versions are similar at their core, there are differences. We will take a closer look at this when we consider objections.

Surrounding this core are two other key details. *First*, there is the Synoptics' placement of the event in association with a Passover meal, a dating John appears to challenge by saying Jesus was crucified when the meal was being prepared (juxtaposing John 13:1, 18:28, and 19:14 and 31 yields this alternate setting). This is another key objection we shall consider in detail later. *Second*, there is Jesus' mentioning that his approaching suffering comes at the hands of a betrayer from within the Twelve. Jesus does not identify the traitor at the meal, but readers who know the story know him to be Judas. These two other key details precede the remarks of Jesus over the bread and cup and appear in Matthew 26:17–25 = Mark 14:12–21 = Luke 22:7–13.

Multiple Attestation of Forms

The reference by Paul to the meal makes the meal and the words said over it some of the earliest attested elements of Jesus' life.

These are mid-first-century CE sources, since First Corinthians is dated in the last half of the fifties. Paul's rooting that material in the tradition makes it explicitly older than the apostle's use of it. The subsequent importance of the meal in the liturgy of the church as the basis of the Lord's Supper gives the sense that this meal made a deep impression on the early church.[2] Paul also notes this connection between the Last Supper and the subsequent celebration of the Lord's Supper in the church.

So in examining this meal, we look at three key features beyond the fact of a meal itself: the naming of the betrayer, the timing and nature of the meal, and what was said at it.

OBJECTIONS

There are four challenges to the narrative of this meal, three of them significant. One is whether such a meal was even held at all, which is the least substantive of the challenges. More important are issues raised about Judas, the nature and timing of the meal, and finally, what was said there. We take the four objections in this order.

Questions about Whether the Meal Actually Occurred

The fact that Paul discusses this meal makes it unlikely that Mark is responsible for the event. Paul's mention predates the gospels and is rooted in the oral tradition of the early church. Nonetheless, some have argued for an origin that creates the event for other purposes, even if Mark is not responsible.

The Meal Is Etiological, Not Historical

Dennis Smith argues that the scene is etiological, not historical—an etiology being a story that explains the origin of something (usually a disease), but here we are speaking about the origin of a church practice, the Lord's Supper. Smith argues that because the account explains this practice in the church, we do not have a historical account.[3] However, he does not make clear why a real event cannot be the root of a practice. Most holidays we celebrate today commemorate something that actually took place—for example, Americans celebrate Independence Day, commemorating the signing of the Declaration of Independence on July 4, 1776. So the claim that the event functions with a purpose for the church does not preclude it from having an origin in a real event. Given the depth of testimony that exists for such a decisive final meal, with attestation in Mark, John, and Paul, as well as appearing in multiple forms (narrative, epistle, traditional creed), Smith's argument is not persuasive.

The Meal Is Imitative

Another challenge takes into account the way disciples found a room for the meal by Jesus' instruction according to Mark 14:12–16, seeing this as evidence that the meal reflects a created scene, not a real event.[4] The argument is that this aspect of the story is imitative of 1 Samuel 10:1–8. So in order to assess the validity of this objection, we need to compare the details of the Samuel passage and the account of the preparation for the meal to see if imitation is present.

In 1 Samuel 10, after Samuel anoints Saul, the prophet tells Saul that he will meet two men who will tell him the donkeys he was looking for have been found. Then Saul will meet three men who have goats, bread, and wine. Saul will receive bread from them. After this, Saul meets with prophets and shares in their inspiration before going on to Gilgal, where he is to wait for Samuel to offer sacrifices. Only by combining three distinct Jesus events (Jesus' entry into Jerusalem, the anointing of Jesus by a woman, and the meal preparation) do we actually get an "imitation" with this Samuel-Saul account. This three-event linkage is how we get some of the details in the story to appear to correspond. However, the entry scene and the presence of donkeys are in Mark 11 and the anointing and meal scenes are in Mark 14—an unusual distance for an imitative story. Beyond this, there are other differences that show the two events are not parallel. The anointing of Jesus is with myrrh, while Saul was anointed with oil. Saul meets men who tell him about a donkey. Jesus sends for men to get a donkey. Saul never has contact with the donkey, while Jesus does (but in Mark 11, not here). There is no meal in the Saul story and only bread is mentioned. There are no goats in Jesus' story. In sum, there don't seem to be any convincing parallels to persuade one that the event is an imitation.

The Meal Is Not Connected to Jesus' Death

Some say there may have been a meal, but we can know little about what took place there beyond the fellowship Jesus had. Crossan grants that a meal is authentic, a staple of the ancient world, but he argues that there was no Passover, Last Supper, or connection with Jesus' death.[5] A unique part of Crossan's argument appeals to how the meal is handled in *Didache* 9–10. This early Christian work is dated either to the end of the first century or early second century CE. Crossan argues that this contains the earliest of the Lord's Table traditions, and there is no hint of Passover, Last Supper, or passion symbolism in it.

By contrast, Marshall notes twelve points of overlap between the *Didache* and Paul. These connections suggest that the two traditions are less competing than Crossan argues.[6] Marshall agrees with Crossan that *Didache* lacks explicit reference to the body and blood of Jesus or a death "for you," but Marshall does note that *Didache* spiritualizes the meaning of the bread as about the life and knowledge Jesus made known. This is like John's "bread of life," which assumes such a salvation meaning to the event. Marshall argues the perspective of *Didache* is more reflective of a later period than an early view of the meal, as the symbolism is more complex. In addition, *Didache* is later than Paul and describes what is taking place at the time of its writing. In other words, the *Didache* tells us nothing about any earlier meal because it makes no effort to describe that event. Thus, Crossan's appeal lacks the connection it needs to make his point. More than that, it lacks any real rationale for why a meal would have been recorded and recalled at all. Jesus would have had many general meals. Why elevate this one unless there was something unusual about it? All of this points to a meal that Jesus had that yielded a special significance worth recalling.

Other challenges against the final meal go to specifics within the event to raise objections. These challenges involve questions about Judas, the nature and timing of the meal, and what was said at the table.

Questions about Judas

So is the role of Judas at the meal credible? We have already defended the idea of Judas betraying Jesus in discussing the selection of the Twelve. In that treatment we rooted the defense of the authenticity of Judas' betrayal in the criterion of *embarrassment*. Why create a story that has one of Jesus' own betray him if it did not take place? There is no solid reason why this would be done. If one is making it up, there are many other simpler ways to get Jesus arrested than to suggest the one who did it was an intimate friend Jesus had chosen.

Some object to the detail that Judas entered into a contract with the Jewish leadership to betray Jesus. This detail is said to be the result of the church trying to increase blame on the Jews for the crucifixion and excuse the Romans.[7] In this scenario, what some Jewish leaders did was urge Pilate to execute Jesus; but otherwise, they did nothing. However, it is not clear why Pilate would take the initiative to have Jesus arrested, since Jesus posed no military or political threat to Rome. Jesus' tensions were with the Jewish leadership.

Others contend that the evangelists do not agree on why Judas did betray Jesus, leading them to question the gospels' portrayal.[8] Matthew 26:15 has Judas betray Jesus for greed, namely for thirty pieces of silver, an allusion to Zechariah 11:12 cited in Matthew 27:9–10. This is another claim of scriptural imitation. The detail is said to create the fulfilled prophecy. There is no way to corroborate this detail either way; however, the detail need not preclude the likelihood that money played a role. Mark 14:4 has Judas react to the waste of money in the preceding scene of the woman anointing Jesus. Judas there offered a protest that the anointing with expensive oil from a now broken vase was a waste, something John 12:6 also notes. Now, these accounts are not as far apart as critics suggest. Mark, Matthew, and John all have Judas concerned with money and its use. There is *multiple attestation* about Judas' concern for money. John 6:70–71, 13:2, and 27 see Judas as demon-possessed, a theme Luke 22:3 also notes. So John and Luke share the idea that sinister forces were at work. The detail is multiply attested, since L and John are seen as distinct tradition strands. Such a view of Judas is only natural for those who felt allied to Jesus and saw the betrayal as wrong, especially if they viewed Jesus as sent by God. In other words, the gospel writers' diverse content reflects a mix of themes that seem to be a part of the tradition that was already there. They chose what to use. A different choice does not mean creating a new story.

Questions about the Nature and Timing of the Meal

So what about the nature and timing of the meal? Was it a Passover meal or not? Mark 14:12–16 and Luke 22:15 describe the meal as tied to Passover. John has a meal but in no part of his account does he record anything like the Last Supper scene. It is important to note that John tends to present fresh material about Jesus and there is no doubt he is aware of the Last Supper tradition by the time he writes at the end of the first century, since the Lord's Table was a rite in the church. What we seem to have in John's gospel is a simple choice not to include an event that was already well known. One must be careful using arguments from silence when explanations for absence exist.

What makes a Passover meal difficult is John's seeming association of Jesus' death with the time of Passover. John 13:1, 18:28, and 19:14 and 31 point to this potentially alternative timing. The argument is that if Jesus is slain during Passover, then this cannot be the Passover meal. John 13:1 says Jesus moved to hold the meal "just before the Passover feast." John 18:28 notes that the priests on the day after the meal refrained from going into Pilate's residence because they feared being defiled for the Passover meal. John 19:14 says it was the day of Passover preparation when Jesus was presented to the crowd before his crucifixion. John 19:31 gives the same timing in discussing why the crucified bodies could not remain upon the cross.

Four basic explanations of this difference have been given.

Option 1: John Talks of a Weeklong Celebration

One is to see the remarks of John in a different light.[9] John 13:1 is about the timing of what led Jesus to have the meal and not the timing of the meal itself. John 18:28 is not about the specific Passover meal, but other unleavened-bread meals associated with the weeklong celebration of Passover. There is precedent for such a general use of the term *Passover* in Josephus. *Jewish War* 5.99 speaks of the feast of unleavened bread on 14 Nisan, which is the actual day of Passover. The two texts in John 19 are seen to involve the day of preparation for the Sabbath tied to the Passover week. A similar reading would see the same ambiguity of reference in John 18:28, only here it is a Passover-Sabbath connection, not a Passover–unleavened bread connection. John would be choosing to mention Passover because it is the dominant feature of the entire week. A modern analogy would be that people celebrate Christmas office parties before the event—rarely on Christmas Day.

Option 2: Different Calendars Possibly Used

Others appeal to the presence of different calendars used within Judaism, so that John's reckoning is based on a dating system distinct from that of the Synoptics. These options come in two basic forms.

One appeals to a different calendar reckoning between Galileans-Pharisees and Judeans-Sadducees.[10] The Galilean calendar went sunrise to sunrise, while the other went sunset to sunset. This would result in a twelve-hour difference in reckoning the days. The Synoptics use the Galilean-Pharisaical method, while John is on the official Judean-Sadducean calendar. However, we lack specific evidence for this option. Variations on this option do not reckon with an alternative way of counting the days, but are simply distinct calendars for distinct groups on analogy with the solar-lunar calendar distinction between the Qumran community and official Judaism.

Option 3: Two Days of Sacrifice

And others speak of sacrifices being permitted over two days to deal with the large number required at the time.[11] The key text for this view is from the later *Mishnah* (*m. Zevahim* 1:3), where some rabbis permitted an earlier sacrifice, although other rabbis rejected this option. Since the temple was destroyed when the *Mishnah* was compiled, the discussion of this option appears to be old. The premise here is that an early sacrifice on 13 Nisan would lead to a meal early on 14 Nisan just after sundown, since keeping food overnight would be dangerous. Here what exists is evidence for the early sacrifice but not specifically for an early meal on the day. This latter scenario is quite possible but does not have all the corroborative pieces.

Option 4: A Passover-like Meal

A final option favors John's chronology but accepts the Synoptic sense of the meal. This view argues that the meal has a Passover feel to it or was presented like a Passover meal even though it was not technically a Passover meal offered on the official day.[12] Again this option is possible, but also lacks any external evidence. Jesus is capable of this type of innovation and the season is such that the association would not have been far away.

✦ ✦ ✦

The chronological differences we see in the Last Supper discussion also apply to the timing of the crucifixion. Almost all scholars accept the fact that Jesus was crucified around Passover time, despite the debate on the exact timing in the materials. But the details about exactly when certain events took place do not rise to a sufficient level to doubt the event itself—both of Jesus' death and the timing of the meal. The exact timing may be less transparent in the record of the tradition than the event is, but it does not reach to such a problematic level as to question the event itself.

However, regardless of timing, do the details of the meal give indication that it is a Passover meal? The scholar Joachim Jeremias makes the strongest case.[13] Jesus held the meal in Jerusalem (Mark 14:12–16), even though he was staying in Bethany. This follows the pilgrims' practice of having this special meal in Jerusalem. Paul speaks of what Jesus said on the evening he was betrayed (1 Corinthians 11:23), which would fit with a Passover meal, which was a specially held, evening meal. John 13:10 has them in a state of purity, which would have been a requirement for Passover. The association with singing after the meal is a part of the Passover tradition (*m. Pesahim* 5.7, 10.6–7), as was interpreting the elements of bread and the cup (*m. Pesahim* 10.1–7). The cumulative effect of these correspondences is that we should see a Passover meal here.

Why is the sorting out of the timing and nature of the meal so important? The Passover meal commemorated the night on which Israel was delivered from Egypt (Exodus 12), celebrating the day of Israel's salvation. When Jesus connects his upcoming suffering and death with this day of Israel's history, he is doing so within the context of God saving his people from Egypt. He is comparing one defining act of salvation with another, which he will bring. That much comes just with the timing of the meal. But it was more than just timing; it was also the words Jesus said.

Questions about What Was Said at the Meal

Textual Differences in What Was Said

To begin analyzing what Jesus said at the meal, let's look at the key differences between the accounts. Remember we have two basic versions, Mark/Matthew and Paul/Luke. First, Mark/Matthew speaks simply of Jesus giving the bread with a command to take and him noting that this is "my body." Paul/Luke explains the body is "for you" and remarks about doing this in remembrance. With the cup, Mark/Matthew has Jesus say that this wine is "my blood of the covenant." Mark says it more succinctly, since Matthew has a command for all to drink. They also share the idea of the blood being "poured out for the many." The "many" is likely an allusion to Isaiah 53, where the Servant acts to deal with the sins of the "many" in 53:11–12. Matthew adds an additional explanation, mentioning that the pouring out for the many is "for the forgiveness of sins." Paul/Luke has Jesus present the cup as "the new covenant in my blood." This addition simply specifies the covenant intended by the act, since Jesus brings the new era. Luke adds, "that is poured out for you." Paul adds a note about remembering as often as you drink it.

Needless to say, with these differences there are variations in how scholars see the original wording. Some prefer Mark's simple version (Jeremias).[14] Others prefer the early attested version of Paul (Dunn).[15] Others opt for a mix between the accounts (Marshall).[16] We could examine the detailed discussion here, but the fact is that the variety of views will continue to be held because of the complexity of the questions and variety of plausible options. Marshall's conclusion here sums it up best: "Scholarly uncertainty on the precise wording will continue to exist, but the different accounts testify to a basic core of motifs that existed in the varied wording."[17] Dunn argues that the variation is typical of what happens in oral tradition.[18] It also fits how liturgy works. It can bring out explicitly what was implicit in an earlier saying. It is important to note that these differences are merely elaborations of what is inherent in the core. In other words, the variations in the traditions make explicit what the simplest form of Jesus' wording says implicitly. They say the same thing; the longer version simply says it more clearly.

Jesus' Death Was "For You"

The core claim affirms that Jesus' death was a participation in the salvation of others. It was "for you," as the disciples represent all those who benefit from Jesus' death. It instituted a covenant and involved his death for the many/you. How explicitly Isaiah 53 and its key Suffering Servant figure is in the original background is debated, but covenantal inauguration is clearly intended. So it is not a great step to connect that new-era cleansing work to a death and the saving image of the Servant. Part of the reason for the debate involves answering the question whether or not Jesus alluded to the figure Isaiah 53 and associated this Suffering Servant with himself. Mark 10:45 appears to make such a connection with its idea of ransom drawn from the Isaiah 53 passage. Luke 22:37 has Jesus cite the image of the Suffering Servant figure in terms of his being reckoned with sinners. So Jesus' use of the

Servant song as part of what describes his mission is *multiply attested*, being in Mark and Luke. This makes an allusion here to the same basic portrait quite possible.

Borg and Crossan see a recognition by Jesus of the disciples' participation in Jesus' death, but deny any representative or substitutionary meaning in that affirmation.[19] They note correctly that Passover evokes images of protection, but not guilt or sin. Nonetheless, this is a case of a both-and. Jesus is affirming the disciples sharing in the protection of his death like Passover pictures, but he explains it is possible because he represents them in acting for them. This is part of the point in Jesus speaking of inaugurating a covenant for others ("covenant for you"), even if Isaiah 53 is not explicitly in view. Covenants are inaugurated with sacrifices.

The move from an old covenant to a new one points to a need for purification and reform. Jesus' ministry is about the bringing of this new era of realization. This inevitably points to sin and guilt. If Isaiah 53 is in view, then "dying for the many" makes the connection explicit in the picture of a ransom and substitution. Isaiah 53:11b–12 reads, "My servant will acquit many, for he carried their sins. So I will assign him a portion with the multitudes, he will divide the spoils of victory with the powerful, because he willingly submitted to death and was numbered with the rebels, when he lifted up the sin of many and intervened on behalf of the rebels." So whether Isaiah 53 is in view or not, the presence of a fresh covenant has the premise of a cleansed start. Jesus' death both protects and cleanses.

Jesus Brings New Kingdom Era

What is said here coheres with other elements of what Jesus has taught. He brings the new era of the kingdom. He not only announced it; he made it possible. His upcoming death would clear the way for a covenant inaugurated in his act of sacrifice. The explicit nature of explaining his suffering fits within the theme introduced at Caesarea Philippi, that the Son of Man would suffer—an idea the disciples initially did not expect of the end-time delivering figure. At the table, Jesus explained what his suffering meant. Like the Exodus event of Israel, it would be for the salvation of God's people. This is a part of bringing the eschaton. At the table, Jesus proclaims a second Exodus, a second salvation experience that brings delivery of the new era promised long ago by God. Jesus stands at the center of those events. Despite the objections, the case for Jesus expressing these ideas at this meal is strong.

MEANING OF THE LAST SUPPER

First, as was just noted, this event shows Jesus depicting his death as "part and parcel of the process whereby the kingdom of God comes."[20] When we juxtapose the Exodus setting with Jesus interpreting afresh the elements of the bread and cup, we see him evoking deliverance by a new means. Salvation becomes rooted in Jesus' death. One action opens the door of access to God for many people. That Jesus announces this at the table may also invoke the picture of the messianic banquet. Fellowship in Jesus' act means a place at the end-time table.

As Jesus said, this meal was a statement about his death. The early community took that statement and made it a central act of their worship. This is an indication of the importance they gave to Jesus' death and his explanation of it. It culminated in the only rite believers observe regularly that has its roots in Jesus' ministry.[21] With a positive response to Jesus' death, this meal gave meaning to an event that opened the way for people to become members of the new covenant and the new era.

Not to be missed in all of this is yet another crucial point. Jesus took standard liturgy from the nation of Israel, a celebration mandated by the Hebrew Scripture, and he gave it new meaning. Now, this is not merely taking old liturgy and adding to it with elaboration. This is not an act by a prophet, nor a worship leader. This was taking one of the most fundamental of events in Israel's history and placing alongside it a new act of God, pointing to oneself. It was moving the center of God's deliverance from the Exodus to the cross.

The point is this: Who has the authority and right to do something like this? Who has the right to play with sacred liturgy like this? The theme of authority is one that continues to grow as we look at these events. Jesus has authority over the Sabbath. He has authority over transcendent forces. He claimed authority in the face of many gods when he was confessed as the central delivering figure at Caesarea Philippi. He has authority over the most sacred space of the temple. Now he has authority over sacred liturgy. This portrait is no accident, because Jesus portrayed himself as more than a messenger and prophet of God. His acts spoke of the unique role he had in bringing the new era of God.

Jesus claimed at the Last Supper that this authority was so great that even death could not stop it. That is where our story turns now. Jesus has told his disciples he will suffer and die for them. But how did that story unfold? Can one make the case by the rules for these final decisive events of the last week? Our last three events look at this question as we examine the Jewish examination of Jesus, the sentence by Pilate, and the disciples' belief in an empty tomb and resurrection.

The Examination by the Jewish Leadership:

Sacred Presence and Authority

THE EXAMINATION of Jesus by the Jewish leadership is another event that has generated much discussion.[1] Here there is not only discussion about whether the event took place but how one could determine what may have been said there. In addition, there is discussion about what the exact offense was. Can one make sense of this scene in the cultural background of Second Temple Judaism? Here again we will spend some time dealing with objections to the event, as well as tracing the relevant background.

RULES THAT APPLY TO THE EXAMINATION

Jesus' relationship to the Jewish leadership in Jerusalem is an important element in the events that closed his ministry. Events like his entry and the temple incident were a challenge to their control over the faith. His potential popularity with the crowds meant Jesus' challenge could not be ignored. This led to the attempt to stop Jesus. The Jewish leaders' examination of him was an opportunity to gather the material necessary to take Jesus to Pilate so Rome could use its power against him.

Multiple Attestation

The idea that something like this examination took place is multiply attested. Not only do we have the material in Mark 14:53–65, Matthew 26:57–68, and Luke 22:54, 66–71, but also a brief note in John 18:13–14, 19–23. There is also a remark by the Jewish historian Josephus that some of the leadership and Pilate were responsible for Jesus' death. *Antiquities* 18.64 in part reads, "and when Pilate, at the suggestion of the principal men among us, had condemned him to the cross, those that loved him at first did not forsake him." Obviously the "principal men among us" refers to those who were leaders. The Johannine remark simply has Jesus defend the public nature of his ministry and suggests it is unjust that the Jewish leaders are examining him. It is very brief, so it does not help us consider what caused the leadership to examine Jesus nor does it fit the rules in any of its specifics beyond saying such an event took place. So, even if we could verify John's scene specifically according to the rules, it would not help us other than to confirm such an examination. This means we are left with what Mark, Matthew, and Luke tell us.

However, the gospel texts are not the only passages that point to some kind of an examination or major role for the Jewish leadership in Jesus' demise. Acts 4:23–26 alludes to such a role, and 1 Thessalonians 2:14–15 offers a generic charge against the "Jews who killed Jesus and the prophets." This linkage of Jesus and the rejection of the prophets is something that appears in one of the most important of Jesus' parables, the Parable of the Wicked Tenants (Matthew 21:33–45 = Mark 12:1–12 = Luke 20:9–19). This parable is an allegory about Israel's history of unfaithfulness that

Jesus told during his last week, in the midst of the key confrontations that took place at that time. He was warning them about their rejection of him and that it fit a historical pattern, alluding to Psalm 118 and the rejection of the keystone. The linking of Jesus' treatment to past rejection of the prophets also appears in Stephen's speech in Acts 7.

Three gospels outside the four we are most familiar with also weigh in on the presence of this kind of event.

First, the *Gospel of Thomas* 66 has an allusion that parallels what the Parable of the Wicked Tenants says. It reads, "Jesus said, 'Show me the stone that the builders rejected: that is the keystone.'" "Builders" refers to the Jewish leaders. If *Thomas* is independent of the gospels, then this detail is multiply attested. If not, many still defend the parable as going back to Jesus.[2] There is only one question in thinking through the authenticity of this specific theme about linking Jesus' rejection to that of the prophets. That question involves making a judgment about whether Jesus anticipated his possible rejection as he came into Jerusalem. The precedent of John the Baptist's death at the hands of Herod shows that one could anticipate death if the political and social leadership rejected one's claims. Jesus' public entry, declaration, and temple act involved a risk; and it is likely Jesus knew that.

Second, there is the *Gospel of Peter*, which picks up with the Roman examination but notes that "none of the Jews washed their hands," an allusion to those who had brought Jesus to Pilate. One should not make too much of this, since the detail about washing looks to build off of Matthew's depiction of Pilate's response to the situation in Matthew 27:24. It may show that the tradition Matthew used was known to the author of *Peter*, if he did not know the gospel of Matthew itself.[3]

Third is the *Gospel of Nicodemus*, also known as the *Acts of Pilate*. It attributes some responsibility to the Jewish leadership for bringing Jesus to Pilate. This gospel looks like it appeared later in the chain of development about the trial scene. Here the debate is over Jesus' claim to be Son of God and Sabbath healings. Ten key Jewish leaders are even named. What these other gospels do suggest is a memory of an official encounter between Jesus and the leadership. So multiple attestation of both *sources* and *forms* (epistles, narrative, parable) points to such an event.

Rejection and Execution

A second rule, the criterion of rejection and execution, also authenticates that this event or something like it occurred. Rome had no reason to take the initiative against Jesus. He had no army. His movement was religious. As long as it was nonviolent and caused no major stir, he might be watched but need not be stopped. These criteria of multiple attestation and rejection point to the authenticity of the general event but cannot in themselves suggest anything about the specifics.

The specifics of the scene leave us largely with assessing the scene as it appears in Matthew, Mark, and Luke. As with other events, Mark's version is regarded as our oldest. With an event as important as this, we should recall that there was probably some oral tradition circulating not only in the church but in official Jewish circles about what had taken place. Each side would have made their version of the events known to those in Jerusalem. The core features of this memory are very similar in these gospels. They needed to be reasonably accurate to retain any credibility in the subsequent public debate about Jesus. In other words, the public nature and significance of this dispute operated as a kind of constraint over how such a meeting was reported and circulated in the early tradition.

The core of the scene in the three gospels is similar. All three gospels have Jesus queried on whether he is the Christ. Mark 14:61 has the question in a more explicitly sensitive Jewish form, "Are you the Christ, the Son of the Blessed?" This roundabout way of saying "Son of God" reflects Jewish respect for speaking about God in formal settings. Matthew 26:63 says it more directly: "I charge you under oath by the living God, tell us if you are the Christ, the Son of God." Luke 22:67 has "If you are the Christ, tell us." The point is the same, while the variation reflects what is common in renderings rooted in oral tradition. The key query shared in all versions is that Jesus was asked if he was the Christ, the Messiah.

Jesus responds by citing Psalm 110:1 in all three gospels, affirming that the Son of Man will be seen at God's right hand. This is a claim that God accepts and vindicates the Son of Man, who is Jesus, since Son of Man is Jesus' favorite way to refer to himself. Matthew and Mark also have this Son of Man figure riding the clouds, an allusion to Daniel 7:13–14. In Daniel, the Son of Man receives dominion authority from the Ancient of Days, who pictures God. Matthew and Mark note that Jesus' reply brought an assessment from the leadership that Jesus had blasphemed against God, pictured in their tearing their robes. Luke simply notes that what Jesus said led to his being taken to Pilate. I shall treat the Son of Man title in more detail later as it is a key to appreciating what is being said here.

When it comes to the details, we need to consider the objections and issues they raise. Most important here is to focus on the judgment that what Jesus said was seen as blasphemous by the leadership. Something like this can explain how Jesus ended up before Pilate.

OBJECTIONS TO THE JEWISH
EXAMINATION SCENE

We will deal with six objections in total. Five deal with the core scene, the key issues of the event. The last objection accepts the core event but raises a question about whether and to what degree we can know the details of Jesus' answer. This is a complex discussion, but required because of the event's importance to the overall understanding of Jesus' ministry. Much of what has been said in the events up to this point, however, comes together into a coherent account about Jesus. In other words, a close look, as complex as it is, will be worth it.

Five Objections to the Core Scene

The five objections to this core scene come at various levels.

First, it is claimed the charge of blasphemy does not fit the Jewish understanding of that offense, since the pronunciation of the divine name is required and Jesus does not do that.[4] This kind of specific verbal offense is stated in the *Mishnah, Sanhedrin* 7:5. Even for some who recognize that blasphemy need not involve a disrespectful use of the specific divine name, there is a question about what was blasphemous in what Jesus said, given that claiming to be Messiah or even Son of God in itself does not qualify.[5] Almost all scholars agree that claiming to be Messiah was not seen as blasphemy.[6] So the blasphemy must be something else. A variation on this objection, then, is whether anything Jesus says actually fits what he might have said about himself, and if so, would it be seen as blasphemous. In other words, would Jesus say something so directly about himself as is portrayed here?

Second, the scene is said to be unrealistic, considering that the priests would have to be scrambling to meet and get to Pilate in the middle of the busy Passover holiday season, while others note correctly that normally a trial could not have been held at night or over a holiday.[7] Another version of this objection simply argues that placing the major blame for Jesus' death on the leadership as a whole or on Jews in general reflects a scene depicted with "later Christian apologetic concerns" and not the history of what took place.[8]

Third, a question is raised about where the witnesses for this scene would have come from, since no disciples were present to know what was said.[9] The closest anyone gets are Peter and John (John 18:15), but they are outside the room where Jesus is examined.

Fourth, some question whether a trial is present, since Jews did not have the authority to execute anyone in a Roman context. This point about who had the right to execute is correct.[10] This will require a careful look, since it will cause us to ask if the scene is a trial, as many have claimed, or whether the scene reflects a different kind of meeting.

Finally, some see the scene as formed by Mark or the early church in order to give an example about how to face suffering and persecution.[11] Thus, for some, the scene is regarded as a creation motivated to show disciples how to stand in the face of rejection.

The last argument is the least compelling. Jesus' defense here is unique and tells the disciples nothing about how to stand up for Jesus. Jesus' reply is about himself. The only things Jesus models are courage in the face of questioning and willingness to suffer and die for seeing himself as the Christ, the Son of God. But there is nothing particularly instructive in how Jesus goes about this. Other than giving confidence to stand and suffer, which the scene does show, the account does little more in this regard. So this explanation cannot be the rationale for the full scene. The issue of whether apologetic creates the detail (the second objection) or knowledge from the tradition is more complicated.

Objection: Information about the Meeting Was Unavailable

What suggests the input of tradition reaching back to the real scene? Is there a chain of witnesses available for the scene in response to objection three? There is no sense in discussing whether we are dealing with creative detail or history until we can assess if a witness stream exists. Although at first this looks like a strong objection, in fact, it is a decidedly weak challenge to the scene. The rise of a community of Jewish followers of Jesus in Jerusalem after his death is a historical given that virtually no one doubts. This community would have immediately been in running public debate with other Jews and the official Jewish leadership. We know this because three decades later a descendant of the high priestly family of Annas I and Caiaphas, Annas II, is responsible for the death of James, a member of Jesus' family. Caiaphas was the high priest during Jesus' life and would have been the high priest during the time of any examination of Jesus. Annas I was the patriarch of the family and was the father-in-law of Caiaphas. Once one realizes these family connections in the leadership of both sides of this religious dispute, then one can see that a family feud existed in Jerusalem for a long period. Each side would have made its case for or against Jesus in the running debate. The official position regarding Jesus would have been publicly known in a city that was not that large, given that the population was under one hundred thousand. This kind of public and official conversation would have fed the core tradition. The public nature of the debate and its long-standing duration over several decades operated as a check against confusing the official positions of each side with any rumors or speculation about the events.

More than this, some members of the leadership appear to have had sympathetic relations with the new believers. Here, figures like Nicodemus and Joseph of Arimathea can be mentioned. They would have known and could well have related what took place at the examination.

Even more transparent is that Paul, as a former persecutor of the new community from its earliest days, would have known the official Jewish position against the new movement. So the idea that access to the information at this meeting was and is unavailable is excessively hard to believe. It ignores the vast network of relationships and debates that would have inevitably been a part of those earliest confrontations over who Jesus was within the Jewish community in Jerusalem. Access to information from such an event would have existed and not been a problem to obtain.

Finally, it appears Josephus had access to information about trials and deliberations, if his summary of the situation of James is any indication about his access to sources. And there are examples of letters being sent with those under custody that give official indication of the charges (Acts 23:26–30). This means there could have been types of official records somewhere. If there were access, information could be obtained. Someone like Paul could have had such access to official Jewish information.

Response to Questions about the Core Scene

So what about the second objection about the creation of events or details out of apologetic concerns? It is fallacious to claim that the presence of apologetic negates the presence of historical detail. The debate of the new Jesus community with Jews who did not believe was about Jesus. Such a debate would have inevitably been contentious and apologetic from the moment there was a rejection of Jesus' challenge to the Jewish community. Jesus had asked the community to turn to God *and* presented his authoritative role in that claim. Thus the presence of an apologetic element involving Jesus in the material is not an automatic reason to reject the historicity of the presence of such elements of debate. It would come with the territory.

The remaining issues are whether what Jesus is portrayed as saying is consistent with his ministry, the cultural context for blasphemy, and whether there would have been such a meeting in the midst of a busy holiday season. If there was such a gathering, what kind of meeting was it? Would such a meeting have been held during a busy week? The short answer is yes, if one appreciates the kind of meeting this is and the special circumstances that applied to this situation. So we look at part of the second and fourth objections here.

Understanding the Kind of Meeting This Was

First, it is important to appreciate what this meeting was and was not. It was not a trial where a verdict of death could be rendered. Rome kept the right to execute in its own hands. Events like the later martyrdom of Stephen or the later slaying of James were independent acts by a crowd and a high priest respectively. In fact, Annas II was relieved of his high priesthood for executing James outside of the authority he had (Josephus, *Antiquities* 20.197–203). It proves that the leadership could not legally execute Jesus; only Rome could do that.[12] So this is not a trial in the technical legal sense. This point is important because *trials* could not be held at night or on holidays (*Mishnah, Sanhedrin* 4:1). The scene in the gospels is at night and during a holiday. This misidentification of the event as a "trial" has been one of the reasons some have challenged the historicity of the scene.

Second, as an event, this meeting would have been more like collecting evidence to take to Pilate. Its parallel today is the American grand jury process where the decision is made whether or not to proceed with prosecution. It also allows some informality in how material was gathered. So critics' claims that the account shows trial irregularities from those reflected in the later *Mishnah* are exaggerated since there is no trial. So, for example, it is not a problem nor is it an irregularity for an examination scene to have no defense witnesses called, as the later *Mishnah* required for a trial. In *m. Sanhedrin* 4.1, a capital case begins with the case for acquittal. That requirement was not necessary here. This was merely a meeting to see if Jesus was "worthy of death" (Mark 14:64).

The very presence of a discussion that Jesus had claimed to destroy the temple, a detail only in Mark's version, fits this examination setting (14:55–59). If Jesus had announced a potential act of violence against a sacred site, then he could have been brought before Pilate. The very fact the text argues that this initial tack failed shows that the account is careful by not suggesting that the Jews simply stacked up charges against Jesus. When it was determined that a convincing case could not be made around this charge, it was dropped. This may well explain why Matthew and Luke do not include it. It ultimately became irrelevant.

The dropping of the temple charge also could be understood this way. The leadership's arrest of Jesus was the one chance the leaders might have to get Rome to deal with Jesus. They needed the best and clearest case they could gather. Nothing could have been worse than for them to take Jesus to Pilate and have the prefect either let Jesus go or simply reprimand him in some way. That result would have been terrible, since then Jesus and his followers could have made the case that Rome had examined them and found nothing seriously wrong. Thus it was important to try to bring a charge for which they could make a real case. Since the temple charge could not be put together in a compelling way, it was dropped. Failure to gain a conviction from Rome was not an option.

That some of the leadership wanted to bring Jesus to Rome receives support from an earlier incident involving Jesus. There Jesus is asked about paying taxes to Rome in an effort to trap him (Mark 12:12–16). If Jesus had denied paying Rome taxes, he could have been charged with insubordination and sedition. Pilate was in Judea in part to oversee the collection of taxes for Rome and enforce her sovereignty over the people. The question did not yield the desired result, but that such an effort was made is credible. It fits the indication of an intention to see that Jesus is brought to Pilate.

Third, the special circumstances made it convenient to expedite matters. Pilate was already in town, but would head home to Caesarea Maritima soon. The less time Jesus was held, the better, because of his popularity with some. There are later texts about the leadership seeking justice for deceivers of the people that allow both for exceptional examinations and for a quick resolution of the deceiver's fate if the judgment is that he is guilty.[13] Jesus' situation fits into this kind of a special scenario. Charges of Jesus being seen as a deceiver by opponents are multiply attested, including a later Jewish source (Luke 23:2; Matthew 27:63–64; John 7:12, 47; *Babylonian Talmud* 43a).[14]

This meeting, far from being a formal trial, was an examination to prepare a case for Pilate. It was held quickly because of the special circumstances and concerns that leaders had about keeping Jesus. They had the chance to get Jesus to Pilate for a quick decision and took it. This is why the meeting could take place at night and on a holiday. In fact, holding it at this time of night meant the meeting did not get in the way of the celebrations of the week. So the fourth objection helps us to better appreciate what is taking place here, but does not mean the event should be questioned.

Understanding What "Blasphemy" Is

So what about the charge of blasphemy? What exactly was it that could have gotten Jesus into trouble and led to his being brought to Pilate so that the prefect executed him? This leads us to the first objection. Does the account give evidence of a potential act or utterance that the leadership could have understood as blasphemous given how they saw Jesus?

In fact, it does. Unlike common popular opinion, the blasphemy was not the claim to be Messiah. There are records of numerous messianic figures in the first century, and none of them was accused of blasphemy.[15] Josephus notes several figures who raised hopes of the arrival of the end, and none of them was accused of blasphemy (*Antiquities* 18.85–87, 97–98; 20.167–88). Some of these figures had names or nicknames, such as the Samaritan, Theudas, and the Egyptian, while other texts just refer to unnamed prophetic figures. So what is blasphemy? What did the leadership see in what Jesus said?

Blasphemy is a saying or act that shows intense disrespect for God. What we might call slander. Blasphemous speech could take many forms. To use the divine Name in an inappropriate way is certainly blasphemy and is punishable by death (Leviticus 24:10–16; *Mishnah, Sanhedrin* 6:4 and 7:5; Philo, *On the Life of Moses* 2.203–6). At the base of these ideas about blasphemy lies the command of Exodus 22:27 not to revile God nor the leaders he appointed for the nation.

Acts of blasphemy concentrate on idolatry, a show of arrogant disrespect toward God, or the insulting of his chosen leaders. Often those who blasphemed verbally acted on their feelings. God manages to judge such offenses. Examples in Jewish exposition are Sisera (Judges 4:3 and *Numbers Rabbah* 10.2; disrespect toward God's people), Goliath (1 Samuel 17 and Josephus, *Antiquities* 6.183; disrespect toward God's people and worship of Dagon), Sennacherib (2 Kings 18–19 = Isaiah 37:6, 23; disrespect for God's power), Belshazzar (Daniel 3:29 in Theodotion's version and Josephus, *Antiquities* 10.233, 242; disrespect for God's presence in the use of temple utensils at a party), Manasseh (acting against the Torah; *Sifre§* 112) and the Roman general Titus (*Talmud, Gittin* 56, and *Aboth Rabbi Nathan B* 7; entering, defaming the temple, slicing open the curtain, and taking the utensils away).[16] Acting against the temple is also blasphemous (1 Maccabees 2:6; Josephus, *Antiquities* 12.406). Significantly, comparing oneself with God is also blasphemous, reflecting arrogance according to Philo (*On Dreams* 2.130–31; *Decalogue* 13, 14.61–64). At Qumran, unfaithfulness in moral action by those who pretend to lead the people (*Damascus Document* 5.12) or the act of speaking against God's people (1Q *Pesher to Habakukk* 10.13) are blasphemous. Within Israel, the outstanding example is the golden calf incident (Philo, *On the Life of Moses* 2.159–66).

So let's define blasphemy. When applied to God as object, blasphemy represents an offense against God and a violation of a fundamental principle of the faith that gives glory to him.

Attacking God's people verbally is a second class of blasphemy (Sennacherib; Goliath). Those who challenge the leadership God has put in place for his people can also be seen as attacking God himself. So blasphemy refers to a wide range of insulting speech or activity. This is crucial background to how blasphemy might relate to Jesus in the leadership's view. Behind all of this is the idea that God's glory and honor are unique and should be protected and preserved.

When Jesus claims God will bring him as Son of Man into God's presence and either seat him at God's right hand (alluding to Psalm 110:1) and/or have him ride the clouds (alluding to Daniel 7:13–14), this was heard by the leadership as robbing God of his unique honor and glory. They saw it as blasphemous, even though, as we are about to see, Jews at that time debated the idea of someone being able to sit with God.

How might Jesus' claim to sit at God's side have been seen in Judaism? It depended on who was hearing it. In some wings of Judaism, such an idea could be entertained for a great like Moses or a future figure like the Son of Man in *1 Enoch* 37–71.[17] But other Jews objected to such ideas. In *3 Enoch*, the angel Metatron claims to be the "Lesser Yahweh" and is punished by God for having the nerve to make such a comparison.[18] There also is a well-known tradition repeated more than once involving Rabbi Akiba. In this account, Akiba suggests that David can sit next to God in heaven. However, the other rabbis object, rebuking him and saying, "How long will you profane the Shekinah [that is, the glory of God]?"[19] They are reminding him he is blaspheming in their view.

Now, the bulk of the Jewish leadership at the time of Jesus was made up of the Sadducean party. They were traditional conservatives who focused on what the Torah or first five books of their Scripture taught. They disliked additions to the tradition such as those reflected in *Exagoge* or *1 Enoch*. They would have found it hard to believe that this Galilean teacher could share God's direct presence in the manner he was suggesting. Jesus' remarks fit the cultural context of what would be seen as blasphemy, given the leadership's rejection of those remarks.

Examining Whether What Jesus Said Was Consistent with His Message

This leaves us with a final set of remaining objections (part of objection one)—that what Jesus says here is something Jesus would not have said. This argument is made in one of three ways. *One*, Jesus had never presented himself in such terms. He focused on the kingdom, not himself. More than that, he showed hesitation, at least in public, to use key titles such as Christ and Son of God.[20] As we shall show, this claim may come down to what one does with the title Son of Man. *Two*, Jesus did not use Scripture in the way he is portrayed as doing here.[21] This kind of scriptural reflection is the product of the early church looking back at Jesus. *Three*, Jesus may have said something like this and may even have used one of the two passages alluded to, but he did not use both of them together.[22] Jesus did not use Scripture in this way; that is, he did not link texts together as we see here. In this version of the argument, unlike the first above, Jesus did refer to himself as Son of Man and predicted a divine vindication, but he did not appeal to sitting at God's right hand from Psalm 110. That part is the early church talking.

It is important to note a key difference between the third form of this argument and the first two. In the first two forms of the objection, Jesus did not say anything like what he is claimed to have said. We are not in touch with the historical Jesus at all. In the third version, Jesus did make a claim, and even one that caused the offense of blasphemy. He just did not say as much as the text has him say. So we have a point of contact with the historical Jesus, but one that the early church amplifies.

So, did Jesus refer to himself as a key figure in God's program?

First, our look at previous events has shown that Jesus having a self-reference in God's program is not merely a matter of what

Jesus said, but what he *did*. Claims of authority in action stand at the center of God's promise of kingdom through several public events. Jesus talked less about who he was and chose instead to highlight his role through what he was doing.

Second, we have argued that Jesus came to Jerusalem and became more public once he got there. This represented a change from his previous strategy.

Third, Jesus did consistently point to his status—though rarely referring to himself as Messiah and Son of God because of how those terms could be misunderstood. His title of choice was Son of Man—and even when confessed as Christ, Jesus spoke of the Son of Man. This requires a closer look at the Son of Man title than we have given up to now, for in this examination scene, Jesus responds to questions about who he is with the title Son of Man.

Remember that the expression has two roots. On the one hand, in Aramaic it is an idiom referring to a human being. Just as the son of David is David's son or son of Sarah is Sarah's son, so son of man is the son of a human being, simply meaning a person. The second root comes from the expression "one like a Son of Man" in Daniel 7:13. Here the expression is not a title, but a description of a figure who rides the clouds and comes to the Ancient of Days to receive dominion from God. What is interesting is that although the everyday idiom points to a human being, the use in Daniel 7 points to a transcendent figure, since in the Hebrew Bible the only beings who ride the clouds are either God or the gods (Exodus 14:20, 34:5; Numbers 10:34; Psalm 104:3; Isaiah 19:1). Heaven and earth meet in this description.

The expression was not a formal title at the time, although its use in *1 Enoch* 37–71 at about this time shows that some Jews were beginning to think in such terms.

More interesting is the usage of the general expression in the New Testament. Son of Man appears eighty-two times in the gospels, and in every case but one (John 12:34), it is used by Jesus.[23] The one exception describes someone reflecting on what Jesus has said, so it is not really an exception. This is not a term the church or people use to describe Jesus. It is a term he uses about himself. It is consistently rendered as "the Son of the Man" in Greek. This means that it is not a generic use in this rendering. The claim that this idea is a product of the church faces two questions that bring the claim into doubt. First, how is it this title appears only on Jesus' lips at different tradition levels if it comes only from a church creation? In other words, who made up the rule that the different strands of tradition reflect that this title would be placed only on the lips of Jesus? And second, if this title is an early church creation as a major title for Jesus, why do our materials outside the gospels show so little use of it? Why do they show not a single use as a confessional title for Jesus? The only four uses outside the gospels are Acts 7:56, Hebrews 2:6, and Revelation 1:13 and 14:14. This is unlike other titles, like Christ or Son of God, which show up often in the epistles and Acts as well as in the gospels.

All of this makes it far more likely that Jesus referred to himself with this title than that the church created it for him. Its use here fits the thrust of his ministry disclosure patterns and his use of this title.

Understanding Jesus' Use of Scripture

On the objection that Jesus did not use Scripture in this manner: this is a variation of the previous objection that argues that this kind of complex allusion to texts from the Jewish Bible, what is called a *pesher*, comes from the early church and not from Jesus. One form of this objection says an appeal to either Scripture (Psalm 110 or Daniel 7) did not go back to Jesus, because he did not defend himself with such scriptural appeal. Much of what we have already said applies to this objection. It is simply unreasonable that Jesus did not reflect on Scripture in considering his mission, especially when he saw that mission as tied to the plan of God. So it is difficult to justify a rule against historicity that says if a passage refers to Scripture or a group of Scriptures in a reflective way, it must be the early church's invention. Jesus' ministry claimed that God had promised things that were now being realized. Where would those promises be but in the sacred texts of the community?

There is nothing in the evidence of the use and availability of Psalm 110:1 or Daniel 7:13 that demands a use limited to the post-Easter period. Daniel 7 imagery, especially, was circulating in Jewish texts such as *1 Enoch* 37–71. Jesus shows signs of using Daniel 7 in the discourse on the end that appears in Mark 13, Matthew 24, and Luke 21. Psalm 110:1 appears very ambiguously in Mark 12:35–37 = Matthew 22:41–46 = Luke 20:41–44, where Jesus uses the text not to refer to himself directly but simply to ask why David referred to the one to come as Lord rather than his own son. The cultural tension in Jesus' question is *How does the ancestor in a patriarchal society show such respect to a descendant that he gives this far younger relative the title "my Lord"?* The question is left unanswered in its use in Mark 12, something to ponder. The text has that inherent ambiguity that supports historicity.[24] The use in Mark 14 picks up the issue.

These two Hebrew Bible texts (Psalm 110:1 and Daniel 7:13–14) did make a deep impact on the early church, being their most cited texts. Some suggest that wide use points to the likelihood that the church inserted the references here for apologetic reasons. However, the depth of that impact suggests the connection had roots in the community's founder. One need not choose between apologetics and history or between christology and history. These categories in the early church were not either/or categories, but both/and.[25]

Both Hebrew Bible passages were available for Jesus to use at his examination. Nothing Jesus does or says at the trial represents a stretch for his usage of these sources, even read critically by the rules. If Jesus used either Psalm 110:1 or Daniel 7 at this scene, then the point of offense was made. His opponents would have seen the use of either text claiming God's defense and vindication of the Son of Man as a blasphemous claim of close association with God's glory. If Jesus claimed either that he as Son of Man was to be seated in God's presence as a result of divine activity, or that he would ride the clouds to receive authority, then the claim of sharing divine glory was made and the reaction of his opponents rejecting the claim would have followed. If either text was used, then the core historicity of the event stands. This leaves us with one final form for this objection. Can one make the case that Jesus used both texts together?

In this objection, Jesus alludes to Daniel 7, since the evidence for his use of Daniel 7 is so extensive, but he does not use Psalm 110:1. The key to this objection is the idea that Jesus rejected the messianic title for himself, so the use of Psalm 110:1 reflects the early church and not Jesus. To a significant degree we addressed this issue in discussing Jesus' declaration at Caesarea Philippi— Jesus gave the title Christ a qualified acceptance in terms of popular understanding, recasting the term for his followers.

Yet another factor leading to an objection here involves the differences in Jesus' replies in Matthew, Mark, and Luke. When asked if he is the Christ, Jesus says in Matthew 26:64, "You say." The same question in Mark 14:61–62 yields the reply, "I am." Luke 22:67–68 has Jesus respond that if he says they will not believe and if he asks they will not answer. Is Jesus reluctant to answer, does he affirm the title, or does he qualify the question? The ambivalent response in two of the versions indicates that the question is formed in a way that Jesus does not entirely accept. His answer in all three accounts suggests that being the Messiah alone does not say enough. In other words, in all versions, he trumps the question. They want to know about the Messiah, but he responds with a full divine vindication. However, this is not a rejection of the title. It simply points out that what it means is far more than was realized. In that sense, Mark's crisp "I am" affirms what is accepted. Jesus is the anointed one of God in terms of authority and rule.

The idea that Jesus rejected the title of Christ faces a major hurdle much like the discussion on the Son of Man—but in reverse. It is clear that the early community accepted this title for him, so much so that Christ became a key part of his name in all of the earliest materials we have. If Jesus had rejected this title, it is hard to know why the church would have ever affirmed this, given that such a claim of kingship created so many problems for them in terms of both persecution and social acceptance. The criterion of embarrassment applies here. Why create a title that brings with it problems? The better explanation is that Jesus accepted the title, although the handling of the sources shows he did so with some qualification.

Dunn argues that at his examination and in his ministry as a whole, Jesus answered this question about being the Messiah with a "qualified no."[26] So Jesus did not use Psalm 110:1. My position is one step over. I think he answered the messianic question with a qualified yes. Dunn claims he never uses the title of himself, never unequivocally welcomes its application to him by others, and refuses the dominant royal militaristic association. Dunn is right about Jesus having a concern about a militaristic understanding; however, some scenes argue some acceptance of the title. These scenes include the healing of the blind man who cries for help from the Son of David, parallels with David in discussing the Sabbath, and the meeting involving the Samaritan woman. They show Jesus responding positively on these occasions to this association (multiply attested theme: Bartimaeus from Mark 10:46–51 = Matthew 20:29–34 [so from Mark], two blind men = Luke 18:35–42 [so from L]; David and Sabbath, Mark 2:23–27 = Matthew 12:1–8 = Luke 6:1–5 [so from Mark]; Samaritan woman, John 4 [so from John]). The same conclusion also emerged from the Caesarea Philippi scene. For me, the apocalyptic Son of Man pictures the authority to rule and judge that the royal militaristic Messiah possessed. So a militaristic Jesus is a part of the portrait, but not the whole story, and Jesus qualifies any expectation that sees a militaristic thrust as all there is to the Messiah. In addition, Jesus is now acting or speaking more directly about who he is, as the temple incident and entry scenes showed. So in this examination scene, Jesus used both ideas together with the title Son of Man and cited a royal psalm (110:1).

Despite the challenges, this scene has a coherence that, once carefully understood, makes sense. None of the objections blocks our path to understanding what took place here. Jesus made a remark that his opponents rejected. When Jesus claimed that the divine presence was on his side and he shared a place with that authority, his opponents thought he had affirmed that he was the anointed one of God and that his exalted claim had offended the unique honor due to God in the process. What they saw religiously as blasphemy, they translated into a political charge to take to Pilate. In the end, Jesus gave the word himself that led to his death.

MEANING OF THE EXAMINATION

Our study contends by the rules that what we have is not merely story or preaching. The core materials can be trusted to give us a glimpse of Jesus as he was, even of Jesus as he presented himself.

This event is key to discovering who Jesus was. In it, all the forces pro and con surrounding Jesus meet. In what Jesus says here there is reflection of what the story has been and where the story now is inevitably headed. Divine promise, presence, and authority meet in the ministry Jesus presents. Jesus' claims of divine vindication and sharing in heavenly glory set the stage for all the church would say about Jesus. The bridge was built on Jesus' previous actions of authority along with what he says here about what God will do for him. Jesus claimed God would show his hand in the dispute between the Jewish leaders and himself, and that what God was about to do would affirm what God had been doing through Jesus. These events as portrayed have a strong claim to authenticity, a far stronger claim than that Mark or the earlier church made up this scene or the other events we have traced.

In the end, this examination event stands up to historical scrutiny. There is a coherence in what Jesus does and says here. Jesus appeals to both Psalm 110:1 and Daniel 7 to make his point. Jesus answers the question about whether he is the Messiah by affirming and predicting that God will vindicate him as the Son of Man. This figure will sit with God and will ride the clouds. This vindication will show that Jesus as the Son of Man has a heavenly role in God's plan that includes his residing at God's side, including sharing that authority and glory. In the dispute between the leadership and Jesus, this vindication will be the indication of which side of the dispute God is on. The leadership read this reply as blasphemy, because in their view God shares his glory with no one and in Jesus' response was the inherent criticism that the leaders were not God's chosen representatives for the faith. Both of these reasons qualified as blasphemy in Second Temple Judaism. What Jesus claimed was God's initiative in exalting him, the leadership saw as blasphemy. So they see Jesus accepting the claim to be king and take that political dimension of the charge to Pilate to seek Jesus' death. Given the leadership did not accept Jesus' claims, their response makes complete logical sense in terms of how they should proceed.

The leadership and Jesus were traveling on the same train track in opposite directions. What Jesus saw as divine support and vindication, the leadership saw as blasphemous. When they finally decisively met, what resulted was a complete collision of views.

12

The Examination by Pilate and Crucifixion:

Death for Sedition

ONE OF the least doubted events of the historical Jesus' life is that Pontius Pilate ordered Jesus to be publicly executed.[1] For this reason, this chapter will spend less time on objections and more time on the cultural context of the rule of Pilate and the meaning of crucifixion. We will explore questions such as: Why did the Romans crucify him, and who was responsible for Pilate acting as he did? Jesus was ultimately crucified at the direction of Pontius Pilate for the charge of being "king of the Jews."[2] What does this tell us about Jesus' ministry? The short answer is more than one might think.

RULES THAT APPLY TO PILATE'S EXAMINATION AND THE CRUCIFIXION

Multiple Attestation

That Jesus suffered a public death is multiply attested. Galatians 3:1 speaks of Jesus being publicly exhibited as crucified, while

5:11 speaks of the offense of the cross to refer to how he died (also 6:12, 14).[3] The offense is seen in experiencing the curse of "hanging from a tree" (Deuteronomy 21:22–23, Galatians 3:13). There recently has been some controversy about whether the translation "cross" is best for the terms associated with crucifixion.[4] The terms Paul uses simply refer to some form of public death involving an object on which one is suspended. However, the gospel accounts mention that Jesus was nailed to this object (Luke 24:39, John 20:27). The two texts come from distinct traditions, so the detail is multiply attested. That detail makes it likely the shape was some type of T or †. In terms of dating, these references from Paul represent our earliest recorded sources and date to within sixteen to twenty-five years of Jesus' death, since Galatians is dated anywhere from 49 CE to somewhere in the fifties, while the date of the crucifixion is placed usually between 30 and 33 CE.[5]

The Q tradition also has a reference to the cross (Luke 14:27 = Matthew 10:38).[6] The picture of bearing the cross sees Jesus' suffering in rejection as an example to follow. A variant of this saying appears in the *Gospel of Thomas* 55. Other New Testament materials testify to his death. Hebrews 12:2 and 1 Peter 2:24 mention the cross, while Revelation 11:8 speaks of Jesus being crucified.

Of course, the gospels themselves narrate the crucifixion scene in much detail. The scene covers twenty-five units in the gospel narrative.[7] A paragraph-like unit in a gospel is called a *pericope*. Specific references to the cross that may reflect independent witnesses are found in Mark 15:24 and John 18:18.

In the nineties, Josephus testified to Jesus' death under Pilate in *Antiquities* 18.63–64. The text, as we have it, has certain clear Christian additions. For example, in one place the text calls Jesus the Messiah, something Josephus as a Jew and not a Christian would never have said. Still, most historians believe that the bulk of the passage we have is authentic. They argue that Josephus wrote, "Pilate, due to an accusation by the leading men among us, condemned him to the cross."[8] This remark is important because it gives a major Jewish witness to the idea that the Jewish leadership had a role in contributing to Jesus' death.

The Roman historian Tacitus, writing in the early second century, speaks in *Annals* 15.44 of "Christus, the founder of the name [Christians], had undergone the death penalty in the reign of Tiberius, by sentence of the procurator Pontius Pilate." Some skeptics suggest Tacitus is merely repeating what Christians were saying, but the tie to Tiberius is a detail nowhere mentioned in the New Testament materials we have noted. In addition, Tacitus' further description of Christians is very negative, calling the Christians a "pernicious superstition" and a "disease." This shows a critical engagement with whatever information he had, so that what he passed on he viewed as having taken place.[9] Most important, Tacitus uses the technical Latin term to describe the sentence, *supplicium*. This term describes Jesus' death as a capital punishment involving suffering like crucifixion.

A final piece of evidence is a piece of graffiti found in 1857 on some stone on the Palatine Hill of Rome. It portrays a man with the head of an ass with hands outstretched on a cross. Another man is said to worship this figure, as the picture has the inscription "Alexamenos, worship God!" This piece of satire shows how skeptically Romans saw Christians. The drawing has been dated to somewhere between the first and third centuries.

So, the nature of Jesus' death is multiply attested by at least six independent *sources* (Paul, Q, Mark, Josephus, Tacitus, Alexamenos inscription). Five other sources could be independent (Hebrews, 1 Peter, Revelation, John, *Thomas*). This attestation also involves multiple *forms*—narrative, epistles, apocalyptic genres, and inscriptions, as well as testimony from outside Christian circles. In fact, three of these witnesses come from non-Christian sources. Evidence like this with this type of spread makes almost all historians very confident that Pilate ordered Jesus' execution.

Embarrassment

The criterion of embarrassment also applies to this scene. To acknowledge that Jesus died as a criminal subjects the movement to public social shame, as the just-cited remarks by Tacitus showed. This embarrassment works on three levels, two involving Jewish concerns and one that reflected Greco-Roman attitudes.

First, for Jews crucifixion was a hurdle to accepting that Jesus was the Messiah as the earliest Christians preached. In all forms of Jewish expectation, the Messiah was a figure of power, not of shame. So why create such an event if it did not happen? To create the event gains nothing and encumbers the church with much baggage.

Second, it gets even worse. To "die on a tree" was seen as being cursed of God in Second Temple Judaism, as 1 Corinthians 1:23, Galatians 3:13, and the key text, Deuteronomy 21:22–23, show. Deuteronomy reads, "If a person commits a sin punishable by death and is executed, and you hang the corpse on a tree, his body must not remain all night on the tree; instead you must make certain you bury him that same day, for the one who is left exposed on a tree is cursed by God. You must not defile your land which the LORD your God is giving you as an inheritance." So to have created such an event would not make sense. It would have created too many problems.

We have near-contemporary testimony to how such a death was viewed. The Qumran text 4Qp Nahum frag. 3–4 1:6–8 describes the reaction to such a death. This text is a pesher (or exposition) of Nahum. It describes an action by Alexander Jannaeus, called "the Angry Lion," when he hung eight hundred for rebelling against him in the first century BCE. Josephus describes this event in his *Jewish War* 1.96–98 and in *Antiquities* 13.380. Alexander hung these rebels alive from a tree as a lesson to others, an action the pesher called horrible and like what was done in ancient times in Israel.[10] A second text from Qumran, 11QT[a]

64:9–13, also teaches that a man who curses his people should be hung on a tree and that God has cursed those so hung. To be crucified was to experience what was seen as a horrible form of death. If carried out justly, crucifixion was viewed as reflecting God's rejection.

Third, crucifixion was seen in Greco-Roman circles as a shameful form of death. It was reserved for the lower strata of society and for criminals. When Philippians 2:8 and Hebrews 12:2 portray Jesus' death as a humiliation, this cultural attitude is what is being described. The just-described Alexamenos inscription reflects well the Roman attitude, subjecting such a death to satire.

Palestinian Environment

So the rule of embarrassment gives credence to the authenticity of this event. In fact, it does so in a way that accurately reflects the Palestinian-environment criterion, since the perspective of how this death was accomplished under Pilate's authority in Judea fits the Roman and Jewish setting so well.

All of this makes an examination by Pilate to render such a verdict likely, since only he could render a verdict of death.[11] That Pilate was responsible for Jesus' death also is multiply attested in terms of texts and forms. This testimony involves Christian sources (narrative: Mark 15:1–15, John 18:28–19:16; epistle: 1 Timothy 6:13; Ignatius [early 2nd century], *Magnesians* 11; *Trallians* 9:1; *Smyrneans* 1:2) and non-Christian sources (historical narratives: Josephus, Tacitus).

Embarrassment also applies here, because rejection by Rome raises questions about the character of the movement, something the Christians had to constantly deal with in their early history. Again, why create such trouble, if a sentence under Pilate did not take place?

Rejection and Execution

The criterion of rejection and execution also is relevant here. The fact that Pilate had Jesus crucified tells us something about the nature of the charges against him, because such a sentence occurred for a very limited range of crimes. This power, known as the *imperium*, belonged to the Roman emperor and his agents alone. It was reserved for crimes against the state. So Jesus' execution would have been a Roman political act against someone accused of undercutting the state. The crime would have been sedition.

OBJECTIONS TO THE TRIAL OF PILATE AND CRUCIFIXION

Any objections to this scene apply not to the fact that Jesus was crucified or to the idea that Pilate examined him, but to details attached to these events. Before looking at specific objections, we need to set the historical context of Pilate's authority and the issues tied to a death sentence.

Pilate had several responsibilities in his office as prefect. He functioned much like what we might call a governor, especially in the old sense of the British Commonwealth. Pilate represented Rome and the emperor in Judea. He had to protect Caesar's interests, collect the taxes for Rome, keep the peace, and select the high priest.

We know of several incidents during his rule where Pilate exercised his authority, because various writers tell us of them. Josephus writes about several of Pilate's actions that caused offense to the Jews in *Jewish War* and in *Antiquities*. The placement of shields with symbols seen as icons to the gods caused offense to Jews who shunned such images because of the First Commandment, not to have any images of God nor any other gods (*Jewish*

War 2.169–74, *Antiquities* 18.55–59). Pilate backed off from this standoff. The Jewish philosopher Philo also tells another account of an incident involving icons (*Embassy to Gaius* 299–305). This encounter caused the emperor Tiberius to write a letter of rebuke to Pilate, telling him to show more sensitivity. Another time Pilate caused offense by taking money from the temple treasury to build an aqueduct (*Jewish War* 2.175–77, *Antiquities* 18.60–62). Luke 13:1 tells of a time when Galileans were slain in the temple area. Finally, after the time of Jesus, when Pilate handled a Samaritan uprising harshly, he was removed from his office (*Antiquities* 18.85–88). Tiberius had finally had enough. These incidents show that Pilate could and did wield his power. Pilate also was the first Roman ruler in the region to issue coins affirming Roman power versus adorning coins with simple agricultural imagery. Pilate could act aggressively and did so to show Caesar's authority.

Pilate's examination of Jesus would have been a judicial inquiry to see if Jesus was worthy of death because he was guilty of sedition. Pilate was charged with keeping the Roman peace, or *Pax Romana*, which the previous emperor Augustus had solidly put in place. When more lowly people in the empire committed a crime that required a ruler's attention, the process was called *extra ordinum*, that is, "outside the List [of State Judgments]." Inside-the-list judgments involved people of high status and required a tribunal or jury. Lower classes were handled less formally and quickly. Pilate's examination of Jesus was of the *extra ordinum* type and involved a simple judicial inquiry known as the *cognitio*. Here the prefect acted as judge and jury to determine the facts and render the verdict. Executions required such an inquiry, as the letters of Pliny the Younger to and from Trajan show. In Pliny's collection of epistles (*Epistles* 10.29–30), the emperor Trajan tells Pliny that the examination of two slaves still requires a *cognitio*, if the prospect exists of their being executed. The circumstances with Jesus are similar.

Our historical concern here revolves around the core events

tied to the examination by Pilate and the resulting execution of Jesus. In particular, we are most interested in the charge against Jesus. Of what did Pilate judge him to be guilty?

In seeking to get corroboration of detail here, the task is more complicated. For the details, the gospel sources on which we depend are less independent. Most of what we see comes to us from Mark or John. Q has no passion material, so we have lost one of our sources.

Questions about Attestation

Several things are singularly attested and cannot be corroborated. So most of them must be left to the side.[12] Most significant here are some Matthean details, such as the warning by Pilate's wife, Pilate's washing his hands, the crowd's willingness to have Jesus' blood on their hands, and some details in Luke, such as the sending of Jesus to Antipas and details about the charge. Some of them, such as the charges Luke lays out, make sense in the context without much difficulty. The Jewish leadership brings Jesus to Pilate and presents Jesus as a troublemaker and a regal claimant. Pilate must deal with these charges to do his job. These additional charges cohere with the accusation about Jesus being a king that emerges at the end of the process. The key evidence for such a judgment involves what is written on the placard that is brought along with the cross when Jesus is executed. So Jesus was judged for claiming to be a king Rome had not appointed, something Rome clearly did not like.

Questions about Portrayal of Pilate

There also are differences in emphasis in the portrayal of Pilate. In Mark we see Pilate very much in control, while in Matthew and Luke—in part because of unique material they have chosen to include—there is more of a sense of Pilate wavering about what to do. The portrait of Mark is like the unhesitating use of power we see Pilate exercise in Josephus and Philo.[13] In particular, Dunn sees the tendency of the later gospel sources to place greater blame on the Jewish leadership versus Pilate as the result of political considerations versus historical ones. He speaks of Pilate "being in effect bullied" in those accounts.[14] Here it may be the relative brevity of Mark's version that leads to the distinct impressions about Pilate. A shorter text can lead to a less complete impression. As to whether Pilate was bullied or lobbied, that is a matter of characterizing the narratives we have. Dunn is anxious that the responsibility for Jesus' death not be overly applied to the Jewish leadership in light of what he calls the gospels' anti-Jewish tendency.

However, given a Jewish examination and initiation of the process, which we have shown to be likely and credible, it certainly was in the Jewish leaders' interests that they be successful here. If Pilate had acquitted Jesus, it would have been a public relations nightmare for the leadership. If Pilate was at all hesitant, one can be sure the leaders made their case as strongly as they could. And there is some reason for Pilate to hesitate. Jesus has no army and is not a real threat to Rome. He also has a popular following and so to exacerbate the situation may not be politically wise. His initial solution to whip Jesus as a warning makes some political sense. Jesus is put on notice, but no death takes place to embolden his followers. Pilate was a politician whom the emperor had instructed to be more sensitive to local concerns. Under such oversight, Pilate might well initially have liked such a compromise approach. As such, it is not clear that what looks like hesitation and waffling by Pilate is something else. It may be an initial, genuine political assessment with strong Jewish advocacy rising up in response. It may be no more than a politician calculating to split the difference, generating an understandable counterreaction from a side that wants a clear resolution.

Questions about Witnesses to Examination by Pilate

One objection that can be raised here, as it was at the Jewish examination, concerns who were the potential witnesses to this event so that information could get out. No followers of Jesus were there. The women from Galilee, who could testify to what happened to Jesus on the cross (Mark 14:40–41 = Matthew 27:55–56 = Luke 23:49; John 19:25), were not at this event. All that remains is that word leaked out from either Romans or Jews who were present. Here there is not as much to go on as at the Jewish examination, but the likelihood still exists that the Jewish leadership would have known and reported on the results. As was mentioned in the Jewish examination scene, contacts did exist in the Sanhedrin and in Herod's entourage extending up to Herod's steward (Mark 14:53, Luke 8:3). After all, it was in their interest to give as much responsibility to Rome for Jesus' execution as they could. In the end, to be able to say Rome did it and why would be a protection against any who wanted to hold the Jewish leaders significantly responsible. Nothing explicit is here, because most of our sources throughout do not identify explicit sources for the events they portray. Still, the possibility of obtaining information about this scene existed and would naturally surface in the context of later public debate over these events.

What is being suggested is that the outline of the Roman examination events from the gospels makes sense, but being able to clearly show the details is more difficult in a corroborative model. One can construct a plausible scenario for what the gospels give us here in detail, but it is harder to show by the rules.

MEANING OF THE EVENT

But what about the core issues of the scene? Can we go deeper? What was the significance of Jesus' execution, not as a theological act, but in terms of its historical cause?[15] Two questions dominate our focus. Was there Jewish leadership participation? What was the final charge and Pilate's verdict? These reveal the meaning of the event from the side of Rome.

Jewish Involvement

There is an example for this kind of Jewish involvement in a possible Roman execution from an incident some thirty years later, in the sixties. When Jesus, son of Ananias, stood in the temple and repeatedly proclaimed a woe on Jerusalem, the "leading men" arrested him, had "magistrates" examine him, and then turned him over to the governor, Albinus (Josephus, *Jewish War* 6.300–305). Albinus examined this Jesus, decided he was crazy, and let him go. So as in the case of Jesus of Nazareth, there was Jewish leadership involvement, examination on the Jewish side, and then examination by the Roman representative, who gave a final verdict.

Here we have not only the likelihood that Jewish leaders would have kept an interest in what took place with Pilate, but multiple attestation that they were involved (Mark 15:1, John 18:28–30, Josephus, *Antiquities* 18.63–64). So there is no reason to think that having worked so hard to get Jesus before Pilate, they would have handed him over to the prefect and walked away. There was too much at stake.

The shift of the charge from blasphemy to kingship is not a problem. It is simply translating the charge into a form that would be of concern to Pilate. Pilate would not care if Jesus had said something offensive to Israel's God. He would have become concerned only had it caused a major disturbance of the peace. Pilate also would care if Jesus made a claim to be a king whom Rome had no role in appointing, especially if Jesus was drawing interest.

The Charges

When it comes to the charges, the gospels have various details. Mark stays focused on Jesus' claim to be king (Mark 15:1–3, 9, 12, 18—the last verse in mockery). Matthew does the same (Matthew 27:1–2, 11–12, 17, 22, 29—the last verse in mockery). Luke 23:2 expands the issues. The charges here are (1) subverting our nation, (2) saying we should not pay taxes to Rome, and (3) saying he himself is the Messiah, a king. Despite this expansion, Luke makes nothing of the first two issues. Pilate's examination treats only the third question as relevant, even though the Jewish leadership continues to bring up the charge of disturbing the peace by misleading and inciting the people (23:5, 14). Now, one can easily argue that inciting the people is nothing but a natural elaboration of claiming to be king, since kingship would raise the expectation of deliverance and excite those who wanted to see a new era. So we probably have nothing more here than an elaboration of the kingship charge, one that says Jesus disturbs the Roman peace and so you must deal with him, Pilate. So this is a difference without a real distinction.

John has no formal charge, but Pilate also pursues the kingship question, asking Jesus if he is king of the Jews (John 18:33). This theme continues in other texts (John 18:36–38, 39; 19:3, 12, 14–15). In the deliberation that follows Pilate's conversation with Jesus, the Jews say Pilate must act because Jesus has claimed to be "the Son of God" (John 19:7). If this was raised, however, in a Greco-Roman environment, this might have been heard by Pilate to be a claim to be another Caesar, since this was a title given to the emperor.

In the *Gospel of Peter*, it is kingship of Israel and sonship with God that are mentioned (*Peter* 3:7, 9). This follows the same track as our more familiar gospels.

Thus, the charge of king of the Jews is *multiply attested*. It runs through the whole of the sources.

All of this fits with the inscription placed with Jesus on the cross to publicly explain the charge. This placard on which the charge is publicized is formally called the *titulus*. This Latin term refers to something inscribed with a notice, an ancient billboard of sorts. Other Roman sources describe such notices in other settings (Suetonius, *Caligula* 32.2—with the execution of a slave; Cassius Dio, *History of Rome* 54.3.7—of another slave who wore his titulus as he headed to his death). This was not a universal practice as is sometimes claimed, but it did serve as a humiliation to the one who was being executed, as well as a warning to others not to do the same or else risk facing the same result. The closest modern analogy to this scene is when the Nazis forced Jews and others accused of crimes to walk in public with placards around their necks describing what they had done. This was part of the public shame associated with crucifixion, and the lesson it was designed to teach others.

The *titulus* is *multiply attested* in Mark 15:26 and John 19:19, as well as in *Peter* 4:11. The claim to be king also does not fit the normal early church confession of who Jesus is. In the epistles, king is not a title for Jesus, Messiah/Christ is. This difference speaks to its authenticity.

The exact wording of the *titulus* is less clear, since Mark 15:26 has "the king of the Jews," Matthew 27:37 has "this is Jesus, king of the Jews," Luke 22:38 has "The king of the Jews [is] this [man]," John 19:19 has "Jesus of Nazareth, King of the Jews," and *Peter* 4:11, "This is the king of Israel." It seems clear that king of the Jews was in the inscription, and three of the five refer to Jesus or "this man," but the differences make it likely that one or more of the gospel writers explained or clarified what the *titulus* said. As with the narrative about the charge, the *titulus* argues that Jesus died because he was found guilty of being the king of the nation. It was a charge of sedition against Rome.

The title of king is important culturally. *First,* Rome had given Herod the Great this title, so to call Jesus king was to make him a competitor to the officially recognized line of Herod. *Second,* the tie to kingship in Israel led back to David and forward to a hope of an end-time delivering figure as a text like *Psalms of Solomon* 17–18 shows. In these psalms, likely written in the aftermath of the Roman general Pompey's taking Jerusalem in 63 BCE, 17:21 cries out for a king of Israel, "the son of David, to rule over your servant Israel in the time known to you, O God." In v. 32, the call for a king continues, saying, "their king shall be called the Lord Messiah." The *Psalms* hoped for a delivering figure who would remove the Roman presence.

Third, such expectation fueled movements that had the eschatological hope of God's deliverance of his people. This eschatological thread is something we have traced through many of the previous key events. As such, this claim was a challenge to Rome. Rome appointed her kings. She did not care for the rise of independent claimants.

This charge of kingship is significant for a variety of reasons and serves as the core element in appreciating the historical cause of Jesus' death. *First,* the claim to be king invoked the claim of the kingdom of God. This rule by God stood in contrast to the kingdom of Satan, as our look at exorcism showed, and also reflected a community distinct from Rome. The contrast with the kind of kingship Rome had shows up in Jesus' exchange with Pilate in John 19. These remarks are singularly attested but they fit the character of Jesus' ministry. Jesus' lack of direct political engagement with Rome throughout his ministry and his lack of gathering any type of army show him operating in a distinct way. Jesus is never portrayed as going to Tiberius or Sepphoris, the largest Roman-oriented cities in his home region of Galilee. So the character of Jesus' ministry shows that the kind of kingdom he is arguing for is different from normal politics.

Second, the charge of kingship connects to two other events we have considered: Jesus' atriumphal entry into Jerusalem and his temple action in overturning the tables of the money changers. The first event made a claim to kingship, while the second involved a cleansing of the city that the promised ruler was supposed to perform. So there is coherence between the charge and these earlier actions by Jesus. The account of events holds together.

The Verdict

So Pilate sentenced Jesus to death for claiming to be king. This verdict recognized that Jesus was about more than being a prophet. As with the many other events we have traced, Jesus appears in this event as standing at the center of a movement that hoped for the promised rule of God. For Pilate, this claim and the crowd it was gathering was a threat not so much to the political power of Rome as to the public peace, the *Pax Romana*. The reaction of those Jews closest to Pilate made this clear. Pilate had appointed Caiaphas as high priest in each year that Pilate was prefect, and Caiaphas had brought Jesus to him. Although on one level Pilate may have thought that Jesus was not a real threat to Rome because of his lack of military presence, in the end the prefect followed the insistence of his appointee—even if he had a sense the action was excessive. Jesus did have the potential to invoke large crowds. Roman rulers viewed such popular followings with suspicion. They knew the regions of Judea and Galilee to be full of trouble. So by putting Jesus to death, Pilate thought he was stopping any potential for public conflict. He also was standing behind the one he had appointed to help him on Jewish political affairs.

In the end, Pilate's act made Rome ultimately responsible for

Jesus' death. However, those who followed Jesus never forgot who got the ball rolling. This is why responsibility for Jesus' death by the new community is always portrayed as a shared act. The early church saw the refusal of many of the Jewish people to embrace Jesus' claims and the initiative of the leadership to put Jesus to death as the cause of an innocent Jesus' death. The claims of authority have stretched back in Jesus' work, whether one thinks of his work of exorcism to show the presence of the kingdom of God, his work on the Sabbath, his entry into Jerusalem, or his temple cleansing. All of these public acts, some of them authenticated by unusual means, made a claim that was now being rejected by the leading representatives of Rome and of the people of Israel. The action, it was thought, would put an end to Jesus and the movement he was generating. In fact, because of what happened next, Jesus' death was only the end of the story's opening chapter.

13

The Women Discover an Empty Tomb:

Fabrication, Metaphor, or Something More?

Those who know anything about the Jesus story and Christianity know that its turning point is the claim that God raised Jesus from the dead.[1] The presentation of a resurrection three days after Jesus' death is at the core of the Jesus movement's message. The image of the resurrection is that of an empty tomb, the void in the grave testifying to the physicality of the affirmed resurrection. This was no immortality of a soul leaving a physical body. The resurrection involved the hope of an entirely restored person, both body and soul.

This claim stretches the kind of examination history engages in to its limits. Two parts of the event cause this tension. *First*, as a matter of course, people do not come back from the dead. *Second*, how does one show God has acted, even if a body is missing? For many, this claim is too much. Two basic approaches exist to those who question this event. One option is that the account of the empty tomb and appearances are pure fiction, presented as legend or myth. The other option, often taken, is that these accounts authentically represent a genuinely transforming, psychological experience those in the community had after Jesus died. The experience is often chalked up to a response of grief relieved. For those who had this intense experience of Jesus' presence, Jesus lived. An empty tomb and sudden personal appearances were how to describe and portray it. In this chapter special attention is given to the idea that this story was created as legend or is only a reflection of some type of internal experience. We focus on the account of the empty tomb, because that claim is the starting point of the story. An empty tomb also assumes something other than a private experience, which appearances alone could represent.

I depart from the way the other chapters have been laid out. The objection that legend is present in these accounts is discussed while presenting the case for this event's authenticity. How one sees the material is so basic to how one reads its content that we must deal with this objection up front. The rest of the discussion follows along the lines of the other chapters—the objections section treats the remaining challenges to the accounts' details before coming to the event's meaning.[2]

In the end, this chapter focuses on one key issue. Is the empty tomb a fabrication, metaphor, or something more?

RULES THAT APPLY TO THE EMPTY TOMB AND RESURRECTION

Strictly speaking, this is not an event of Jesus' ministry in the normal way we think of ministry events. He does nothing. Everything reported about this event spins around him. The women find the tomb empty. His body is gone. Others announce that he has been raised. Only with the appearances does Jesus do something by appearing and interacting with those around him. In part, it is the peculiarity of this event that is the point. Something very unusual is taking place. In the ancient world, there was a hope of resurrection at the end of time or a belief in immortality of the soul at death—there was even the belief of the spiritual exaltation of an emperor like Caesar, seen as a soul alive in a comet during the time of Augustus and known as the "Julian star" (in Latin, *sidus Iulium*; the belief in such a transformation into divine exaltation is called an *apotheosis*).[3] However, this was the first claim that a physical resurrection had happened in the midst of active history.[4] This stood in contrast to the common Jewish view of a resurrection at the end, which enabled a final judgment of the righteous and unrighteous. The resurrection event affirmed something without real precedent for a human being.

So can any of our rules apply to this scene?

Single Attestation and Varying Details

There are singularly attested parts of the account. The most important of these involves the discussion of the presence of guards at the tomb in Matthew 27:62–64 and 28:4, 11–15. As we have done with other such details, the fact that the presence of the guards is singularly attested means we cannot substantiate its authenticity by the rules.

One detail that varies is who gives the report to the women about what happened in the empty tomb. Matthew 28:2–7 speaks of a single angel. Mark 16:5–7 has a single man in white, which can be read as attire for an angel (2 Maccabees 5:2; Josephus, *Antiquities* 5.277; also Revelation 7:9, 13; 10:1). Luke 24:4–7 has two men in dazzling attire around a throng of women. Another detail that varies is who receives the report of the empty tomb. Luke 24:4–7 has a larger group of women than the other gospels note (Luke 24:10—three women named plus "other women" [Mary Magdalene, Joanna, Mary the mother of James]; Mark 16:1—

three women [Mary Magdalene, Mary, mother of James, and Salome]; Matthew 28:1—two women named [Mary Magdalene and the other Mary]). There is agreement on Mary Magdalene and a second Mary. Is Joanna a second name for Salome, in analogy with second names for Saul/Paul or Simon/Peter, or is she a distinct person? That is not clear. Either is possible, since Luke has more women present than he names, so that distinct figures are likely. John 20:8–11 has Mary see Jesus at some point after discovering the empty tomb and two angels seated there. The accounts agree on an empty tomb, but do differ on these details.

John often has events the other gospels lack, because John writes at a time when the events of death and resurrection like those we see in the other gospels would have been circulating in the church for a long time. John may have thought the appearance to Mary by Jesus trumps the already well-known report of the angels to the women and so alludes to the angels while telling the Jesus account. Jesus' conversation with Mary is singularly attested and so we cannot corroborate it by the rules.

This leaves one final difference. It involves the remarks about one (Matthew, Mark) or two figures (Luke) from the empty tomb reporting to the women. This could simply be a matter of differing selection of detail at different points of the experience. The number is told in passing. Most scholars say Matthew knew at least Mark, as did Luke. The remainder of scholars argue that Matthew is first and was known to Luke. So, either way, the key difference is the one Luke introduces. His larger group of women may explain the difference, showing he goes into more detail. For him, one angelic figure serves as a greeter with another alongside. In the accounts where one is noted, we are simply told about the one who speaks. However, none of this can be confirmed or corroborated. So we are left with the difference unresolved by the rules as a historical detail.[5]

Three criteria are relevant to the empty tomb scene itself: multiple attestation, multiple forms, and details associated with the first-century cultural background that show the criterion of embarrassment.

Multiple Attestation of Sources and Forms and the Nature of This Event

Multiple attestation of sources and forms appear because the resurrection is asserted in texts that reflect traditional creedal content, narratives of the empty tomb and appearances, as well as declarations in Acts and the Epistles. The list of texts making this claim are extensive, since this was a hub claim of the early faith: Galatians 1:1; 1 Thessalonians 1:10; Romans 1:2–4, 4:24, 6:4, 8:11, 10:9; Colossians 2:12; Ephesians 1:20; 1 Peter 1:21; Polycarp, *Philippians* 2:1; Acts 3:26, 10:40, 13:33; 1 Corinthians 6:14, 15:15; 2 Corinthians 4:14. Sources include Paul, Peter, the testimony of Acts, and Polycarp. In noting these sources, we do not even count the attestation in the gospels themselves that involve many distinct, independently presented events.

More Than an Internal, Psychological Event

In 1 Corinthians 15:3–5, Paul speaks of "passing on" to the Corinthians what he "also received." This is the language of tradition. So the claim predates Paul's letter to Corinth. This faith in resurrection has to be in place for Saul to change his religious allegiance when he has the experience of the raised Jesus appearing to him in a vision. This is because only a belief in resurrection would allow him to accept that he saw the raised Jesus and now can preach him as raised. He attests to this event as a revelation in Galatians 1:12. Acts 9:3–8, 22:6–9, and 26:12–18 describe this scene as more than merely an internal psychological event, since those around Saul also sensed something was taking place, hearing sounds and standing in the light projected by the raised Jesus. Of course, Saul becomes the apostle Paul as a result. So we have the rare case of having solid ancient testimony about this experience rooted in multiple sources. Paul's experience dates to the middle thirties, so we are virtually in touch with the time of the crucifixion and claims of resurrection itself. This appearance likely took place within a couple of years of Jesus' death. Paul was in Jerusalem during these early years after Jesus' death, well aware of what the official Jewish position on Jesus was, as he was an official persecutor of the church for the leadership. As we shall see, no one doubts that early Christians affirmed a resurrection by Jesus and that it impacted the direction of many lives among the earliest followers of Jesus. What gets debated is the nature and meaning of that testimony.

The Nature and Meaning of the Testimony

The type of event in view can be determined from the early creedal statement of 1 Corinthians 15:3–5. That text reads:

> For I passed on to you as of first importance what I also
>   received
> that Christ died for our sins
>   according to the scriptures,
> and that he was buried,
> and that he was raised on the third day
>   according to the scriptures,
> and that he appeared to Cephas, then to the twelve.

I have laid this text out so you can see the balance in the lines. This shows the material to be tradition, passed on in a form that can easily be memorized. This is official teaching. Four events are presented: the death of the Christ, his burial, a resurrection on day three, and appearances. In fact, the list of appearances goes on through verse 8.

The way this is laid out is important. *First*, the name of Jesus is simply the Christ. This shows the messianic focus of the statement. *Second*, the idea that a divine plan has been followed appears in the idea that the Christ's death and resurrection were according to Scripture. *Third*, all the events operate on the same "event" plane; that is, the death and burial are treated as events and so are the resurrection and appearances. There is nothing in how this is said that suggests we have moved to some type of metaphorical level or mere private experience with the resurrection and appearances. In fact, a private experience is ruled out in the list, since five hundred are said to have seen Jesus at once. So we are clearly referring to a resurrection and appearances as real events in a chapter defending *physical* resurrection, which is what the creed in 1 Corinthians introduces. The belief in a material element in the resurrection, namely that the body was involved, strongly suggests a belief in something like the empty tomb (1 Corinthians 15:35–58). Burial in the statement of the tradition points to death and a grave. That grave becomes irrelevant after a resurrection and a series of appearances.[6] Two other observations also are of significance here.

No Debate about an Empty Tomb

First, there is no record in the debates between Christians and Jews of any appeal after the claim of resurrection that there was an undisturbed grave in which Jesus still remained nor is there any appeal to the existence of a body or its decayed remains. The best we can tell, the opponents' claim was that the disciples had stolen the body and moved it, a claim that assumes an empty tomb.[7]

This claim of stealing the body stretches across two centuries, appearing in Matthew 28:15 and in Justin Martyr's debate with his Jewish opponent Trypho in the middle of the second century (*Dialogue with Trypho* 108). In that text Justin says the reaction to the preaching of resurrection is "you have sent chosen and ordained men throughout all the world to proclaim that a godless and lawless heresy had sprung from one Jesus, a Galilean deceiver, whom we crucified, but his disciples stole him by night from the tomb, where he was laid when unfastened from the cross, and now deceive men by asserting that he has risen from the dead and ascended to heaven." Note how the report of Justin's opponent, Trypho, acknowledges a Jewish role in Jesus' death. This Jesus was one "whom we crucified." Trypho goes on to call the new faith a heresy and affirms the taking of the body as the reason a resurrection, ascension, and empty tomb are preached. So Trypho not only sees the resurrection-ascension as a silly teaching, he also explains a Jewish position about the empty tomb.

No Indication That the Empty Tomb Was a Holy Site

Second, there is no indication among early Christians of reverence for the tomb as a holy site.[8] This is most unusual as it is often the case that such religious locales became holy sites. The debate today about the exact location of the tomb—at the Church of the Holy Sepulchre or at Gordon's Tomb in Jerusalem—underscores the point. The tomb had become irrelevant to early Christians. The tomb had become empty in their view.

The point about the empty tomb is important because some scholars argue that the empty-tomb tradition and appearance traditions involve independent ways to discuss and defend resurrection. Further, they argue that the empty-tomb tradition came later, after the resurrection was transformed into a more physically oriented event. That these accounts may be independent is possible, but that the empty tomb emerged later among the genre forms is unlikely because of the early evidence we have just traced. Whatever the early Christians believed about resurrection and whatever caused that belief, the resurrection was seen early on as physical and as involving an empty tomb. We shall see shortly that the physicality of resurrection matches what most Jews who held to resurrection taught about it. This serves as support for the idea that to speak of burial and resurrection also meant to refer to an empty tomb and a departed body, so that the resurrection in view had physical dimensions. However, for now the only point being made is that the resurrection is multiply attested in terms of sources and forms with both empty-tomb and appearance traditions occurring early. There is more evidence that we shall look at shortly that nails down the physical aspect of the expectation.

Embarrassment

Another key element in the empty-tomb tradition involves the criterion of embarrassment. In fact, this criterion is the one that most contradicts the idea that what we have is a fabricated account, a created story that is mere myth or legend. The key factor here is the unanimous testimony in the gospels that women were the first to discover the empty tomb.

What is important in this detail is the ancient culture's lack of appreciation of women. In this culture, a woman's testimony often counted for nothing. Josephus testifies to this view in *Antiquities* 4.219 when he says, "From women let no evidence be accepted, because of the levity and temerity of their sex." The *Mishnah, Yebamot* 16:7, shows some permitted women's testimony to attest to a death but others do not. So their role was debated. In the *Mishnah, Ketubot* 2:5, and *Edduyot* 3:6, a woman's testimony about her marital status is to be rejected if another witness speaks to the contrary. These texts show that women were not highly regarded as witnesses in the first century.

So if the Jesus community is trying to sell the unpopular idea of a resurrection to a skeptical audience, why would it do this by opening such a difficult story with witnesses who do not count as witnesses culturally? If you are creating the story, why would you create it this way? A created story would have had male witnesses at the start. The idea that this story was created lacks cultural credibility, as evidenced in the starting point for this account. The women's being in the story and remaining there in all the gospel versions speak to the authenticity of this detail and of the empty tomb. No one would have put them there had they not already been there.

Interestingly, some of the accounts reflect this nervousness about female testimony. Mark 16 ends before reporting any message to the disciples. Luke 24:11 says those who initially heard the women thought they spoke "nonsense." In fact, the second-century skeptic Celsus mocks the report's credibility, speaking of Mary Magdalene as a "half-frantic woman" (Origen, *Celsus* 2.59). All of this reinforces that the criterion of embarrassment is applicable to this account. The combination of multiple attestation and embarrassment appears to attest to concrete events, not legend. But to show this, we need to work through some key challenges and examine the kind of resurrection that was expected in Judaism.

Differing Lists

Some challenge the women's presence because the lists differ about which women were present. As already noted, Mark 16:1 has three (Mary Magdalene; Mary, the mother of James; and Salome). Matthew 28:1 has two, lacking Salome. Luke 24:10 has the two Matthew names, also lacking Salome while adding Joanna and "other women." John 20:1–2 mentions only Mary Magdalene but presents her reports about the empty tomb to the disciples with her saying that "we" do not know where the body is. Interestingly, the accounts show independence in this difference. There is no collusion in the versions we have. Mary Magdalene is obviously the key player, and the other Mary serves as a second witness. In Judaism, two witnesses were required to guarantee authenticity (Deuteronomy 19:15). So all our lists go this far. The rest was choice about whom to include. Only if one insists that such lists have to be exhaustive, and that is an assumption, is there a real irreconcilable problem.

Other Varying Details

Other details also cause some to question the account's authenticity. For example, the texts' descriptions of when the women started out to go to the tomb vary. Mark 16:1 has "very early on the first day, at sunrise." Matthew 28:1 reads "at dawn on the first day of the week." Luke 24 says, "Now on the first day of the week, early in the morning." John 20:1 notes it was "very early on the first day, while it was still dark." The one account that differs slightly is from John. The detail shows the independence of the accounts and reflects a choice about how to describe the dawn during a journey when the sun was rising. It is hyperliteralism to argue that there is a real difference in terms of the timing. One could well speak of it being first thing in the morning with it being darker when they started than when they arrived.

Another issue often noted is that Jesus commissions the disciples to meet him in Galilee in Matthew 28:18–20 while telling them to stay in Jerusalem in Luke 24:49. These locations are said to be irreconcilable. This difference belongs to the appearance scene more than the empty-tomb accounts, but is important enough to note. There is good reason to suggest that as the disciples waited in Jerusalem, some of them went back to Galilee to collect things for the stay. Those who had traveled to Jerusalem had planned to be there only for the weeklong Passover feast. So it is not unreasonable to suggest that some returned to prepare for the longer stay of the group in Jerusalem. Now it must be said that this explanation fills in a gap between the accounts, and cannot be corroborated, but the suggestion also shows how the claim that these two versions are incompatible is not a foregone conclusion.

The short ending of Mark 16:1–8 has the women so shocked they are afraid to say anything. This is an open literary ending by Mark—it is clear the women overcame their fear and testified to what took place, because the story of resurrection gets told and the resurrection is what the church preached. People in the church aware of the tradition at the time of Mark would have known that larger story. The point of Mark's ending is for the reader. The resurrection has taken place. It is a stunning event. It is a fearful thing to contemplate in terms of what God had done. So the question becomes what will one do with this unique event? Mark ends abruptly, almost surprisingly so, leaving the reader to ponder how to respond.[9]

How Resurrection Was Seen in Judaism

Before turning to other objections, we need an overview of how resurrection was seen in Judaism. This also helps us understand what was being claimed about this event in the texts.

In the Hebrew Scriptures, the key texts on resurrection tell us very little about what exactly was expected. Ezekiel 37 uses the image of dry bones coming to life to picture the restoration of the nation. This use, however, is illustrative. Daniel 12:1–2 speaks of resurrection but gives no details. The idea of God rendering a final judgment after death supposes some type of conscious survival after this life. The Daniel passage speaks of being awakened to face either everlasting life or condemnation. So this tells us very little. This could involve the spirit or soul only or a body and a spirit.

Despite the lack of detail in the Hebrew Scripture, the concept had developed significantly by the time of Jesus, with three different views emerging.

First, some Jews denied resurrection. Josephus tells us that the Sadducees did not believe in it, arguing that "souls died with their bodies" (*Antiquities* 18.16; also repeated in *Mishnah, Berakot* 9:5, where heretics are said to believe there is no world to come, so that this view is rebuked and rejected there).

Second, other Jews held to immortality of the soul, where only the invisible part of the person lived on as the body decayed.

4 Maccabees 10:4 speaks of being able to apply torture to the body but that such torture "cannot touch my soul." (4 Maccabees 13:13, 16:13, and 18:23 also speak of a preservation of the soul.)[10]

Finally, the majority of Jewish texts that hold to resurrection hold to a physical dimension that involves the soul and some type of restored physical element. This is clearly displayed in 2 Maccabees, especially in the martyred death of seven brothers in chapter 7. Here one of the brothers, as they are being executed in sequence, exclaims they can destroy his body, but that God will give it back to him one day. 2 Maccabees 7:10–11 reads, "After him, the third was the victim of their sport. When it was demanded, he quickly put out his tongue and courageously stretched forth his hands, and said nobly, 'I got these from heaven, and because of his laws I disdain them, and from him I hope to get them back again.'" That some type of physical restoration is in view could not be clearer.

Paul's View of the Resurrection

This is also the view of the Pharisees. Paul testifies to this idea in an argument he makes in 1 Corinthians 6:12–20, where he argues that what we do morally with our bodies matters because God will restore those bodies one day, an act that shows the body is holy and should be treated as such.[11] In Acts, the indication is that what Paul defends in terms of resurrection is something the Pharisees also believe. Acts 23:6–8 says, " 'I am on trial concerning the hope of the resurrection of the dead!' When he said this, an argument began between the Pharisees and the Sadducees, and the assembly was divided. (For the Sadducees say there is no resurrection, or angel, or spirit, but the Pharisees acknowledge them all.)" Acts 24:15 reports Paul saying, "I have a hope in God (a hope that these men themselves accept too) that there is going to be a resurrection of both the righteous and the unrighteous." What is said in Acts matches what Paul says in 1 Corinthians 6.

It also reflects the belief of the Pharisees, the Jewish group Paul belonged to before he became a believer in Jesus. So when Paul defends the resurrection in 1 Corinthians 15, it is the more physical view of resurrection that he is defending, not immortality of the soul.[12]

By contrast, most Greco-Roman expectation either held to death being the end or to an immortality of the soul dwelling in a place known as Hades. Physical resurrection seems at best an exception to this rule in texts such as Plato's *Symposium* 179b, Aeschylus' *Eumenides* 723–24, and the story of Callirhoë. But these texts are debated in terms of whether they affirm this much.[13] So, when speaking of resurrection in a Jewish context, the most common view involved some kind of material dimension to that new life. It was more than immortality of the soul.

We have shown that the empty tomb is multiply attested in both form and sources, as well as meeting the criterion of embarrassment because of the lead role of the women as witnesses. We have argued that belief in the empty tomb points to the most popular view of Jewish resurrection, some type of total resurrection involving body and soul. We have argued it is an early tradition, standing behind the views Paul had when he was converted within a few years of Jesus' death. We also have argued that this is a noninternal event. So the early church preached and argued for a resurrection of Jesus that involved the raising of his soul and body. This they proclaimed as God's vindication of Jesus. It supported his message about the arrival of the new era with its hope of complete deliverance.

What are the remaining objections to this view of these events? Beyond the core worldview issue of whether God can act this way, which obviously impacts how one reads these accounts, what other objections remain?

OBJECTIONS TO THE EMPTY
TOMB AND RESURRECTION

Beyond the claim that these accounts are simply created myth or legend, there are three key objections to the empty tomb. The *first* is a claim about the genre or type of literature we are seeing in the resurrection claims. The *second* challenges what the theological point is in defending a vague concept of resurrection. The *third* challenge raises a historical-context question about Jesus' burial. Again we present them first and then assess them.

The first objection is that the experience in view should not be seen as a historical event. The stories differ too widely and the language is not that of history.[14] The account is better read as a parable about new life. One sentence from Crossan and Borg states their view clearly: "But we are convinced that an emphasis on historical factuality of the Easter stories, as if they were reporting events that could have been photographed, gets in the way of understanding them." History, they say, is "to report publicly observable events that could have been witnessed by anyone who was there." Parables "can be true—truthful and truth-filled—independently of their factuality . . . Its point is its meaning." Finally, they say, "Believe whatever you want about whether these stories happened this way—now let's talk about what they mean."[15] This view operates much like the view that legend or myth is present, but it is stated in a way that makes a distinct claim about the literary form. So this challenge needs to be independently assessed and not simply combined with the idea that myth or legend is present.

The second objection argues that 1 Corinthians 15 is not about a defense of a physical resurrection. It is about contending for apostolic power and authority.[16]

And finally, the third objection is that Jesus would not have been buried in a personal tomb, but would have been dumped in a common grave pit as a common criminal. He would have been left to rot. No one knows what happened to his body or where it was laid.[17] In this scenario, Joseph of Arimathea is a completely made-up figure. At one point, wrapping up his argument, Crossan says, "With regard to the body of Jesus, by Easter morning, those who cared did not know where it was, and those who knew did not care."

Objection Concerning Jesus' Burial Place and Body

Let's look at the third objection first. There are major problems with having Joseph of Arimathea be a made-up figure. Any story told about what happened to the body that presented "fictional" witnesses and actors could and would have been immediately challenged by opponents. We already noted the nature of the opponents' response to the empty tomb. These opponents do not make any claims about where Jesus was laid to rest or that his remains could be found. They argued that the body had been stolen. To use Crossan's words, those "who knew where Jesus had been put but did not care" would have been made to care in the context of the earliest preaching in Jerusalem of a resurrection. The preaching's stirring up of controversy in the city compelled a response. Those who had supposedly disposed of the body merely would have needed to say that they put Jesus' body in a specific location or that they dumped it with all the others. Those who knew those who had disposed of the body needed only to refer to that report and then declare that the disciples' resurrection and tomb story was false. Yet our witnesses to the controversy do not go there. They claim the body was taken, which assumes that the disciples did know the locale of burial and that all knew the tomb was empty. In the view of this Jewish response, the disciples fabricate only the claim of resurrection, not the empty tomb. All of this assumes on both sides that a dispute about real events is going on, not the telling of a parable in place of history.

Dunn makes the case for Joseph of Arimathea being a "very plausible historical character."[18] He notes that Joseph is attested in all four gospels (Mark 15:43–47, Matthew 27:57–60, Luke 23:50–56, John 20:38–42) as well as in the *Gospel of Peter* (2:3–5). It is worth remembering that we are in a context where increased blame is being placed on the Jews for the death of Jesus as we move across how the gospels tell the story. So is it likely that a story would be created making one of them a sympathizer of Jesus? More than that, the specific locale of Arimathea is obscure, carrying no biblical symbolism to lead to its mention and being so small we are not sure of its location today. All of this points to a real Joseph who acted on Jesus' behalf.

On top of all this, everything about the burial fits Jewish practice. Bodies in Jewish context were not left out overnight, because it was seen to risk leaving the city in an unclean state (Deuteronomy 21:23; 11Q Temple 64.7–13a = 4Q524 frag. 14, lines 2–4). Indeed, criminals could be released to families but were not allowed to be buried in a family tomb. In the *Mishnah*, *Sanhedrin* 6:5, we are told, "And they did not bury [the felon] in the burial grounds of his ancestors." This was a way of dishonoring the criminal. The tomb of Joseph did not belong to Jesus' family and so qualified.[19] In such circumstances, private grief is allowed, but not public mourning (*Mishnah*, *Sanhedrin* 6:6). So what is described in the texts fits what is possible for the practices we know about the burial of one executed as a criminal.

Objection Concerning Paul's Defense of the Resurrection

Now let's look at the argument related to 1 Corinthians 15. If Paul is interested only in apostolic authority, he has gone to a great deal of trouble as a sidebar to defend resurrection! The entire chapter is about the necessity of believing in this teaching and that not believing in it as an event leaves Jesus in the grave so that the preached Christian hope is futile. 1 Corinthians 15:12–19 speaks for itself here:

> Now if Christ is being preached as raised from the dead, how can some of you say there is no resurrection of the dead? But if there is no resurrection of the dead, then not even Christ has been raised. And if Christ has not been raised, then our preaching is futile and your faith is empty. Also, we are found to be false witnesses about God, because we have testified against God that he raised Christ from the dead, when in reality he did not raise him, if indeed the dead are not raised. For if the dead are not raised, then not even Christ has been raised. And if Christ has not been raised, your faith is useless; you are still in your sins. Furthermore, those who have fallen asleep in Christ have also perished. For if only in this life we have hope in Christ, we should be pitied more than anyone.

The issue here is the reality of the resurrection.

Also, Paul has already expressed himself in 1 Corinthians on how he sees resurrection. In 6:12–20, Paul challenges the Corinthians, arguing that sexual immorality in the use of the body matters long-term. It matters because the body does not merely decay as most Greeks taught. In vv. 13–15a, Paul says, "The body is not for sexual immorality, but for the Lord, and the Lord for the body. Now God indeed raised the Lord and he will raise us by his power. Do you not know that your bodies are members of Christ?" This physical dimension of resurrection and its sacred link to Christ are why what happens to the body matters. In vv. 19–20, Paul concludes his argument this way: "Or do you not know that your body is the temple of the Holy Spirit who is in you, whom you have from God, and you are not your own?

For you were bought at a price. Therefore glorify God with your body." The purchase Paul has in mind is of the body and soul, the entire person. So when Paul affirms resurrection a few chapters later in the same letter, it is this view that includes a physical dimension to resurrection that is being defended.

One can choose to disbelieve the empty-tomb idea and the resurrection the early followers of Jesus held to, but it is important to be clear about what they contended for in proclaiming resurrection. They argued that this event involved the whole person of Jesus, body and soul, just as it will in the future for those who are resurrected at the end. This was the core hope they affirmed and preached. God's vindication of Jesus pointed to their future hope. God would bring them back to life as a whole person.

Objection Concerning the Historicity of the Resurrection

All of this brings us to the first objection, the parable-history debate. The summary of all we have explored indicates that the disciples intended to portray real events, acts that were more than internal psychological experiences or mere visions generated in the mind. Had cameras been present at that time, believers would have taken press photographers to the tomb to show them it was empty. Everything we have laid out in terms of the cultural background and a presentation of those arguing for resurrection supports the idea that something concrete happened, not a schizophrenic model that says Jesus was raised but only through a psychological experience. Some of these appearances, such as to the five hundred at once (1 Corinthians 15:6), are not merely internal visions unless we foresee five hundred individuals having the same experience at the same time (very unlikely). Paul's experience in Acts blinded him for a time, according to Acts 9. This is not merely an internal event, but a revelation (Galatians 1:12). Resurrection belief is not the expression of a grieving heart turning to hope. Paul and the disciples saw Jesus as alive from the dead, a down payment on the hope they now preached to others that one could know God and his promise forever. These texts do not force us to choose between meaning and history. For the disciples, the two belonged inseparably together because God was reaching out to the entire person as part of his intention to deliver people into life.

The account of the empty tomb is more than a story. For the disciples, it was a surprising and marvelous act of God. It testified to hope and all Jesus had said and done. By their own testimony, this event transformed them from dejected followers of a movement that had met failure in Jesus' crucifixion to confident believers in a unique message of hope for which they were willing even to die. As Osborne summarizes, "It is clear that the disciples were radically changed by these events, and they and the early church believed Jesus had visibly appeared to them after his death. They also presented this material as realistic historical claims and not as fictive legends." [20]

MEANING OF THE EMPTY TOMB
AND RESURRECTION

So what does it mean? At his examination, Jesus had predicted a divine vindication of his ministry that would culminate in his presence with God. The resurrection is that vindication—not only of his life but also of his claims. This Jesus who suffered death actually stood at the center of God's promise and now had authority over life. Thomas Neufeld says it clearly: "Early followers would have seen Easter as God's final word of approval regarding what Jesus said and did and regarding his willingness to give himself even in death." [21]

The resurrection proclaimed Jesus' authority over death and over the sin that leads to it. Jesus' claim over life in the announced kingdom of God is also a claim to be able to nullify all that stands against it: injustice, hate, sin, death, and forces that seek to distort what God has created. In affirming the rule of God, Jesus was pointing to overcoming that which demeans and damages what God has created as sacred and in his image.

Our study has traced the extent of authority claims Jesus made in his ministry through his various actions and words. In this final event, the empty tomb is evidence of the vindication of such claims. We have authenticated these events and their meaning by the rules of historical Jesus scholarship. In those events, Jesus claimed authority to create a new community, authority over how to extend fellowship, authority over the Sabbath, authority over transcendent forces, authority over the temple, authority over liturgy, and authority to be given a unique place in God's presence. In other words, Jesus had authority to offer and manage the promised new rule of God. The Jewish leadership saw this claim as blasphemy; Rome judged it as a seditious claim. The resurrection is God's vote of vindication for Jesus. The claims Jesus made and the actions he performed show that this authority, in all its various spheres of expression, came with divine blessing and power.

CONCLUSION

Who Is Jesus by the Rules?

Pointing to the Rule That Matters

I<small>T IS</small> a unique story that has captivated many over many centuries: Jesus, born on the edge of a large empire in a small village that was far from the center of world activity. In a handful of months his ministry generated a movement that grew to become one of the great expressions of faith and spirituality the globe has seen. That story has been investigated, critiqued, and deconstructed over the centuries; it has led to praise and inspired many, transforming the direction of their lives. Many things have been done in his name—good, bad, and ugly. It all started right here with the events surrounding his life.

Usually when Jesus is handled by the rules, much of what is said and written about him is cast aside, like chaff being shed from the wheat. We have examined why this is the case and have challenged whether this story deserves to be so completely deconstructed. We have taken a different path, but have argued for it using the same corroborative rules others use in studying Jesus. Those rules of historical Jesus study have been applied to twelve significant events or themes. We have examined the reason these accounts can be trusted, as well as the objections raised against them. These are not the only twelve events we could discuss to get at who Jesus was and what he did, but they do constitute central events that together tell a coherent story. We have explored what discussion of the historical Jesus entails and why it is controversial. We have weighed those opinions and attempted to place Jesus in his historical context. Out of that study we can see a unified portrait of a figure claiming to bring with him a fresh reflection of God's presence. In what he did and said, Jesus presented the promised rule of God and placed himself at the center of its arrival. In those acts, there was a consistent claim of authority displayed that gave all pause—some in embrace, others in rejection. There was no place for a kind of middle ground. Either Jesus brought the kind of era he proclaimed, or he did not.

The twelve events we have studied together tell us a lot about Jesus. The first three events set the table for what Jesus was bringing. Event 1: Jesus affirmed the ministry of John the Baptist and the claim that the new era of God was approaching, which also brought with it an accountability before God that required a response. Event 2: He collected twelve key followers around him, symbolizing the restoration of a promise for a community with a rich history of involvement with God. Event 3: He associated with sinners to demonstrate a place for forgiveness in helping people to find their way back to God.

Controversy followed him, because the actions he performed reflected great, unusual claims. What Jesus offered was new and challenged the way things were being done. Jesus was more than a prophet or religious teacher. His claims went beyond simply pointing the way to God. His claims involved a personal level of authority through which God was revealing himself.

Event 4: In claiming to be Lord of the Sabbath, Jesus showed how pausing for a day of sacred reflection was never meant to prevent one from showing mercy or meeting daily needs. Event 5: By casting out demons, Jesus showed that his message was about more than the politics of Rome. Jesus challenged and faced off against forces that sought to rip out our humanity from within. Event 6: In accepting with caution Peter's declaration that he was the Christ (or Messiah), Jesus began to teach that the kingdom he would bring was different than the anticipated raw display of power his disciples had expected. It involved suffering for him and for those who followed his path.

Confirming this different kind of kingdom, in event 7 Jesus rode into Jerusalem on a donkey. There in the central city of his faith he issued a challenge that would lead to his death. This was a kingdom that would not force itself on people. It would just be what it was, walking with faithfulness in the direction that had been set. Event 8: However, this kingdom is not timid. In the temple action, Jesus affirmed an authority over sacred space and reminded people that life is about more than participation in a bazaar.

Event 9: Sitting at a table with his followers at a final meal, he completed the salvation story of his people. He transformed the deliverance of Passover into a story of how God would use him to deliver. His death would become the opportunity to bring anyone into a fresh connection with God who sought the forgiveness he offered as a sacrifice.

Event 10: Before the Jewish leaders, he predicted a vindication that would exalt him into God's presence, sharing directly in the divine rule. That testimony sealed his short-term fate and led him to Pilate. Event 11: There the Roman ruler, using the power of his mighty state, put Jesus to death for sedition. Pilate executed Jesus for claiming to be a king Rome had not appointed. That painful crucifixion was supposed to be the end of the story.

Event 12: However, what Jesus had promised, the empty tomb delivered. Women, who had no business being witnesses, discovered that the dead body they had gone to anoint was gone. Risen and alive, the one who stood at the center of God's kingdom was vindicated. His claims of kingship, heavenly rooted authority, and God's kingdom stood firm. Life triumphed over death. The disciples' grief became conviction. The offer of life had found in him a fresh central focal point—forever. The disciples taught what Jesus had preached. They proclaimed the new promise of God. They shared that life had come in the message and person of Jesus. Resurrection not only meant new life for Jesus, but the offer of new life to the world.

These twelve events belong together. They tell us of a figure who mixed authority and humility. They reveal a power that invites and inspires. They affirm to us that the Jesus of history links to and discloses the Christ of faith. Jesus Christ was sent to reveal the living God and point us into the way of life. That is who Jesus was—and is.

The bridge we discussed in the introduction to this book can be crossed. To cross it leads not only to the historical Jesus but to the cross and the Christ. That bridge points to the anointed one of God who sits at the hub of God's promise, ready to deliver on God's promise of forgiveness, enablement, and life to those who seek it. That link takes us into something whose reach extends into heaven. To bring us to this opportunity for life, his followers tell of the events faithfully in every sense of that word. Through these events, Jesus' followers answer the question *Who is Jesus?* Our culture has an array of answers and questions about this question, as we have seen. But, as we have also seen, the answer of his followers points to his authority and uniqueness. Using the rules to examine who Jesus is points to the one question that matters: *How should we relate to the God Jesus so authoritatively discloses?* The disciples told the story this way, because the message about God, Jesus, and us is so life-changing. It is something we can see powerfully only after we link the Jesus of history with the Christ of faith.

ACKNOWLEDGMENTS

A BOOK LIKE this does not happen because of a single author. There are several people who deserve thanks.

The first is the IBR Jesus Group, which met faithfully for a weekend each summer for more than a decade to discuss the issues tied to the historical Jesus and to produce the original body of technical essays. At one time or another we had fifteen participants, but in any year had at least six of the group present. The participants came from three continents and all had to have previous published expertise in Jesus studies to participate. Extra thanks goes to my co-chair, Robert Webb, editor of the *Journal for the Study of the Historical Jesus*, who was a major conversation partner in the project and spent much time in organizing the group each year. Financial support for that original effort came from Joe Head. Without them, this study could not have been done in the collaborative manner in which it was undertaken.

Appreciation goes to the German government and its generous Humboldt Stiftung (Scholarship) program, which provided three months support for my study at the University of Tübingen as I wrote the draft of this book in 2010–2011. Prof. Dr. Hermann Lichtenberger was my university host, and every other Monday during the semester hosted a stimulating English-language symposium that discussed issues like the ones in this book.

Dallas Theological Seminary has a generous sabbatical program that also freed me up for a year to go to Germany and write this book. So the administration of the seminary, especially Mark

Bailey, John Grassmick, and Buist Fanning, have my gratitude for granting the time to do this.

Finally, there is the editorial team at Howard and Simon and Schuster for the willingness to take on a technical subject and allow it to be brought to the public square. Jonathan Merkh, Becky Nesbitt, Philis Boultinghouse, and Andy Meisenheimer lent their publishing expertise to this effort with skill and patience. What faults remain are strictly mine. They were an encouragement throughout the process.

In a category all her own stands my faithful friend, wife, and companion, Sally. She has had to put up with a lot over the years, including We are going *where* for a year? What about the language difference? So she learned enough German to function and has come to love the people here as I do.

I write this on the last full day of my time in Tübingen, a place that has become our European home after four sabbaticals (over four years total) spent here at different times from 1989, when the Wall came down, to 2011. It is hard to leave, but the time here has been a time for reflection as well as composition. Of all the people here, our closest friends have been Mark and Irina Werth, who helped us negotiate German life each time we came and whose children grew up with ours. Linking the Jesus of history with the Christ of faith is in large part about friendships like these that know no boundaries and span both continents and time.

DARRELL L. BOCK
TÜBINGEN, BADEN-WÜRTTEMBERG, GERMANY
JULY 26, 2011

NOTES

INTRODUCTION

1. Rudolf Bultmann, *Jesus and the Word* (New York: Scribners, 1958 translation of a 1926 German work).

2. Another clear example of this distinction also comes from Germany: Martin Ebner, *Jesus von Nazaret: Was wir von ihm wissen können* (Jesus of Nazareth: What We Can Know about Him) (Stuttgart: KatholischesBibelwerk, 2007). He says the gospels are "the early Christian preaching and proclamation—and speak not about the historical Jesus" (p. 13, translation mine).

3. We made our case in a series of very detailed essays on each of these events in a full technical study of Jesus published in 2009 with the internationally known New Testament series *Wissenschaftliche Untersuchungen zum Neuen Testament* (Scientific Investigations on the New Testament) entitled *Key Events in the Life of the Historical Jesus*, recently released in the USA in paperback through Eerdmans. Robert Webb and I edited that volume. The essays on the twelve events came with a full introduction on method in studying Jesus, as well as introductory and concluding essays.

4. I am relying on the work done by my colleagues, who will be named with each essay.

5. In choosing these twelve events we are not saying these are the only key events one can defend. We simply selected these twelve as significant. Their relationship to one another gives us major clues about Jesus. If the core of these events took place, then we can say much about Jesus.

CHAPTER 1

1. In our technical study, Robert Webb wrote this chapter about the criteria of authenticity, what I am calling *the rules*. Webb is sessional lecturer at McMaster University in Hamilton, Ontario, Canada. He co-chaired our Jesus study group. He also is the editor for the *Journal for the Study of the Historical Jesus*. In the technical chapter, Webb also includes a detailed look at doing history and the philosophy of history. He treats in far more detail some of what I have said about corroboration and how claims about the supernatural are handled in Jesus studies. He stresses how history inherently

involves interpretation for the historian, both ancient and modern. This is because the historian chooses how to present and evaluate the narration of cause and effect, the choices about what to include in the account, as well as the literary means by which to say it.

2. Q is a contested hypothesis for many. So some scholars might challenge the existence of Q, even if they think Mark wrote first. Those that do will not appeal to this source. Others may see Matthew as the first gospel written and also see Luke using Matthew. They also will not make use of Q.

CHAPTER 2

1. In our technical study, Robert Webb also wrote this chapter. Webb had done technical study on John the Baptist in his published dissertation, *John the Baptizer and Prophet* (Sheffield: JSOT Press, 1991). He also produced an initial version of this technical essay, "Jesus' Baptism: Its Historicity and Implications," *Bulletin for Biblical Research* 10 (2000): 261–309.

2. Another fragment Jerome discusses is the *Gospel of the Nazareans* (in *Pelagius* 3.2). In this account, Jesus objects to being baptized and refuses to do so with his mother and brothers because he has committed no sin. This clearly looks like a later theological addition, but it assumes discussion about baptism did exist.

3. Morris Enslin, "John and Jesus," *Zeitschrift für die neutestamenliche Wissenschaft* 66 (1975): 1–18.

4. The text is cited in the beginning of the next section.

5. This is multiply attested to in Mark 1:4 (= Luke 3:3), as also seen in John's preaching, Q: Matthew 3:8 = Luke 3:8, as well as the Josephus text from above.

6. Josephus tells us that "baptism would certainly be acceptable to him [God] if used . . . for the purification of the body . . ." (*Antiquities* 18.117). The Jewish *Sybilline Oracles* 4:165–67 calls on people to "wash your whole bodies in perennial rivers. Stretch out your hands to heaven and ask for forgiveness from your previous deeds." This work dates to after the time of John and Jesus, in the later part of the first century.

7. *Mekilta* is a Jewish midrash (exposition) of Exodus dating from the third century CE but containing older traditions.

8. Robert Webb, *John the Baptizer and Prophet*, 333–46.

9. John Dominic Crossan, *The Historical Jesus* (San Francisco: HarperSanFrancisco, 1991), 232.

CHAPTER 3

1. Scot McKnight, Professor of New Testament Studies at North Park University, Chicago, Illinois, wrote this chapter in the technical volume. He has written works on Jesus entitled *A New Vision for Israel* (Grand Rapids: Eerdmans, 1999) and *Jesus and His Death* (Waco: Baylor University Press, 2005).

He also was a member of the steering committee for the Historical Jesus section at SBL. An earlier version of this technical chapter was published as "Jesus and the Twelve," *Bulletin for Biblical Research* 11 (2001): 203–31.

2. The *Mishnah* took Jewish oral traditions on topics and set them out in written form.

3. John Dominic Crossan, *Who Killed Jesus?* (San Francisco: HarperSanFrancisco, 1995), 71.

4. John Meier, *A Marginal Jew, Volume 3: Companions and Competitors* (New York: Doubleday, 2001), 128–47, has a full discussion of the case for authenticity.

5. Robert Funk and the Jesus Seminar, *The Acts of Jesus* (San Francisco: HarperSanFrancisco, 1998), 71.

6. Ibid.

7. E. P. Sanders, *Jesus and Judaism* (Philadelphia: Fortress Press, 1985), 373, n. 32. On p. 101, Sanders asks, "Why should the church invent the number twelve and then produce lists of names that disagree?"

8. Lloyd Gaston, *No Stone on Another* (Leiden: Brill, 1970), 417. Also Robert Meye, *Jesus and the Twelve* (Grand Rapids: Eerdmans, 1968), 200–201.

CHAPTER 4

1. Craig Blomberg, Distinguished Professor of New Testament Studies at Denver Seminary in Denver, Colorado, wrote this chapter in the technical volume. His previous work in Jesus studies includes *Interpreting the Parables* (Downers Grove, IL: InterVarsity Press, 1990) and *Contagious Holiness: Jesus' Meals with Sinners* (Downers Grove, IL: InterVarsity Press, 2005). His essay in that volume was a summary of this larger work on Jesus' table fellowship. An earlier version of this technical chapter was published as "Jesus, Sinners and Table Fellowship," *Bulletin for Biblical Research* 19 (2009): 35–62.

2. In a rare example of agreement across the spectrum stand John Dominic Crossan, *The Historical Jesus*, 344, E. P. Sanders, *Jesus and Judaism*, 174–99, esp. 174, and N. T. Wright, *Jesus and the Victory of God* (Minneapolis: Fortress, 1996), 149. Sanders accepts the theme as authentic but goes on to question specific sayings because the church could generate such sayings on the basis of what Jesus had done.

3. Dennis Smith, *From Symposium to Eucharist: The Banquet in the Early Christian World* (Minneapolis: Fortress, 2003). Blomberg challenges this symposium connection in his essay in Bock and Webb, *Key Events in the Life of the Historical Jesus*, 219–27, discussing Jewish meals. Smith makes too little of this Jewish background.

4. Kathleen Corley, *Private Women, Public Meals: Social Conflict in the Synoptic Tradition* (Peabody, MA: Hendrickson, 1993) and *Women and the Historical Jesus: Feminist Myths of Christian Origins* (Santa Rosa, CA: Polebridge, 2002).

5. So a sample abbreviation would be *m. Berakot* 1:1. It means Mishnah, tractate (or chapter) with the topic's name (*Berakot* means "on blessings"), then the chapter and paragraph number.

6. These other sources also contain discussions of rabbinic issues related to being faithful to God and the Law that come from centuries after the *Mishnah*. The initial abbreviations for these works are *t.* and *b.*, respectively. They share topic names with the *Mishnah*.

7. Meier, *A Marginal Jew* 2:149.

8. Ben Meyer, *The Aims of Jesus* (London: SCM Press, 1979), 160.

9. Sanders, *Jesus and Judaism*, 178.

10. So Meier, *A Marginal Jew*, agrees; 2:150.

11. See the incomprehension, Luke 15:29–30 as portrayed in the parable of the prodigal son; dismay, Luke 15:2, 19:7; Matthew 20:11; derision, Matthew 11:19 = Luke 7:34; and exhortation not to follow Jesus' example, Mark 2:16; Ben Meyer, *The Aims of Jesus*, 295–96, n. 105.

12. James Dunn, *Jesus Remembered* (Grand Rapids: Eerdmans, 2003), 526. On p. 527, n. 179, he observes it is unlikely the church would create a saying where there is a seeming lack of concern for the righteous. This vivid and shocking way of putting things sounds more like Jesus than a community saying. Later on p. 527 and n. 181, he sees echoes of the saying in 1 Timothy 1:15, *Epistle of Barnabas* 5:9, and *Oxyrhynchus Papyri* 1224. These later witnesses from the first and second century point to a deep impression made on the church. His entire discussion is of value, pp. 526–34.

13. Blomberg in Bock and Webb, *Key Events in the Life of the Historical Jesus*, 244.

CHAPTER 5

1. Donald Hagner wrote this chapter in the technical volume. Until his recent retirement, he was the George Eldon Ladd Professor of New Testament Studies at Fuller Theological Seminary in Pasadena, California. His major work related to Jesus is his two-volume commentary on Matthew for the Word Biblical Series, *Matthew 1–13* and *Matthew 14–28* (Dallas: Word, 1993–95).

2. Very orthodox groups today still keep practices that move outside of the oldest written laws of the Pentateuch.

3. Text and numbering are from Jacob Neusner, *The Mishnah: A New Translation* (New Haven: Yale University Press, 1991).

4. John Meier, *A Marginal Jew*, uses this picture in his volume on the Law and Jesus; 4:40.

5. For details, see ibid., 4:327–28, n. 130. Only in the later *Talmud* is this connection made (*b. Menahot* 95b–96a).

6. Meier, *A Marginal Jew*, 4:276–77.

7. Israel Abrahams, *Studies in Pharisaism and the Gospels* (New York: Ktav, 1967 ed. of 1924 book), 134.

8. Meier, *A Marginal Jew,* 4:277–78.

9. Casey, *Aramaic Sources of Mark's Gospel,* SNTSMS 102 (Cambridge: Cambridge University Press, 1998), 151–52.

10. The text here is Mark 2:23–24 = Matthew 12:1–2 = Luke 6:1–2. These texts merely note that when the Pharisees saw the disciples do this they reacted. The description of the Pharisees following Jesus and keeping watch on him is scholarly commentary on this wording. But it may merely be that some Pharisees happened to be present when this took place and they noted their reaction. In other words, we may have an example of hypercriticism here.

11. Gerd Theissen and Annette Merz, *The Historical Jesus: A Comprehensive Guide* (Minneapolis: Fortress, 1998), 367–68. For example, in this very text, Mark 2:27 has "The Sabbath was made for man, not man for the Sabbath." Matthew and Luke do not have this text at all. In another text, Mark 1:43 speaks of Jesus sternly charging the healed leper not to say anything about his healing other than to go to the priest. Matthew and Luke do not have this instruction at all. I speak with uncertainty here about a claim for an independent version in these examples because there is so much overlap in these events and the idea of a distinct version of this event is not strong.

12. The fullest discussion appears when we treat Jesus' examination before the Jewish leadership.

13. If these events all develop the point, then multiple attestation will be present again.

14. James Dunn, *Jesus Remembered,* 670–71. These texts qualify as multiple attestation because even if the stories reflect what the gospels treat, they show the acceptance that a class of events took place with Jesus that needed explaining. The reply was not that those things did not happen.

15. Dunn, *Jesus Remembered,* 670. His remarks come taking into account all of these sources.

16. This argument is made by Leonard Goppelt, *Theology of the New Testament,* vol. 1 (Grand Rapids: Eerdmans, 1981 translation of 1975 German ed.), 144.

17. It is this positive and negative feature that undercuts the otherwise potentially credible objection that often in the ancient world wonders are attributed to a major figure to enhance the luminary's status. In what follows we will examine this line of objection more closely.

18. Two examples involve Julius Caesar and Vespasian. (1) Waters are calmed as Julius Caesar crosses a treacherous stretch of sea. This one story of danger is told several times by the ancients but not always in ways that suggest anything miraculous (Dio Cassius, *Roman History* 41.46.1–4; Lucan, *The Civil War* 5.476–699; Plutarch, *Lives: Julius Caesar* 38.2–6; *Moralia*; *The Fortune of the Romans* 6; Appian, *Roman History* 8.56–57, 21.148; Suetonius, *Twelve Lives of Caesar: Julius Caesar* 58.2; Florus, *Roman History* 2.13.35–38). It is not really a nature miracle but an account of how the gods protected Caesar by preserving him in the midst of great danger. The version in Suetonius simply speaks of surviving, making no special claims at all. (2) Vespasian

performs two healings, one involving a blind man and the other a crippled hand (Tacitus, *Histories* 4.81–82; Suetonius, *Twelve Lives of Caesar: Vespasian* 7.2; Dio Cassius, *Roman History* 65.8). In fact, most miracles in the Greco-Roman world involve the gods, not humans. For the whole host of miracles tied to the Greco-Roman world, see Wendy Cotter, *Miracles in Greco-Roman Antiquity: A Sourcebook* (London: Routledge, 1999). Cotter's reference to Dio Cassius in referring to the Julius Caesar story on p. 147 is incomplete.

19. Geza Vermes, *Jesus the Jew* (Minneapolis: Fortress, 1981), 58–82, presents the material on Honi and Hanina. Many of these sources are late, but still one should look at what Honi and Hanina are said to have done.

20. On Apollonius, who is often portrayed as the closest parallel, see the effective critique of Martin Hengel and Anna Maria Schwemer, *Jesus und das Judentum*, 194, n. 6; 257–58; 481–82. His miracles are chronicled in the "biography" written by Flavius Philostratus (170–c. 249 CE). Note how much later this account is written from the first-century figure it is said to chronicle. The gospels have a much tighter date-to-event window.

21. Hagner in Bock and Webb, *Key Events in the Life of the Historical Jesus*, 270.

22. Ibid., 276.

CHAPTER 6

1. In the technical volume, Craig Evans wrote the chapter on this theme. He is Professor of New Testament Studies at Acadia Divinity College, Wolfville, Nova Scotia, Canada. He has written numerous books and individual technical articles on Jesus. He is completing a full commentary on Mark, with *Mark 8:27–16:20* (Nashville: Nelson, 2001) already published. A collection of his essays is gathered together in *Jesus and His Contemporaries: Comparative Studies* (Leiden: Brill, 1995). An earlier form of the technical essay is "Inaugurating the Kingdom of God and Defeating the Kingdom of Satan," *Bulletin for Biblical Research* 15 (2005): 49–75.

2. Gabriele Boccaccini, ed., *Enoch and Qumran Origins* (Grand Rapids: Eerdmans, 2005) presents a series of technical essays on the significance of this figure in some segments of Second Temple Judaism.

3. *1 Enoch* is actually five pieces of material stitched together over time. The last segment of the Parables, even though it is in the middle of the book, is seen to be the most recently written section. It is dated to either the second half of the first century BCE or to the first century CE. I am currently editing a technical book with James Charlesworth of Princeton arguing for the earlier date, but most Second Temple Judaism scholars see this portion as Jewish and likely earlier versus later on the date spectrum. See the discussion by Charlesworth, "Can We Discern the Composition Date for the Parables of Enoch?" in *Enoch and the Messiah Son of Man*, Gabriele Boccaccini, ed. (Grand Rapids: Eerdmans, 2007), 450–68.

4. Wright, *Jesus and the Victory of God*, 194.

5. Ibid., 195. The brackets in the citation reflect my addition.

6. David: 1 Samuel 16:14–23; Josephus, *Antiquities* 6.166–68; *Pseudo-Philo* 60; 1Q5 27:9–10 (= 1QPsᵃ); Solomon: Wisdom 7:20; Josephus, *Antiquities* 8.45; 11QPsᵃ column 1, especially *Testament of Solomon*; also see Dunn, *Jesus Remembered*, 667.

7. Note especially *Testament of Solomon* 15:14, which says the purpose of the book is for Solomon to pass on such knowledge to the sons of Israel.

8. There is a slight wording difference here as noted in Luke 11:20 and Matthew 12:28. We shall discuss this in treating the remark.

9. The date of this work is disputed, but many scholars place it in the first or second century CE. More interesting is that the gospel's Greek wording about Satan's kingdom coming to an end matches (after translation) the Latin wording of the Jewish *Testament of Moses* exactly. So the expression of the idea is very Jewish. "The Testament of Solomon," in J. H. Charlesworth (ed.), *The Old Testament Pseudepigrapha* (New York: Doubleday, 1983), 1:935–59, has the discussion on the dating.

10. Rudolf Bultmann, *The History of the Synoptic Tradition* (Oxford: Blackwell, 1972), 13–14.

11. The Jesus Seminar had a color-based rating system for sayings. Red meant Jesus said exactly this. Pink meant Jesus said something very close to this. Gray meant this was not Jesus' words, but the saying could be rooted in something Jesus said. Black meant Jesus did not say this at all. More than 50 percent of Jesus' sayings in Scripture are rated black by the Seminar. The Seminar also agrees with us about the direction of the word change here. Robert Funk et al., *The Five Gospels* (New York: Macmillan, 1993), 329–30.

12. Rudolf Bultmann, *Jesus and the Word* (New York: Scribner, 1934), 173–74.

CHAPTER 7

1. In the technical volume, Michael Wilkins wrote this chapter. He is Professor of New Testament and Dean of the Faculty at Talbot Theological Seminary in La Mirada, California. La Mirada is a suburb of Los Angeles. His key technical work is entitled *The Concept of Disciple in Matthew's Gospel: As Reflected in the Use of the Term Μαθητής* (Leiden: Brill, 1988). He also has written a full commentary on Matthew for the Zondervan NIV Application series.

2. This may point to multiple attestation for this idea, if the John account is a distinct event.

3. Also important to the context of the synoptic event of Peter's declaration are Jesus' following remarks that he will suffer (Mark 8:31–33 = Matthew 16:21–23 = Luke 9:22). John's gospel does not have such an explicit prediction of suffering (John 3:14–15 is an allusion to such suffering). However, Jesus foreseeing his suffering appears in other texts Mark uses plus some other passages (Mark: Mark 9:31 = Matthew 17:22–23 = Luke 9:44; Mark

10:33–34 = Matthew 20:18–19 = Luke 18:31–33; Mark 10:45 = Matthew 20:28; Mark 2:20 = Matthew 9:15 = Luke 5:35; Mark 14:7 = Matthew 26:11; Parable: Mark 12:1–12 = Matthew 21:33–46 = Luke 20:9–18; L: Luke 13:32–33; 17:25; 24:7, 21, 46). The theme of Jesus' suffering is multiply attested, while the memory of Peter making a key declaration has a kind of soft multiple attestation because of the account in John.

4. Dunn, *Jesus Remembered*, 644, says, "There are several indications that Mark has been able to draw on a well-rooted memory, with variations between the Synoptists characteristic of performance flexibility." What Dunn means by performance flexibility is that the gospel material was rooted in oral tradition. These accounts were retold, but not always in the same words. What was retained was the gist of the story. Dunn responds to the claims of Bultmann that the scene is a transposed Easter story, that is, a resurrection appearance retrojected back into the ministry. Dunn responds that no resurrection appearance is portrayed as taking place so far north in the land. Dunn asks two important questions: (1) Why would the disciples be there after the crucifixion? (2) Why have a resurrection appearance attributed to this region? Bultmann, *History of the Synoptic Tradition*, 259; Dunn's response, 644–45.

5. Meier, *A Marginal Jew* 3:236–38, argues that the Satan remark is historical but cannot be connected credibly to a larger context to get its full sense. We shall argue that if the "messianic secret" misleads us to think of this theme as Marcan, then upon retrieving the proper historical setting we regain a coherent context for this remark. This will be the point of our discussion in the objections section.

6. See our coming chapter on Jesus' death for details.

7. The brackets indicate a break in the manuscript where text is missing. The sense is supplied by the context.

8. In line 1 of 4Q521, there is discussion about whether one or more messianic figures are in view, as well as whether the stress is on a messianic or prophetic figure as the one through whom God works. John Collins, *The Scepter and the Star: The Messiahs of the Dead Sea Scrolls and Other Literature* (New York: Doubleday, 1995), 205–6, opts for a prophet who is like the anointed figure of Isaiah 61 as opposed to a royal messiah. Martin Hengel and Maria Schwemer, *Jesus und das Judentum*, 332–33, see a singular reference to a messianic figure here, but they do not discuss the kind of messiah in view. Florentino García Martínez sees a reference to the "davidic Messiah" in "Messianic Hopes in the Qumran Writings," *The People of the Dead Sea Scrolls*, ed. Martínez and Julio Trebolle Barrera (Leiden: Brill, 1995), 168–69. The kind of figure in view in the 4Q521 is not clear, as this debate shows. This is not an unusual situation, as this text is fragmentary, so we do not have a full context to understand it completely. It may be more important to see the text as not telling us who the end-time figure is, but that the activity points to a specific period, the eschatological period of God's decisive deliverance.

9. Dunn, *Jesus Remembered*, 645.

10. Wrede actually expressed some uncertainty about whether Jesus had a messianic self-understanding or not, regarding it as an unanswerable question but becoming more open to it at the end of his life (see citation from him that follows in the next note).

11. A little known fact, even for scholars, is that Wrede articulated before his death, in a personal letter to Adolf von Harnack, that he no longer could hold to a nonmessianic view of Jesus with certainty. Wrede wrote this letter in 1905 about a year before his death. The relevant part of the letter reads, "I am more disposed than I used to believe that Jesus saw himself as the chosen Messiah." This change of opinion is crucial, because Wrede cannot say this without denying the gist of his earlier view. Martin Hengel, "Jesus, the Messiah of Israel," in his *Studies in Early Christology* (Edinburgh: T & T Clark, 1995), 16, reports on this letter. Details about this letter appear in Martin Hengel and Anna Maria Schwemer, *Der messianische Anspruch Jesu und die Anfänge der Christologie: Vier Studien* (WUNT; Tübingen: Mohr Siebeck, 2001), ix.

12. Dunn, *Jesus Remembered*, 626–27, presents this argument. The citation is from 627 and the emphasis is his. The embedded citation in the sentence is from Nils A. Dahl, "The Crucified Messiah," in D. H. Juel, ed., *Jesus the Christ: The Historical Origins of the Christological Doctrine* (Minneapolis: Fortress, 1991 reproduction of a 1960 article), 39–40.

13. Unfortunately for some, this point is made most clearly in a German source, Martin Hengel and Maria Schwemer, *Jesus und das Judentum* (Jesus and Judaism) (Tübingen: Mohr Siebeck, 2007), 521–22.

14. Wright, *Jesus and the Victory of God*, 529, calls the secret if it goes back to Mark a "Markan trick." He also argues this "secret" explanation of its origin cannot work. Some scholars argue that Jesus denies or rejects the title Messiah by his call for silence here and then shifts discussion to the Son of Man. This is very unlikely. First, if Jesus denies the title here, then there is no confession present at all from Peter and the scene becomes meaningless. A denial also cannot explain very easily why Matthew has the title affirmed strongly and why Mark uses the title elsewhere positively (Mark 14:61, 15:32). The call for silence is not a rejection of the title, but has another, better explanation. As I shall argue, Jesus is qualifying how it is to be used.

15. There are probably fifty-one distinct Son of Man sayings in the tradition (out of the eighty-two uses present; reuse in a parallel does not count in getting to the smaller number). Fourteen of these are from Mark. Ten are from Q. Every source has such sayings, so it is multiply attested. Raymond Brown, *The Death of the Messiah*, 2 vols. (New York: Doubleday, 1994), 507. Outside the gospels, the expression does appear as an idiom (not a title) in the sermonic letter Hebrews 2:6, where Psalm 8 is cited and the reference is to humanity; Acts 7:56 (a vision of Jesus standing as Son of Man to receive Stephen); and in an apocalypse, that is, the book of Revelation 1:13, 14:14.

16. As already noted, the date of this work is debated. Many place it around the time of Jesus, if not slightly later because the section containing the title was not found among the copies of *1 Enoch* at Qumran. But the majority of

Second Temple scholars place it at the end of the previous century or early in the first century. See chapter 6, note 3.

17. Excellent summaries can be found in John Collins, *The Scepter and the Star*, and in Jacob Neusner, William Green, and Ernest Frerichs, eds., *Judaisms and Their Messiahs at the Turn of the Christian Era* (Cambridge: Cambridge University Press, 1987).

18. Wilkins in Bock and Webb, *Key Events in the Life of the Historical Jesus*, 366. The reference to Jesus being regarded as a prophet is multiply attested as the citation notes sources in Mark and John. There also is material from L. Luke 4:24–30 compares Jesus with Elijah-Elisha.

19. This is why one of the most famous of recent books on the historical Jesus is called *The Aims of Jesus*. In it, Ben Meyer argues against the idea that seeking to understand how Jesus saw his mission by taking a close look at Jesus' actions and teaching is engaging in an impossible type of historical psychoanalysis. On p. 111, he says it this way: "For the man with 'aims,' the non-drifter, aims are the man. They throw a flood of light on his history and they are the key to his historic selfhood." For Meyer, as for our study, the ambiguity and debate over who Jesus was and saw himself to be can be grasped by looking at the meaning of what he did and the explanation of those acts by those closest to him. The meaning emerges from the study of the background of how acts were seen at the time. The explanation needs to cohere with that background. This event nicely shows that convergence. This potential for historical analysis is why we spend so much time developing the background in these events.

CHAPTER 8

1. In the technical volume, Brent Kinman wrote the chapter covering this event. He is pastor of Heritage Evangelical Free Church in Castle Rock, Colorado. He received his PhD from Cambridge University and wrote his dissertation there on this event, since published as *Jesus' Entry into Jerusalem: In the Context of Lukan Theology and the Politics of His Day* (Leiden: Brill, 1995). An earlier version of the technical essay was published as "Jesus' Royal Entry into Jerusalem," *Bulletin for Biblical Research* 15 (2005): 223–60. His work on this event represents an updating of those earlier studies.

2. This point about the awareness of the background is recognized by Jesus scholars. Marcus Borg and John Dominic Crossan mention it and contrast the entry of Jesus to that of Pilate in their book, *The Last Week* (San Francisco: HarperSanFrancisco, 2006), 2–3.

3. *Titulus* is the Latin word to refer to the placard placed with the cross that displayed this charge against Jesus.

4. E. P. Sanders, *Jesus and Judaism*, 253–54, 272.

5. Some estimates are even larger, hitting as high as 300,000. E. P. Sanders, *The Historical Figure of Jesus* (London: Penguin, 1993), 249–51, and *Judaism: Practice and Belief, 63 BCE–66 CE* (Philadelphia: Trinity, 1992), 125–28. The larger the crowd, the more powerful the point we are making.

6. Kinman in Bock and Webb, *Key Events in the Life of the Historical Jesus*, 413.

7. The original German citation is in *Die Geschichte der synoptischen Tradition* [*The History of the Synoptic Tradition*], 2nd ed. (Göttingen: Vandenhoeck & Ruprecht, 1931), 281.

8. *Jesus of Nazareth, King of Jews* (New York: Alfred A. Knopf, 1999), 250–51.

9. Ibid., 137–42.

10. Hengel and Schwemer, *Jesus und das Judentum*, 551–52. They defend the historicity of the core of this healing scene by noting the use of the unusual term *rabbûnî* in the address to Jesus and the Aramaic-Greek name. The term appears elsewhere only in John 20:16. It also is not common to have the Son of David be seen as a healer in the end time, although as we noted earlier, Josephus (*Antiquities* 8.40–48) attributes healing power to Solomon, who was a Son of David.

11. This parable is not one of our events, but it has been defended as authentic by one of our participants. See Klyne Snodgrass, *The Parable of the Wicked Tenants: An Inquiry into Parable Interpretation* (Tübingen: Mohr Siebeck, 1983).

12. Dunn, *Jesus Remembered*, 641, shows this event is likely historical for other reasons. (1) There are many local details. (2) The acclamation reflects the character of oral tradition. (3) "Hosanna" is a cry firmly embedded in this story but appears nowhere else in the NT. (4) Mark's account is surprisingly low-key. However, Dunn regards Jesus' full intent as unclear. He sees most of the messianic implications as reflecting elaborations on the event. Part of this has to do with Dunn's reading of Caesarea Philippi as involving a subtle rejection of a messianic claim by Jesus, a view I challenged in an earlier chapter.

13. This city was called Caesarea Maritima to distinguish it from Caesarea Philippi. While Maritima was located on the Mediterranean coast, Philippi was located near the edge of Mount Hermon in the interior and farther north within the province.

14. On later reflection, as John's gospel noted, the church connected this event to Zechariah 9:9. Matthew shows the same association in a narrative re-mark tying the event to the passage (Matthew 21:4–5). The fact that this is a narrative remark means it does not belong as a part of the event, but to a description of it. Zechariah pictures a humble king. Behind this royal claim-ant stands a call to peace, something noted in Zechariah 9:10. The claim of Jesus is that he wields a different kind of power with a different kind of goal than Rome's military might in ruling.

CHAPTER 9

1. In the technical study, Klyne Snodgrass wrote this chapter. He is Paul W. Brandel Professor of New Testament at North Park Theological Seminary in Chicago, Illinois. He is editor of the journal *Ex Auditu*, past president of the Institute for Biblical Research, and author of *Stories with Intent: A Com-*

prehensive Guide to the Parables of Jesus (Grand Rapids: Eerdmans, 2008) and a technical study on the parable of the Wicked Tenants, *The Parable of the Wicked Tenants: An Inquiry into Parable Interpretation* (Tübingen: Mohr Siebeck, 1983).

2. Sanders, *Jesus and Judaism*, 11, 61; Wright, *Jesus and the Victory of God*, 405; Borg and Crossan, *The Last Week*, 47–49. Dunn, *Jesus Remembered*, 650, sees a prophetic protest by Jesus and a real event with an eschatological thrust, but beyond this says he thinks that we cannot say much about it. He sees the event as less significant than most.

3. Isaiah 56:7b reads, "My temple will be known as a temple where all nations may pray." Jeremiah 7:11a has "Do you think this temple I have claimed as my own is to be a hideout for robbers?" Zechariah 14:21b says, "And there shall no longer be a trader in the house of the Lord of hosts on that day." When John 2:16 speaks of not making God's house a marketplace, the allusion is to the traders mentioned in Zechariah.

4. Leon Morris, *The Gospel According to John* (Grand Rapids: Eerdmans, 1995), 189–91.

5. Burton Mack, *A Myth of Innocence: Mark and Christian Origins* (Philadelphia: Fortress, 1988), 266, 270, 291–92.

6. David Seeley, "Jesus' Temple Act," *Catholic Biblical Quarterly* 55 (1993): 269–70.

7. *Commentary on John* 10:16. This can be found in Roberts and Donaldson, *Ante-Nicene Fathers* collection, vol. 9, 393–95.

8. Borg and Crossan, *The Last Week*, p. 48, speak of a "symbolic" shutdown, a prophetic act "that intends in macrocosm what it effects in microcosm." They compare it to pouring blood on a single set of files in an office to protest the entire Vietnam War.

9. So correctly, Jerome Murphy-O'Connor, "Jesus and the Money Changers (Mark 11:15–17; John 2:13–17)," *Revue Biblique* 107 (2000): 42–55, esp. 46–50.

10. Daniel Bahat, "Jesus and the Herodian Temple Mount," in *Jesus and Archaeology*, ed. James H. Charlesworth (Grand Rapids: Eerdmans, 2006), 300–308, esp. 304. This article has the details of why we place the location of this activity there.

11. Hengel and Schwemer, *Jesus und das Judentum*, 559–60, speak of a small tumult that does not create a reaction by the soldiers.

12. Victor Eppstein, "The Historicity of the Gospel Account of the Cleansing of the Temple," *Zeitschrift für die Neutestamentliche Wissenschaft* 55 (1964): 42–58, esp. 54–55. Kim Huat Tan, *The Zion Traditions and the Aims of Jesus* (Cambridge: Cambridge University Press, 1997), 49, n. 25, refers to an area known as "Solomon's Stables" under the southern portico. There would not have been many animals here, since they were also available on the Mount of Olives.

13. Horsley, *Jesus and the Spiral of Violence* (San Francisco: Harper & Row, 1987), 298.

14. Sanders, *Jesus and Judaism*, 62–67.

15. For example, Sanders, *Jesus and Judaism*, 66, does not see the scriptural allusions as part of the authentic event, and so challenges a commerce charge.

16. So forcibly argued by N. T. Wright, *Jesus and the Victory of God*, 418–28. Some scholars challenge Jesus' prediction of the temple's destruction in the Olivet Discourse of Mark 13 = Matthew 24–25 = Luke 21:5–38, arguing that the early church created this predication looking back after the temple's destruction in 70 CE. However, such a view underestimates the context. All Jesus needed to believe to predict the destruction was that the nation was unfaithful to God's covenant, so that Israel was subject to the possibility of an exile-like judgment as presented in Deuteronomy 28–32. There unfaithfulness leads to divine judgment of being overrun by the nations. This unfaithfulness, leading to his call for reform, is a premise of his entire ministry.

17. Jacob Neusner, "Money-Changers in the Temple: The Mishnah's Explanation," *New Testament Studies* 35 (1989): 287–90.

18. So Adela Yarbo Collins, "Jesus' Action in Herod's Temple," in *Antiquity and Humanity: Essays on Ancient Religion and Philosophy*, ed. Adela Yarbo Collins and Margaret M. Mitchell (Tübingen: Mohr Siebeck, 2001), 45–61.

19. Ben Meyer, *The Aims of Jesus*, 170, 209, 214.

20. Craig Evans, "Jesus' Action in the Temple: Cleansing or Portent of Destruction?" in *Jesus in Context: Temple, Purity, and Restoration*, ed. Bruce Chilton and Craig Evans (Leiden: Brill, 1997), 395–439.

21. A choice between an act symbolizing destruction and cleansing is not easy. Against the idea of destruction is the remark about what the temple should be. Why mention this at all if the temple is seen to be going away? To opt for cleansing here is not to deny Jesus predicted the temple's destruction elsewhere, because the Olivet Discourse does this clearly. The only question the prediction of a temple destruction leaves is whether that act was seen as involving a permanent or temporary judgment, another complex issue scholars also debate but that does not involve the meaning of this temple action by Jesus.

22. Now some scholars appeal for the destruction view by bringing in John 2:19, where Jesus says to destroy this temple and in three days he will raise it up. However, this text is not relevant, because John tells us Jesus is discussing his body and not the physical temple.

23. This work, written in the first century BCE, has two sets of versification. Thus the brackets and alternative verse numbers.

24. Snodgrass in Bock and Webb, *Key Events in the Life of the Historical Jesus*, 475.

CHAPTER 10

1. In the technical study, I. Howard Marshall wrote this chapter. Howard is Emeritus Professor of New Testament Studies at the University of Aberdeen

in Scotland. He wrote a major study on the supper entitled *Last Supper and Lord's Supper* (Exeter: Paternoster, 1980). The technical essay was an update of that study. He also wrote a major commentary on Luke entitled *The Gospel of Luke* (Grand Rapids: Eerdmans, 1978).

2. This point is made by Dunn, *Jesus Remembered*, 230. He sees the variation in wording as an indication that the scene was passed on initially in oral form with a small amount of variation typical of that process.

3. Smith, *From Symposium to Eucharist* (Minneapolis: Fortress, 2003), 188.

4. See Robert Funk and the Jesus Seminar, *The Acts of Jesus*, 137–38.

5. Crossan, *The Historical Jesus*, 360–67. He sees five stages of development. Only at later stages four and five do we see the themes the gospels made famous. Crossan accepts much of Smith's work cited above. To get here, one must stress a Hellenistic background, not the Jewish one of Jesus' ministry. We covered this background issue in discussing table fellowship.

6. Marshall in Bock and Webb, *Key Events in the Life of the Historical Jesus*, 522–26.

7. Funk and the Seminar, *The Acts of Jesus*, 134–37.

8. Borg and Crossan, *The Last Week*, 105–7.

9. The detailed discussion is in Barry D. Smith, "Last Supper, Words of Institution," in *Encyclopedia of the Historical Jesus*, Craig Evans, ed. (London: Routledge, 2008), 365–68.

10. So Harold Hoehner, "Chronology," in *Dictionary of Jesus and the Gospels*, ed. Joel Green and Scot McKnight (Downers Grove, IL: InterVarsity Press, 1992), 120–21. Others see the sacrifices for Passover starting early simply because of the number of sacrifices required on this day for all the pilgrims present. See option 3 below.

11. So Maurice Casey, "The Date of Passover Sacrifices and Mark 14:12," *Tyndale Bulletin* 48 (1997): 245–48, and David Instone-Brewer, "Jesus' Last Passover: The Synoptics and John," *Expository Times* 112 (2001): 122–23.

12. Scot McKnight, *Jesus and His Death* (Waco: Baylor University Press, 2005), 271–73. Similar but emphasizing the literary association with the time of the Passover is John Nolland, *The Gospel of Matthew* (Grand Rapids: Eerdmans, 2005), 1044–46.

13. Jeremias, *The Eucharistic Words of Jesus* (London: SCM, 1966), 15–88. This was a translation of a German work whose last edition was the fourth, published in 1967. The English translation is of an earlier edition. Jeremias notes all the Jewish texts that tell us about the customs associated with the meal. The *Mishnah* has the practices for the feast described in detail in the tractate on that feast, *Pesahim*. However, there are some signs that some details in that tractate should be dated after the temple's destruction in 70 CE, such as the meal without a lamb, since there is no temple after the destruction to make the sacrifice. It is important to note that many of these later differences deal with the liturgy of what was said at the meal. See Marshall, in Bock and Webb, *Key Events in the Life of the Historical Jesus*, 545, n. 226.

14. *Eucharistic Words*, 173.

15. J. Dunn, *The Theology of Paul the Apostle* (Grand Rapids: Eerdmans, 1998), 607–8, slightly so, but noting that each version has some development.

16. Marshall, *Last Supper and Lord's Supper*, 40–53, but seeing the Pauline/ Lukan version as generally the earliest.

17. Marshall in Bock and Webb, *Key Events in the Life of the Historical Jesus*, 575.

18. Dunn, *Jesus Remembered*, 230–31.

19. Borg and Crossan, *The Last Week*, 101–5. They deny that Mark 10:45 goes back to Jesus as they discuss this point.

20. So George R. Beasley-Murray, *Jesus and the Kingdom of God* (Grand Rapids: Eerdmans, 1986), 269.

21. The other rite, baptism, happens only once to an individual, but believers take the Lord's Supper on regular occasions.

CHAPTER 11

1. In the technical volume, I wrote this chapter. It is a development of two previous pieces. The first was a full book study, *Blasphemy and Exaltation in Judaism and the Final Examination of Jesus* (Tübingen: Mohr Siebeck, 1998). The second was the original essay for this study, published as "Blasphemy and the Jewish Examination of Jesus," *Bulletin of Biblical Research* 17 (2007): 53–114. This essay builds off of that earlier work.

2. Klyne Snodgrass, *The Parable of the Wicked Tenants*, argues for authenticity in this detailed treatment of this parable.

3. *Thomas* and *Peter* are two of the most well known of the gospels that do not appear in the Bible. Both of them are most likely early second-century texts, although almost all scholars accept that some portions of *Thomas* are older and may even preserve some things Jesus said. Neither of these gospels is seen to go back to Thomas or Peter. On these works, see my *The Missing Gospels* (Nashville: Thomas Nelson, 2006). Interestingly, Helmut Koester, *Ancient Christian Gospels* (London: SCM, 1990), 216–20, sees *Peter* using independent tradition. If so, then this is another source attesting the connection.

4. Donald Juel, *Messiah and Temple: The Trial of Jesus in the Gospel of Mark* (Missoula, MT: Scholars Press, 1977), 97–98, notes that the scene does not meet this strict legal requirement, but then notes that most "scholars insist, therefore, that the legal definition must have been considerably broader in the first century." My detailed survey of blasphemy in the study noted at the opening of this chapter sought to prove this point for a broader definition from the ancient materials. There is much ancient evidence for it.

5. E. P. Sanders, *Jesus and Judaism*, 297–99, presents seven objections to this scene, including doubt about such a formal meeting. The most important issues he raises are all summarized in the five objections I pursue here. His core conclusion is that we cannot know exactly what took place here, and

cannot even know if the Sanhedrin met. He sees only an arrest by the high priest and Jesus being interrogated. We can know nothing more. He argues that the disciples did not know why the leaders had Jesus executed.

6. One of the issues here is that claiming to be the Son of God could simply be seen as a claim to royalty (2 Samuel 7:7–17; Psalm 2) and so not blasphemous even if it was regarded as a false claim.

7. Sanders, *Jesus and Judaism*, 298, objections 5 and 6.

8. Paula Fredriksen, *Jesus of Nazareth: King of the Jews*, 254–55, suggests Caiaphas may have urged Pilate to kill Jesus once Rome seized him or may have taken the initiative to act alone. In her reconstruction, Jewish involvement is highly circumscribed. Beyond this, she argues that we cannot know much about what took place.

9. So Borg and Crossan, *The Last Week*, 128. The lack of witnesses means "the trial scene may represent a post-Easter Christian construction and not history remembered."

10. This issue was raised years ago by Hans Lietzmann, *Der Prozeß Jesu* (The Trial of Jesus) (Berlin: De Gruyter, 1931).

11. Borg and Crossan, *The Last Week*, 133. It "involves following Jesus through death into resurrection and a life here below absolutely opposite to the way of the world's imperial normalcy." The imitation is of Jesus' courage. So also Martin Ebner, *Jesus von Nazaret*, 145–46.

12. The ancient texts here are Josephus, *Jewish War* 2.117—the Roman procurator has the power of death received from Caesar; *Antiquities* 18.2; John 18:31, 19:10. See Otto Betz, "Jesus and the Temple Scroll" in *Jesus and the Dead Sea Scrolls*, James Charlesworth, ed. (New York: Doubleday, 1992), 87–88. Such ideas are also reflected in the later catalog of Roman law, *The Digest of Justinian*, which encapsulated what had been a likely, long-held practice in Rome. See *Digest* 1.16.6 and 11. These Roman texts say only a proconsul can issue a death sentence or inflict a severe flogging. Pliny the Younger, *Epistles* 10.30.2, shows the same idea about a century after the time of Jesus. Finally, the Cyrene edicts (lines 63–67 from 7–6 BCE) give the same limitation to capital punishment. This was a long-standing Roman custom. See Webb, "The Roman Examination and Crucifixion of Jesus," in Bock and Webb, *Key Events in the Life of the Historical Jesus*, 728–29.

13. August Strobel, *Die Stunde der Wahrheit: Untersuchungen zum Strafverfahren gegen Jesus* (The Hour of Truth: Investigations of the Criminal Proceedings against Jesus) (Tübingen: Mohr Siebeck, 1980), 85, notes texts from the *Mishnah* (*Sanhedrin* 11:3–4) and the later *Tosefta* (*Sanhedrin* 7:11, 10:11).

14. What the fifth-century *Talmud* attests to is seen in other texts of the first and second century as well. David Neale, "Was Jesus a *Mesith*?" *Tyndale Bulletin* 44 (1993): 89–101; Graham Stanton, "Jesus of Nazareth: A Magician and a False Prophet Who Deceived God's People?" in *Jesus of Nazareth: Lord and Christ*, ed. Joel P. Green and Max Turner (Grand Rapids: Eerdmans, 1994), 164–80; N. T. Wright, *Jesus and the Victory of God*, 439–42.

15. Correctly Sanders, *Jesus and Judaism*, 298.

16. *Numbers Rabbah, Sifre* and *Aboth Rabbi Nathan* are later Jewish expositions of the Hebrew Bible that see these biblical figures as having blasphemed.

17. In the second-century BCE Jewish text of the *Exagoge of Ezekiel*, Moses has a dream and is told to sit on God's thrones. In the Hebrew Bible, only in Daniel 7:9 is God's throne described in the plural. This *Exagoge* text probably elaborates Exodus 7:1. There God promises Moses, "I will make you God to Pharoah." It pictures an incredible authority that includes judgment. In *1 Enoch*, the Son of Man is described as a future figure who sits next to God and judges, a figure later named as Enoch. In both cases we have greats of Hebrew lore who are considered perhaps worthy of such an honor.

18. This Jewish work comes from the second century CE.

19. The story is in *Babylonian Talmud, Hagigah* 14a, 14b; *Sanhedrin* 38b.

20. Sanders, *Jesus and Judaism*, 297, objection 1. He argues that nothing in the public teaching of Jesus would lead to the question being asked to begin with, much less getting an answer from it.

21. Norman Perrin, "Mark XIV.62: The End Product of a Christian Pesher Tradition," *New Testament Studies* 12 (1966): 150–55; Eugene Boring, *Mark* (Louisville: Westminster John Knox, 2006), 413–14.

22. Dunn, *Jesus Remembered*, 749–54.

23. An even closer look at the term shows that there are about fifty-one sayings involved in this usage once one excludes overlaps that reflect parallel uses between the gospels. Fourteen of these are in Markan sources, while ten reflect Q. The rest are divided between material unique to Matthew (M has eight sayings), material unique to Luke (L has seven), and John with thirteen. In other words, this use is deeply multiply attested. It is a title rooted in the tradition that recalls how Jesus spoke about himself. Numbers here are not precise ("about fifty-one sayings") because one can place certain sayings in more than one category and whether in certain cases one has a parallel or not is debated, impacting the final numbers. The distribution across the sources is deep enough that this number difference does not impact the key point about multiple attestation. In fact, scholars like to divide these sayings into three types. Some sayings describe what Jesus does in his earthly ministry. Other sayings deal with Jesus' suffering. The final class speaks of the Son of Man's authority at the end of time or in judgment. This last class is called the Apocalyptic Son of Man sayings. Jesus' reply here about seeing the Son of Man on the clouds and seated at God's right hand is an apocalyptic saying. This class of sayings is also multiply attested. Mark has three such sayings in 8:38, 13:26, and 14:62. The last case is the use in this event.

24. There is a very technical debate over whether Jesus would have said Psalm 110:1 in a way that reflects what we have here. That debate has to do with the use and difference between the Psalm in Hebrew, whether Jesus spoke in Hebrew or Aramaic here, and the differences with the Greek version we have in the gospel text. The disputed line rendered carefully from the Hebrew reads, "Yahweh said to my Lord, 'Sit at my right hand . . .'" The challenge is that only in Greek do we get the ambiguity of the text as we have

it, "The Lord said to my Lord." If Jesus, following Jewish custom, was careful about not pronouncing the divine name, since out of respect the name Yahweh was often avoided in formal public discussion, then this custom would have resulted in a reading, "The Lord said to my Lord." This is exactly what the texts in Mark 12 and 14 have.

25. But Boring, *Mark*, 414, argues for a choice between the categories.

26. Dunn, *Jesus Remembered*, 652–53. This issue is very complex. For a full discussion of a response, see my essay in *Key Events in the Life of the Historical Jesus*. I make only a few remarks here.

CHAPTER 12

1. In the technical volume, Robert Webb wrote this chapter.

2. Dunn, *Jesus Remembered*, 775, is certain of these core facts. He says, "That Jesus was crucified on the direct authority of Pilate himself need not be doubted for a minute."

3. Other texts from Paul include 1 Corinthians 1:17–18, 22–23, 2:1–2; Philippians 2:8.

4. Gunnar Samuelson, *Crucifixion in Antiquity: An Inquiry into the Background of the New Testament Terminology of Crucifixion* (Gothenberg: University of Gothenberg, 2010). This dissertation argues that the terms normally translated "cross" are actually more vague in meaning, referring to a raised pole on which someone is suspended. The shape of that pole is not clear from the term itself. That requires a look at each context. Shapes can be like the letters I, X, or T, or †.

5. The uncertainty as to the year of Jesus' death is because we are not told exactly when in Pilate's rule he was executed and we are not sure exactly how long Jesus ministered (whether it was about three or four years). Pilate ruled from 27 to 36 CE. The timing of John the Baptist's ministry puts us in the late twenties for his work. Jesus' ministry follows right after that.

6. Other texts in the Q tradition merely speak of rejecting the prophets or killing the prophets God has sent. These look like allusions including the rejection of Jesus but are less specific. Among these texts are Luke 6:22–23, 11:47–51, and 13:34–35, and their parallels in Matthew 5:11–12, 23:29–34, and 23:37–39.

7. Webb in Bock and Webb, *Key Events in the Life of the Historical Jesus*, 762–63, has a chart listing the twenty-five units and what they describe. The chart includes material from the *Gospel of Peter*, which includes twelve of the twenty-five scenes of the other gospels. Earlier in his article, Webb argues that whoever wrote the *Gospel of Peter* likely used oral material shared with the other gospels and some other independent tradition. This gospel is late, coming from the early second century CE. As such, its claimed association with Peter is not real. The *Gospel of Peter* 4:10 describes Jesus as crucified between two criminals, a detail that looks to be dependent on Luke 23:33. What the *Gospel of Peter* does show is the nature of some tradi-

tion about Jesus' death that circulated slightly later in settings outside those of the more well-known gospels.

8. One reason most scholars accept the idea that Josephus said this and a few other things about Jesus here is an indirect back reference to the Christ, made when Josephus calls James the brother of the so-called Christ in *Antiquities* 20.200. This later, very short aside seems to presuppose an earlier discussion about the Christ in his work.

9. We make this point against George Wells, *Who Was Jesus?* (Chicago: Open Court Publishing, 1989), 20, who argues Tacitus is just parroting what he heard from Christians.

10. Those telling this story in the pesher to Nahum do not like what Alexander Jannaeus did, but characterize the kind of death as a horrible act reflective of earlier horrific deaths.

11. This evidence seriously challenges attempts to argue that the Jesus story is totally a myth about a made-up figure (so Tom Harpur, *The Pagan Christ: Recovering the Lost Light* [Toronto: Thomas Allen, 2004]) or that Pilate condemned Jesus but then saw to his survival (so Michael Baigent, *The Jesus Papers: Exposing the Greatest Cover-Up in History* [New York: HarperCollins, 2006], 115–32). Such arguments are exercises in historical fantasy themselves, ignoring whole swaths of ancient testimony from various angles.

12. Remember, I have noted that singularly attested material may be historical, but it is hard to make a case for it in a corroborative model.

13. Dunn, *Jesus Remembered*, 774–76.

14. Ibid., 776.

15. Christians preached that Jesus died for sin. This is a theological explanation of the event in terms of its meaning as an act in God's program. One can see and corroborate a death in terms of a historical act, but one cannot see or corroborate a death *for sin* as a matter of demonstrable proof. One can testify only to what happened around the event as a way to point to and support the claims of a theological significance to the act. This is what the preaching of the church did in texts like 1 Corinthians 15:3–5 and its elaboration by Paul. Texts, the character of Jesus' ministry, and divine vindication served to substantiate the unseeable theological claim associated with the act in the disciples' message about Jesus. So this chapter only pursues the historical reasons and verdict that led Pilate to send Jesus to the cross.

CHAPTER 13

1. In the technical study, Grant Osborne wrote this chapter. He is professor of New Testament at Trinity Evangelical Divinity School in Deerfield, Illinois, located just outside Chicago. His published dissertation from the University of Aberdeen is entitled *The Resurrection Narratives: A Redactional Study* (Grand Rapids: Baker, 1984). He also is responsible for the article on the Resurrection in the *Dictionary of Jesus and the Gospels*, Joel B. Green and Scot McKnight, eds. (Downers Grove, IL: InterVarsity, 1992), 673–88.

2. A very recent fine study of the resurrection including a careful assessment of objections to it is Michael Licona, *The Resurrection of Jesus: A New Historiographical Approach* (Downers Grove, IL: InterVarsity Academic, 2010).

3. On this event, see Cassius Dio, *Roman History* 45.7.1; Suetonius, *Twelve Caesars: Julius Caesar* 88. Here is what Dio says: "When, however, a certain star during all those days appeared in the north toward evening, which some called a comet, claiming that it foretold the usual occurrences, while the majority, instead of believing it, ascribed it to Caesar, interpreting it to mean that he had become immortal and had been received into the number of the stars, Octavius then took courage and set up in the temple of Venus a bronze statue of him with a star above his head. And when this act also was allowed, no one trying to prevent it through fear of the populace, then at last some of the other decrees already passed in honor of Caesar were put into effect. Thus they called one of the months July after him, and in the course of certain festivals of thanksgiving for victory they sacrificed during one special day in memory of his name. For these reasons the soldiers also, particularly since some of them received largesses of money, readily took the side of Caesar." Here is Suetonius' report: "He [Julius] died in the fifty-sixth year of his age, and was numbered among the gods, not only by a formal decree, but also in the conviction of the common people. For at the first of the games which his heir Augustus gave in honor of his apotheosis, a comet shone for seven successive days, rising about the eleventh hour, and was believed to be the soul of Caesar, who had been taken to heaven; and this is why a star is set upon the crown of his head in his statue." Octavius and Augustus are two names for the same person.

4. The portrayal of Jesus' raising of Jairus' daughter, his bringing the widow of Nain's son back to life, or of Lazarus coming out of the tomb were not presented as resurrections. They all would eventually die. Those acts were resuscitations out of death, events that showed God's power over death but were not resurrections in the midst of history.

5. Other discussions of this scene appear in William Lane Craig, *Assessing the New Testament Evidence for the Historicity of the Resurrection of Jesus* (Lewiston: Mellen, 1989), 214–15. N. T. Wright, *The Resurrection of the Son of God* (Minneapolis: Fortress, 2003), 641.

6. Dunn, *Jesus Remembered*, 839, speaks of the tradition being interested in an empty tomb or else why mention burial. He argues that this detail "probably reflects the place of tomb narratives—burial but also empty tomb—in the earliest traditions of Easter." He also notes how the preaching in Acts 13:28–31 and 2:29, as well as the account in Luke 23:52–24:7, point to this understanding (in n. 61).

7. Ibid., 836.

8. Ibid., 837, points to how tombs of early rabbis can still be visited today in Israel. For example, I have been to Tiberias and the site of the tomb of Rabbi Akiba, who lived in the early second century CE, where honor is given to him by some visitors.

9. The short end of Mark is part of a larger debate about where Mark origi-

nally ended, at verse 8 or verse 20 or at some point now lost to us. Translations note this difference in the manuscripts of Mark, usually with a note or by placing brackets on vv. 9–20 to express uncertainty about the location of the ending. The shorter ending is the one attested in our earliest manuscripts. Our earlier English translations used manuscripts that had the longer ending in it. This longer ending, running to verse 20, looks to have been added later, since it contains mostly a combination of things said from scenes in the other gospels. Those who find Mark's ending in v. 8 as too abrupt suggest we have lost the original ending. I prefer seeing the short ending as a probe by Mark to ask if one is going to fear or have faith in the resurrection, a theme Mark has earlier in his gospel. For a full discussion of the issues tied to Mark's ending, see David Alan Black, ed., *Perspectives on the Ending of Mark: Four Views* (Nashville: Broadman & Holman Academic, 2008). In that volume, I give details as to why I think Mark 16 ended at v. 8.

10. What is not entirely clear is whether this distinction implies no hope for a restored physical element in the future or merely is a description of the fact that the body now can be destroyed because of its mortality.

11. I will go into more detail on this specific argument below.

12. There was also a physical resurrection hope at Qumran, which likely reflects the Essenes' view within Judaism. A text entitled *On Resurrection* (4Q521) says that God "will heal those defiled and give life to those dead." *Pseudo-Ezekiel* (4Q385, fragment 2) interprets the dry bones of Ezekiel 37 as describing a host of people who "will rise and bless the Lord of hosts who causes them to live." Ezekiel 37 pictured a physical body being brought back to life. *Sapiential Work A* (4Q416 fragment 23.6–8) speaks of "your resemblance will blosso[m foreve]r and in the end you will inherit joy." At the least this points to some form of conscious afterlife, while the idea of praising God, the mention of resemblance, and the picture of Ezekiel 37 point to some type of physical existence. (The brackets in the citation above mean the text is reconstructed but reflects the probable reading at this point. The brackets show where some of the text is missing or not legible.)

13. See Osborne's summary in Bock and Webb, *Key Events in the Life of the Historical Jesus*, 812–14. Also for resurrection in a Greco-Roman setting, Stanley Porter, "Resurrection, Greeks and the New Testament," in *Resurrection*, Stanley Porter, ed. (Sheffield: Sheffield Academic Press, 1999), 52–81; against its presence in that context, N. T. Wright, *The Resurrection of the Son of God*, 32–84, who argues that the exceptions appear only in mythic or fictional stories and are not beliefs held about human life. His conclusion is that death is a "one way street" in the Greco-Roman world (p. 82).

14. Borg and Crossan, *The Last Week*, 191–94. Key differences are already treated above.

15. Ibid. These last four citations are from pages 191, 192, and 193 (the last two citations), respectively.

16. John Dominic Crossan, "The Passion, Crucifixion, and Resurrection," in *The Search for Jesus: Modern Scholarship Looks at the Gospels*, ed. Hershel

Shanks (Washington, DC: Biblical Archaeology Society, 1994), 109–26, esp. 123–25.

17. Crossan, *The Historical Jesus*, 391–94.

18. Dunn, *Jesus Remembered*, 782–83.

19. By the way, if this account and custom are true, then the claim a few years ago about having found Jesus' family tomb in the Talpiot district of Jerusalem cannot be true. Jesus would not have been interred with family members. There is no Jesus family tomb, because Jesus was not buried with his family.

20. Osborne in Bock and Webb, *Key Events in the Life of the Historical Jesus*, 804. Other works go into more detail on seeing the resurrection as a real event than we have space for here, dealing with both historical and worldview issues that impact the discussion. See N. T. Wright, *The Resurrection of the Son of God*; Gary Habermas, "The Resurrection of Jesus and the Talpiot Tomb," in *Buried Hope or Risen Savior: The Search for the Jesus Tomb*, ed. Charles L. Quarles (Nashville: Broadman & Holman, 2008), 152–75; Gary Habermas and Michael Licona, *The Case for the Resurrection of Jesus* (Grand Rapids: Kregel, 2004); Michael Licona, *The Resurrection of Jesus: A New Historiographical Approach* (Downers Grove, IL: InterVarsity Press, 2010); and various studies by William L. Craig, "The Historicity of the Empty Tomb of Jesus," *New Testament Studies* 31 (1985): 39–67; "The Guard at the Empty Tomb," *New Testament Studies* 30 (1984): 273–81; *The Son Rises: The Historical Evidence for the Resurrection of Jesus* (Chicago: Moody Press, 1981).

21. Thomas R. Yoder Neufeld, *Recovering Jesus: The Witness of the New Testament* (Grand Rapids: Brazos, 2007), 283.

Who Is Jesus?

Dr. Darrell Bock

READING GROUP GUIDE

INTRODUCTION

Most people agree that a man named Jesus lived in the first century in the historical regions surrounding Jerusalem. But what about Jesus as one claimed to be the actual Son of God, the Savior of the World? Can anyone know the concrete truth about the Christ of faith? A significant way to crack the Jesus code, especially with those who have questions, Dr. Darrell Bock says, is to follow the rules—rules set not by the Church but by historians.

TOPICS & QUESTIONS FOR DISCUSSION

1. Have you had conversations about Jesus with people you know? If so, have you generally taken the "skeptic" side or the "believer" side in those conversations?
2. Discuss the title *Who Is Jesus?* and how it relates to the contents of the book. If a friend posed that question to you, how would you answer him or her?
3. Were you familiar with the quest for the historical Jesus before reading this book? How did reading this book change your perspective?
4. Do you think that studying the historical Jesus tends to deepen or weaken faith, or neither? Why?
5. What do you think might be the motivation of scholars who undertake serious study of the historical Jesus? To affirm the biblical account? To discredit it? Both? Neither? Does it depend on who is doing the study?
6. Review the Rules for the scholarly study of Jesus on pages 13–25. What do you see as the strengths and weaknesses of these various Rules?

7. Discuss how archaeology, linguistics, and other fields of study have impacted the study of Jesus.

8. Why do you think some Christians might feel threatened or unsettled by serious inquiry into the historical Jesus? Do you think these concerns are valid?

9. Compare and contrast the church's way of studying Jesus versus the historian's way. Do you think there can be a middle ground between these two approaches? Why or why not?

10. Discuss the twenty-first-century view of oral accounts versus the first-century view. Does the fact that Jesus lived in a primarily oral culture affect the reliability of the Bible? Why or why not?

11. What role, if any, do you think that historical sources outside of the biblical canon should play in the study of Jesus?

12. Dr. Bock discussed twelve events in the life and ministry of Jesus. If you could sit down face-to-face with Jesus and/or one of the disciples, which event would you most like to discuss? What questions would you most like to have answered?

13. Has reading this book changed how you think about the Bible? About the scholarly quest for the historical Jesus? About the relationship between theology and history?

Enhance Your Book Club

1. Think of someone in your life who is skeptical about Christianity. Imagine or role-play a conversation with him or her. What might be their objections to Christianity? Rehearse some possible responses.

2. Pray for biblical historians who seek to honor Christ while pursuing rigorous research and scholarship. Discuss the issues and challenges that Christian scholars might encounter.

3. Of the twelve events in the life of Jesus discussed in the book, which one holds the most meaning for you, and why? Discuss your answers with your book club.

A Conversation with Dr. Darrell Bock

1. **Who do you think should read *Who Is Jesus?***

   The book is for anyone who is interested in Jesus and how he is discussed in the public square. It takes a close look at the social context of his life and ministry as well as how certain key events should be seen that can help us understand him.

2. **What inspired you to write *Who Is Jesus?* What concerns or trends in the modern church do you hope to address?**

   I have many conversations with people who have honest questions about how the gospels present Jesus, and there are many debates about him. This can be confusing for people who are interested but hear an array of things about Jesus. So my book summarizes work on this question that involved several scholars over a decade's worth of meetings and conversation. We wanted to give to everyone (not just people in the church) the best information we have about certain key events in the life of Jesus. These events show who he is and deals carefully with issues and questions people raise about those events.

3. **How would you respond to someone who says the Bible is unreliable because it emerged from an oral culture and was not written until long after the events it depicts?**

   I would point out that one of the values of ancient oral culture was that people regarded the living word as more important than a written word. So the church did not write the gospels until they began to lose those witnesses who could tell the story of Jesus. Also, oral culture had ways of remembering that protected the core story and its accuracy, even as it often told and retold the same story with some variation. An example of this in the Book of Acts is that Luke tells the story of Paul's conversion three times. Each account has variation of detail, but the core story is the same. We see the same thing in parallel gospel accounts. All of this fits the oral culture and does not point to unreliability but to the way they passed on material. One more thing, in terms of most ancient materials we have about ancient events, the length of time between the event and the writing of the gospels is not so great a distance in time, within a generation or two, where some people who experienced these events were still alive.

4. **Discuss the rules of sound historical scholarship. Why is it important for Christians to adhere to these rules when studying the life and ministry of Jesus? What limitations does such study have?**

The key element in sound historical work involves having an awareness of your sources, knowing the historical setting, and looking for corroboration. The rules of historical Jesus study look for such elements as well as for corroboration between the various sources. This also has its limits because a single source can have value. It is just that possibility cannot be corroborated. The value of the rules is that it can help in a conversation with those who have questions about the accounts. Here are rules set up by people who were skeptical about the sources. If an event can get over those hurdles, it gives an indication of the credibility of what is reported. Of course, the limits include the point that failure to meet the rules does not mean the event did not take place. It just means it did not meet the high standard of corroboration the rules seek to test.

5. **What are the dangers of overlaying twenty-first-century values onto first-century culture? Do you think some theologians and historians make this mistake?**

The major problem is that the values and approach to things like passing on events do not reflect a written or digitally oriented culture, but one where most communication was oral. In addition, the way certain things were done in the flow of life was different. So we place our expectations on events or how they were told and can misread them. This is why we spent so much time discussing the cultural features that inform the meaning of the key events we treated, including pointing out what those sources are and what they tell us. These are the cultural scripts that inform the meaning of what was taking place and why. It is hard work. So some skip this step or do not give it enough attention. In other cases, they assume the meaning of an event is clear and so do not look to see if ancient practices and attitudes were different.

6. **What approach would you take in discussing Jesus with a skeptic who doesn't trust the biblical account? What are some other resources you would recommend?**

   Well, that is why I wrote the book and why the scholars I worked with took the time to do a detailed study on Jesus. I try to point out why the telling of an event is rooted in good sources and face the questions and objections people raise much as we do in the chapters of the book that treat the events. I take these questions seriously because I shared that skepticism when I was younger. On Jesus, our full study, *Key Events in the Life of the Historical Jesus,* has the full details about these key events. For more general issues tied to the Bible, a recent solid book is *Do Historical Matters Matter to Faith?* (edited by James Hoffmeier and Dennis Magary).

7. **In your view, how important is a strong intellectual life to the ordinary Christian? What can a nonscholarly Christian do to deepen and sharpen his or her intellectual powers and understanding of theology?**

   An intellectual life is vital to keeping the Christian faith fresh and alive, deepening one's appreciation for what life is about as God designed it. With all the resources available, there is much opportunity to pursue such growth. It just takes the investment of time and energy to get there. To the nonscholarly Christian, I would simply note that there are plenty of resources written at a popular level to help them go deeper a step at a time. The place to begin might be with a solid study Bible. Some even focus on history and archaeology to give you notes about important relevant background to the biblical materials.

8. **How have people responded to your teachings on the quest for the historical Jesus? Have you encountered resistance from the church or the academic community?**

   It mostly meets with fascination and appreciation. I often get the response that those details really give depth and a greater understanding to events and the way they connect. Resistance does come as well. Some in the church are nervous about using sources outside of Scripture to help understand it. Others ask if anything good can come out of something set up from a skeptical point of view. The book tries to show that can happen. Some more skeptical scholars also resist what we are doing, saying we always spin the material in a positive direction. This is why I engage questions and challenges directly in the book. That allows the reader to see what the actual conversation is between those who disagree about how we should see the events. So anyone can see the case for themself and assess its value.

9. **What advice would you offer to a young Christian who desires an academic career? Will he or she have to set his faith aside in order to be an effective scholar? How would you advise him or her to prepare?**

My advice is be prepared to work hard, think about things in fresh ways, listen well, and try to be fair to those you disagree with. I do not think one sets one's faith aside, but one's faith can be shaped by the work one does, especially correcting misconceptions one may have had about faith. The result is an enriched faith.

10. **If readers take away one primary message from *Who Is Jesus?*, what do you hope it will be?**

That in the to-and-fro of debate about key events tied to Jesus' life there is a solid case for the events having been faithfully presented even in the midst of genuine skeptical questions about these events. This means reflecting on Jesus and his life as more than a historical matter. What he said and taught about life and God becomes as important a question as one can pursue. I hope that the book causes people to take Jesus and his unique person and message seriously in a cultural context that seeks to relativize him.

11. **What other books or projects are you currently working on?**

I am about to work on commentaries on Matthew and Mark respectively. I also will be launching a weekly podcast for the Seminary where I teach that will deal with an array of issues where God and culture link.